VOTES FOR WOMEN

VIEWPOINTS ON AMERICAN CULTURE

Edited by Catherine Clinton

Viewpoints on American Culture offers timely reflections for twenty-first century readers. A sensible guide to knowledge in a scholarly field, something one can pick up—literally and figuratively—seems to be facing extinction. Volumes in our series will provide intellectual relief and practical solution.

The series targets topics where debates have flourished and brings together the voices of established and emerging writers to share their own points of view in a compact and compelling format. Our books offer sophisticated, yet accessible, introductions into an array of issues under our broad and expanding banner.

Sifters: Native American Women's Lives
Edited by Theda Perdue

Long Time Gone: Sixties America Then and Now
Edited by Alexander Bloom

Votes for Women: The Struggle for Suffrage Revisited
Edited by Jean H. Baker

VOTES FOR WOMEN

The Struggle for Suffrage Revisited

Edited by Jean H. Baker

OXFORD
UNIVERSITY PRESS

2002

OXFORD

UNIVERSITY PRESS

Oxford   New York
Athens   Auckland   Bangkok   Bogotá   Buenos Aires   Cape Town
Chennai   Dar es Salaam   Delhi   Florence   Hong Kong   Istanbul   Karachi
Kolkata   Kuala Lumpur   Madrid   Melbourne   Mexico City   Mumbai   Nairobi
Paris   São Paulo   Shanghai   Singapore   Taipei   Tokyo   Toronto   Warsaw

and associated companies in
Berlin   Ibadan

Published by Oxford University Press, Inc.
198 Madison Avenue, New York, New York 10016

Oxford is a registered trademark of Oxford University Press

Library of Congress Cataloging-in-Publication Data
Votes for women : the struggle for suffrage revisited / edited by Jean H. Baker.
    p.   cm.—(Viewpoints on American culture)
ISBN 0-19-513016-2; ISBN 0-19-513017-0 (pbk.)
1. Women—Suffrage—United States—History.
2. United States—Politics and government—1865–1933.
I. Baker, Jean H.   II. Series.
JK1896. V67 2002
324.6'23'0973—dc21   2001036768

9 8 7 6 5 4 3 2 1

Printed in the United States of America
on acid-free paper

To

Abby Scott Baker (1871–1944), distinguished secretary of the

National Woman's Party, and to her great-great-granddaughters

Abby Elizabeth Bauman and Devin Robinson Munroe

ACKNOWLEDGMENTS

Catherine Clinton had the original idea for this book. Over one of the many lunches we have enjoyed through the years, she persuaded me that a book of essays incorporating new scholarship on the American suffrage movement would prove useful for students and their professors. And so, three years later, *Votes For Women: The Struggle for Suffrage Revisited* has moved from conversational abstraction to material reality. It becomes the third volume in Clinton's series Viewpoints on American Culture, and is intended to provide a practical, handy guide to an important subject. Throughout, Catherine Clinton has herself been the best of guides, casting an experienced eye perceptively and knowledgeably over all the essays that are included. I believe that *Votes for Women* adds to Clinton's many contributions to her larger endeavor of increasing and thickening our understanding of women's history, even as we place it within the widening boundaries of the studied American past. This volume was also immensely improved by Susan Ferber, our diligent and intelligent editor at Oxford University Press, who corrected mistakes of interpretation, fact, and writing.

I am also appreciative of the dedicated efforts of the thirteen contributors who took seriously the mandate to make their essays, in the cliché of our times, "accessible" to different audiences. Their approach to suffrage has been fresh and innovative. They have also made the story of American suffrage dramatic and relevant, as they have moved beyond the traditional retelling of this story to place women's struggle to get the vote where it belongs—in the larger narrative of American democracy and government. From my perspective working on this book has been a collegial, cooperative effort, and I am honored to have worked with all of them.

I am also grateful to several research assistants at Goucher College, especially Paige Young and Candice Hill, who were supported by the Clapp Fund, and Jamie Winter, for support in getting the final manuscript together. As has been the case throughout the many years of our marriage, my husband, Robinson Baker, has listened, read, and commented with frankness and intelligence, and it is to his remarkable grandmother (and our outstanding female grandchildren who will carry on the struggle for women's rights in the new millennium) that *Votes for Women* is dedicated.

September 2001   J.H.B.
Baltimore, Maryland

CONTENTS

CONTRIBUTORS

Jean Baker is Professor of History at Goucher College in Towson, Maryland. Among her books are *Affairs of Party: The Political Culture of Northern Democrats in Mid-Nineteenth Century America* (1983), *Mary Todd Lincoln: A Biography* (1987), and *The Stevensons: Biography of an American Family* (1993). She is a co-author of the recently published *Civil War and Reconstruction*. Currently she is working on a book entitled *Connections: The Lives of the American Suffragists*.

Christine Bolt is Professor of American History at the University of Kent at Canterbury, England. Her publications include *The Antislavery Movement and Reconstruction* (1969), *Power and Protest in American Life* (co-author with A. T. Barbrook, 1980), *Anti-Slavery, Religion and Reform* (co-author with Seymour Drescher, 1980), *American Indian Policy and American Reform* (1987), *The Women's Movements in the United States and Britain* (1993), and *Feminist Ferment* (1995).

Ellen Carol DuBois is Professor of History at UCLA. She is the author of numerous books on the history of the woman suffrage movement in the United States including *Feminism and Suffrage: The Emergence of an Independent Women's Movement in America 1848–1969* (1978) and *Harriot Stanton Blatch and the Winning of Woman Suffrage* (1997). She is also the coeditor, with Vicki L. Ruiz, of *Unequal Sisters: A Multicultural Reader in U.S. Women's History* (2000). Currently she is working on woman suffrage movements around the world.

Faye Dudden is Professor of History at Colgate University. Her books include *Serving Women: Household Service in Nineteenth-Century America* (1983) and *Women in the American Theatre: Actresses and Audiences, 1790–1870* (1984).

Rebecca Edwards is Assistant Professor of History at Vassar College in Poughkeepsie, New York. She is the author of *Angels in the Machinery: Gender in American Party Politics from the Civil War to the Progressive Period* (1997). She is working on a biography of the Western Populist leader and woman's rights advocate Mary Elizabeth Lease.

Linda Ford is co-owner, with her husband, of Half-Moon Books in Northampton, Mass. She received her doctorate from Syracuse University and is the author of *Iron-Jawed Angels: The Suffrage Militancy of the National Woman's Party 1912–1919* (1991). Her most recent publication is *Lady Hoopsters: A History of Women's Basketball in America* (2000).

Robert Booth Fowler is Hawkins Professor of Political Science at the University of Wisconsin-Madison. He is the author of *Carrie Catt: Feminist Politician* (1986), as well as several books on the intersection of ideas and politics including *Contemporary Issues in Political Theory* (co-author with Jeffrey Orenstein, 1985).

Thomas Jablonsky is a Professor of History at Marquette University. His publications include *The Home, Heaven and the Mother Party: Female Antisuffrage in the United States 1868–1920*.

Spencer Jones is working on his doctorate at the University of Wisconsin-Madison.

Nell Irvin Painter, currently Edwards Professor of American History at Princeton University, is the author of several books, including *Sojourner Truth, A Life and Symbol* and *Southern History Across the Color Line*, forthcoming.

Alison M. Parker teaches at the State University of New York, Brockport. She is the author of *Purifying America: Women, Cultural Reform, and Pro-Censorship Activism 1873–1933* (1997) and co-author of *Women and the Unstable State in Nineteenth Century America* (2000). She is currently working on a book entitled *Gendered Reform Strategies: Women and Politics in Nineteenth Century America*.

Anne Firor Scott is the W. K. Boyd Professor Emerita at Duke University. She is the author of numerous books including *One-Half The People* (1975) and *Natural Allies: Women's Associations and American History* (1991).

Allison Sneider is Assistant Professor of History at Rice University. She is the assistant editor of *The Selected Papers of Elizabeth Cady Stanton and Susan B. Anthony*, Vol. 3 (forthcoming) and the co-author of *Knowledge and Postmodernism in Historical Perspective* (1999). Her current book project is "Reconstruction, Expansion, Empire: The U.S. Suffrage Movement and the Re-Making of National Political Community, 1870–1920."

Marjorie Julian Spruill is Professor of History at the University of Southern Mississippi in Hattiesburg, Mississippi. She is the author of *New Women for the New South: The Leaders of the Woman Suffrage Movement in the Southern States* (1993); and she has edited several books on suffrage history including *One Woman, One Vote: Rediscovering the Woman Suffrage Movement* (1995) and *Votes for Women!: The Woman Suffrage Movement in Tennessee, the South, and the Nation* (1995). She is co-editor of *The South in the History of the Nation: A Reader* (1999).

VOTES FOR WOMEN

INTRODUCTION

Jean H. Baker

In the years before the Civil War, American women began a campaign for the vote that lasted nearly seventy-five years. Their battle finally ended in 1920 when the Nineteenth Amendment prohibiting the denial of the right to vote "on account of sex" was adopted. Initially, suffrage was one of several reforms intended to end the significant legal, political, religious, and cultural discriminations against nineteenth-century women. In the 1840s and 1850s, activists targeted injustices ranging from child custody laws that favored fathers to prohibitions against women speaking in public, the denial of equal education, and the existence of a double sex standard. In language and vocabulary familiar to a generation whose parents had lived during the American Revolution and who remembered the Declaration of Independence, women at the 1848 Seneca Falls convention resolved, among other injustices, that "all laws which . . . place her in a position inferior to that of man are contrary to the great precept of nature and therefore of no force or authority."

A necessary transaction in any democracy between the people and those to whom they delegate authority, suffrage emerged in the 1860s as both a powerful symbol of equality with men as well as an instrument of reform. Voting became the essential political utility by which women could achieve other improvements in their status. If women could vote, went the argument of this first generation of suffragists, they would end barriers at the state level that prevented married women from controlling their wages and attending state universities. If women could vote, given their acknowledged position as moral guardians of their homes, they would

3

reform the corrupt practices of American politics. If women could vote, they would end unequal pay.

Following the founding in 1869 of the National Woman Suffrage Association and its rival the American Woman Suffrage Association, suffragists fought for the next fifty-one years against an opposition that at first trivialized their efforts and then circumvented their intentions through legal and constitutional maneuvers, refusing to include black or white women in the constitutional settlement of Reconstruction. Finally, in the second decade of the twentieth century, those opposing votes for women, who now included a group of contrarian women, had become a minority. Women had won their great struggle in the court of public opinion. Passed by two-thirds of Congress in 1918, the Nineteenth Amendment was ratified by three-quarters of the states in the summer of 1920, with Tennessee the thirty-sixth state legislature to adopt the amendment. A campaign—remarkable for its endurance, its development of independent female-led organizations, its leaders, and its tactics, as well as the intransigence of its opposition—delivered the vote to one-half the population and thereby reshaped the United States into a more egalitarian and democratic nation.

Given the utter logic and justice of their cause, suffragists always believed that success was imminent, and so they numbered their amendment to prohibit discrimination in voting on the basis of sex the Sixteenth Amendment. But votes for women came so slowly that they followed changes legalizing an income tax, authorizing popular voting for United States senators, and establishing prohibition. Given the federal nature of the United States government and the tangled jurisdictions over voting between state and national authority, the latter so strikingly evident in the presidential election of 2000, suffragists faced endless campaigns to persuade state legislatures to take the word "male" out of their constitutions. Usually, the procedures for any such change entailed a statewide referendum. In a system that consigned to states authority over deciding who could vote, there was always some battle somewhere that demanded attention. If success did not come in 1890 in South Dakota and Wyoming, then victory would come in New York and Kansas in 1894—or failing that, in 1896 in California or wherever a constitutional convention was held or a state legislature, through its judiciary committee, might bring a resolution for a referendum to the floor of the legislature.

As Carrie Catt, the tenacious president of the National American Woman Suffrage Association (NAWSA), catalogued these efforts: "To get the word 'male' in effect out of the Constitution cost the women of the country fifty-two years of pauseless campaign.... During that time they were forced to conduct fifty-six campaigns of referenda to male voters; 480 campaigns to get Legislatures to submit suffrage amendments to voters; 47 campaigns to get State constitutional conventions to write woman suffrage into state constitutions . . . and 19 campaigns with 19 successive Congresses."[1] And this list does not include efforts to gain an endorsement of woman suffrage in state and presidential conventions held by political parties during the period. There were some successes along the way, notably in the western states of Idaho, Utah, Wyoming, and Colorado, where women's voting was constitutionally authorized by 1890.

The stamina of these optimists represented one of the movement's strengths, as did the longevity of its remarkably energetic first generation of leaders. Lucy Stone died in 1893 at seventy-five years of age; Elizabeth Cady Stanton in 1902 at eighty-seven, and Susan B. Anthony in 1906 at eighty-six. Having joined the suffrage movement as young women, their combined years of service to suffrage added up to nearly 150 years. As the essays in this volume make clear, these women and their followers were sustained not only by the commonsense rectitude of their goal and their growing organizational sophistication but also by their increasing contacts with an international woman's movement that began in the 1830s and brought women from Great Britain, France, and Germany together in a common cause. In 1883, when the crusade in the United States was at a low point, Susan B. Anthony and Elizabeth Cady Stanton organized an international council in London. Thereafter, the council provided a structure for women throughout the world to meet and discuss common issues. Emma Goldman once compared these pioneers of human progress whose life's work crossed national boundaries to seagulls, "they behold new coasts, new spheres of daring thought. . . . They send joyous greetings to the distant lands."[2]

In the United States as in other nations, suffragists sent their joyous greetings not only across space but also through time to a new generation of women. They had nurtured their cause in the early days through a network of friends whom Susan B. Anthony called "the sisters of suffrage." By the end of the century, blood relatives of the pioneers—Anthony's nieces, Elizabeth Cady Stanton's daughter Harriot Stanton Blatch, and Lucy Stone's daughter Alice Stone Blackwell—along with a new group of professional and working women had joined the National American Woman Suffrage Association and the National Woman's Party. Based at first on informal personal associations, in time suffrage women created powerful national institutions, different from most reform organizations because they were female-organized, led and staffed, by women intent on achieving political equality for their sex.

To be sure, there were many disheartening moments, especially during Reconstruction when black males were made citizens in 1868 and enfranchised in 1870 and women—black and white—were not included in what seemed at the time a natural, easily obtained expansion of democracy. As a result of differing positions on the Fifteenth Amendment, which gave black males the right to vote, the suffrage movement divided into two wings—the American Woman Suffrage Association led by Lucy Stone in Boston, who accepted the idea that it was a time to entitle black males during the so-called Negro's hour, and the National Woman Suffrage Association centered in New York and Washington and dominated until the twentieth century by Elizabeth Cady Stanton and Susan B. Anthony, who rejected the Fifteenth Amendment because it did not include women. In the 1870s using one of several strategies, Stanton and Anthony took the position that the Fourteenth Amendment's citizenship clause ("all persons born or naturalized are citizens of the United States") embodied the right to the franchise. Any reasonable interpretation of citizenship meant that women already had a right that was inherent and did not have to be bestowed by state or federal government. But when Susan B. Anthony and other members of the National Woman Suffrage Association registered and voted in the presidential election of 1872, their votes were thrown out. And in Rochester, Anthony was arrested and convicted of a federal felony.

By the 1880s, women appreciated just how threatening their enfranchisement was to what Stanton labeled "the ruling aristocracy of sex," as they increasingly argued for the importance of the vote for women as a collective group rather than as a natural right for individuals. Yet the conviction that women were represented in the political process by husbands, fathers, and brothers and therefore did not need the vote withered painfully slowly. An indication of the significance of the vote, this delay occurred because suffrage represented a systemic challenge qualitatively dissimilar from more benign reforms such as opening up higher education to women or improving kindergartens. For most men, political equality with women cut into their households, endangering domestic arrangements crafted in the understanding that while women might exercise limited degrees of domestic feminism within their homes, men were the acknowledged sovereigns in the public domain. The associated notion that women were ill-suited to participate in public life because of their domesticity has never entirely disappeared. But as Ellen DuBois has shown, the eventual enfranchisement of women has made everything political, or, in the slogan of modern feminists, the personal is irrefutably the political.

By the 1890s, the suffrage organizations merged and began the process of bringing the proposed Sixteenth Amendment before congressional committees. In the early years of the new century, women focused on a federal strategy, which required pressuring the United States Congress and organizing a Congressional Committee of the National American Woman Suffrage Association with the sole function of lobbying members of the Senate and House. By 1915, Alice Paul and a group of militant women had formed the National Woman's Party, which employed confrontational tactics in order to embarrass a vulnerable government during World War I and thereby obtain the vote.

Notable among the weaknesses of the suffrage movement was the fact that, until the twentieth century, women had no core of supporters inside the halls of government. Both propertyless males in the early decades of the nineteenth century and slaves in the 1860s had advocates for their rights. But women were the ultimate outsiders in their struggle for political reform. Accordingly, the story of suffrage is often told as the tale of its exceptional leaders, a great heroes approach—in part because of the longevity and authority of these women, their connections to each other, and the lack of research on the movement's supporters, in part because of the paucity of insiders who made their case, as for example, Senator Charles Sumner did for black males. Even the twentieth-century strategy employed by Alice Paul's activist National Woman's Party, with its array of confrontational tactics borrowed from Great Britain, is no exception. It is Alice Paul (and to a lesser extent her lieutenant Lucy Burns) whom we remember, for she was, in the words of one of her loyal followers, "the Party."

Thus, the essays that follow are threaded together with the collaborations of such women as Elizabeth Cady Stanton and her daughter Harriot, Susan B. Anthony, Sojourner Truth, Carrie Catt, and Alice Paul. Yet today's social history concentrates instead on what William Lloyd Garrison, Jr. once called "the great army of silent workers, unknown to fame, and without whom the generals were powerless."[3] Instead of defensive justification of an unfashionable historical approach, students of the suffrage movement should reconsider the importance of hierarchy as a model for suffrage followers in an age, unlike our own, in which even women's speaking in public was challenged by men. Still, for all their appreciation of the ways to use and retain power, these leaders understood that the movement did not depend on them and was comprised of what Anthony called a "galaxy" of women, who must help them in the battle for public opinion.

No doubt that galaxy needs more study. Today there are historians who take the position that there would have been a vibrant woman's movement without the heroes of suffrage who devoted their lives to the movement. That is perhaps true, though also irrelevant and hypothetical. There are also historians, like those who study slavery from the perspective of slave life, who concentrate on women's culture—that is, women's habits, experiences, ways of doing things, life course, and gender consciousness—as the fulcrum of women's history. Suffrage is viewed as outside this approach, although the development of national associations in which women gained the freedom to express, implement, and achieve their own goal deserves incorporation in perspectives that focus on female culture.

This story of the longest, most important reform crusade in American history has been well-told by historians of women in specialized literature. But in a nation that has placed stories of democratic triumph foremost in its historical imagination, the tales of suffrage have not been center stage and the need to integrate the chronicles of suffrage into the narrative of democracy remains. Until recently, the movement has lacked attention in classrooms, and hence in our national heritage, although at its height millions of American women were involved, some engaged in dangerous acts of civil disobedience. Today there has been a revival of interest in popular forums, heralded by a Ken Burns documentary entitled "Not For Ourselves Alone," along with the establishment of a National Parks Center at the birthplace of the suffrage movement in Seneca Falls, New York. Besides this revival of popular attention in the heroes of the suffrage movement, scholars in women's history have gone beyond simply retelling the story of getting the vote. Today historians are undertaking new and exciting studies that sharpen our understanding of the dimensions of this movement and its impact on the American past.

What follows are eleven essays incorporating recent scholarship on the American suffrage movement. They raise new questions about the movement, some controversial and unresolved, while others revise previous interpretations. The authors have taken suffrage history beyond the place where it is often cloistered with associational histories such as antislavery societies. Instead, they have connected it to larger themes not only of democracy but also of slavery, constitutionalism, modernization, and racism. Thus, suffrage becomes the story of nation-building and citizen-making. These essays display as well the lively historical enterprise of understanding the process by which American women got the vote.

As Alison Parker's essay on the origins of the suffrage movement explains, calls for suffrage did not emerge spontaneously. Rather, their origins rested in the ideas and lives of individual women such as Margaret Fuller, Mary Wollstonecraft, and Frances Wright. But as they would be throughout their battle, American women were also influenced by macro-historical forces such as the Industrial Revolution, evangelism, and even the Cult of Domesticity. The latter, which might intuitively seem to consign women to private lives in their homes, was a double-edged mandate. As Parker makes clear, it also included in its prescriptions a special status for women as moral guardians, inevitably concerned and confronting outside their homes public immoralities such as slavery, drunkenness, and prostitution.

Parker also introduces readers to a more nuanced view of the relationship of suffrage women to the antislavery societies of the 1840s. In the past, concern for suffrage has been viewed as a derivative of antislavery, a place where females learned public roles of speaking and organizing along with, through slavery, a metaphor for their condition. Instead, Parker finds women already susceptible to linking their own deprivation with that of slaves. In fact, their contested presence in male-controlled–abolitionist associations where they sought committee posts split the antislavery movement and was a cause of change in antislavery rather than simply a catalyst for woman's rights. Parker also highlights the neglected annual woman's rights conventions of the 1850s that provided a sustaining structure for women beyond informal visiting and letter writing. Finally, Parker exposes the complex relationship of the largely white, middle-class movement with black women, the latter suffering a double dose of discrimination as blacks in antislavery societies and as females in all-male black conventions.

Nell Painter continues this story, concentrating on two African American women in her essay. Sojourner Truth, born a slave in New York state and freed by the 1820s, became an activist in the 1850s, while Frances Ellen Watkins Harper, born a free black woman in Maryland, became a schoolteacher, poet, and abolitionist lecturer in the same decade. Through the lives of these two women, Painter investigates some of the major themes in suffrage history—the fissure in reform circles over whether to support the Fifteenth Amendment which enfranchised only black men, the subsequent split in the postwar suffrage movement into the National Woman Suffrage Association and the American Woman Suffrage Association, and the often troubled relationship of black and white women. Her essay suggests the ways in which the concerns of black women—as represented by Truth and Harper—diverged from those of white middle-class women, who comprised the principal body of suffrage women.

Neither Truth nor Harper separated their sex from their race, but their emphases and styles were different. According to Painter, Harper found especially repellent the growing elitism of Stanton, who believed in an educated electorate and who condemned voting by ignorant black males whom she called "Sambos." The more diplomatic Truth navigated a different course, remaining closely tied to the Stanton-Anthony wing of the movement. Thereby, as Painter deftly suggests, Truth preserved her place in the critical source, the Anthony-Stanton multivolume chronicle, *The History of Woman Suffrage*, and because of this attention, is today the better known of the two women.

Faye Dudden's article on the "New York strategy" takes a fresh look at the meaning of suffrage to women activists. In the past, historians of suffrage have argued that the Civil War represented a hiatus in women's efforts to get the vote. In this interpretation, directed by the self-sacrificing style expected of proper women, they exchanged their campaigns for women's issues for war work and especially abolitionism. Past interpretations of the Civil War period have assumed that women had to win the vote before they could hope to exercise political influence. Dudden rejects this view. Concentrating on a group of New York feminists, Dudden finds women like Stanton and Anthony using the insider politics of lobbying, writing for publication, influencing editors of newspapers, and making public speeches. To make her case, Dudden focuses on several episodes that depict efforts to affect public events without the ballot— the Tenth National Woman's Rights Convention held in New York in 1860, a tour organized by abolitionists in upstate New York in 1860, the organization of the Women's Loyal National League in 1863, a Custom House scandal, and finally an effort to prevent President Lincoln's renomination in 1864. Activities related to these episodes display women as political actors even without the vote before, during, and after the Civil War. If Dudden's view can be exported beyond New York City, then her perspective is further evidence of the need to move beyond the traditional periodization that grafts male-based chronologies such as the Civil War onto women's history.[4]

In making the case for women as unfranchised political actors, Dudden enters a contemporary controversy. Today some historians demote the importance of the vote and argue that women did not need it to make their voice heard on public matters. The corollary is that once obtained it was unimportant. Fueled by our contemporary distaste for electoral politics, such studies offer alternative routes of influence traveled by women who joined benevolent societies, waved handkerchiefs at political conventions, and used other versions of the insider politics Dudden discusses in New York. No doubt parts of this argument are valid; the vote has always been a blunt instrument. No doubt American women exerted some influence through other activities and associations, in the most significant examples from the nineteenth century, the Woman's Christian Temperance Union and the Federation of Women's Clubs. Yet the importance of getting the vote in relation to other mechanisms of public participation should not be an either/or proposition to which we assign relative weights. As many suffragists emphasized, the movement for human justice took many forms. Anthony was well known for her memberships outside the National American Woman Suffrage Association in labor unions, the New York State Teachers' Association, and the Woman's Christian Temperance Union. But she also believed that without the vote that she variously promoted as a marker of democracy, a tool to achieve other reforms, and a banner of citizenship, women were humiliated and oppressed.

Like Dudden, Allison Sneider's article resituates the suffrage movement, moving it from a traditional interpretative location. Earlier suffrage histories climaxed their analyses in the second decade of the twentieth century with studies of the behavior of Congress and the president. Sneider expands our understanding of what suffrage meant to congressmen and senators from the late 1870s, when the suffrage amendment was first introduced to the United States Senate amid howls of laughter, until 1887, when it was finally voted on and defeated by an overwhelming margin. As the suffrage issue interacted with western expansion, it became entangled with congressional considerations of federalism, states' rights, constitutional authority over territories, and the racial attitudes of southern congressmen.

Sneider shows how congressional decisions about Indian citizenship under the Dawes Act, efforts to deal with polygamy and disenfranchised women in Utah, along with the process of bringing Washington to statehood inevitably brought in their wake discussions over which branch of government—the state or the federal government—had authority over granting suffrage. In Sneider's analysis because, as women argued, the right of citizenship included voting and because the national government (not the states) had enfranchised male slaves, naturalized immigrants, and some Indians and then disenfranchised Mormon women, the federal government clearly had the authority to enfranchise women. Yet in an earlier Supreme Court decision the Court had ruled that the United States had no voters. Contemporary readers will appreciate the continuing saliency of whether states or the federal government have the ultimate authority over the vote. But Sneider's concern with respect to suffrage history is the importance of placing the campaign for votes in a larger framework, in this case linking the suffrage issue to other concerns as congressmen chose their priorities.

The divided authority of state and federal governments, so crucial to Sneider's article, reappears in Rebecca Edwards's analysis of suffrage in the West. Historians have long been mystified by the early success of suffrage in the territories and western states, even though the movement's leadership, associations, and even newspapers were located in the East. The first four stars on the suffrage flag were those of the states of Wyoming, Utah, Colorado, and Idaho, and by 1917, nine other western states had enacted full suffrage statutes, compared with two states east of the Mississippi. Viewed as a case study of American democracy, suffrage moved eastward.

Edwards seeks to explain the pronounced regionalism of suffrage by means of a state-by-state analysis. Her conclusions involve special circumstances—sex ratios and gentility in Wyoming, Mormonism in Utah, and electoral competition of third parties such as populism and socialism in Colorado and Idaho. Edwards argues that electoral competition after 1910, when Progressives and Socialists fractured the usual two-party political map during elections and third parties in some states endorsed suffrage, may explain the behavior of eastern states like New York, which gave women the vote before the passage of the Nineteenth Amendment.

Both Sneider's and Edwards's articles move beyond headquarters history to evaluate the suffrage movement in the context of external events, including changes in party politics and congressional behavior. While the first generation of suffrage students told the story as an institutional account of tireless heroism, the new story is richer and more complex. As these essays show, if suffrage history is to be integrated into mainstream accounts of American history, it needs to be linked to other events in our national experience and not studied in isolation.

This does not mean that the movement did not use certain regional strategies. The articles by Edwards, Sneider, and Marjorie Spruill suggest as much. While Edwards concentrates on the West, where suffrage flourished, Spruill focuses on the South, where it did not. Spruill explains how suffrage women—north and south, black and white, but especially white southern women—tried to persuade white southern males of the expediency of votes for women. Here the spotlight is on the continuing debate about the extent to which suffrage women played the race card. Some historians have argued that the critical argument used in the South was that to enfranchise women was to guarantee white supremacy. But other historians, including Anne Firor Scott, have challenged this interpretation, holding that the white supremacist claim, while used, was not central to the arguments for women's voting.

In an article that is carefully tied to the context of suffrage in a changing South, Spruill demonstrates that during the 1890s, southern white males faced the possibility of an interracial coalition of black and white males in the Populist Party. In such an environment votes for women—albeit intelligent and propertied ones—would neutralize black votes. Certainly, as Spruill makes clear, it made sense for leaders of the movement to argue that enfranchising middle-class white women would dilute the strength of any party dependent on black and white farm workers. But by the end of the 1890s, white conservatives had accomplished the disenfranchisement of most black men through poll taxes and literacy tests without giving votes to any women. When neither Congress nor the courts intervened in this dismal period of race relations, the white male South no longer needed white women.

In the next tactical phase of the suffrage battle, national leaders gave up on the South. Southerners, as Carrie Catt once said, would rather commit harikari than vote for any federal suffrage amendment. Now anti-suffrage women picked up the argument of white supremacy. To women who opposed the vote, suffrage was a threat to southern civilization and states rights. According to Spruill, while everyone used the race card, suffrage women used it defensively and less frequently in the early years of the twentieth century. In any case, southern suffrage women might have been progressive on voting, but most were nonetheless southerners infected with the virus of racism that would forever trump women's issues. Like other essays in this volume, Spruill shows how contextualizing suffrage, in this case placing it in a chronological framework linked to attitudes and behaviors toward black males, invites more complex treatments and connects the movement to larger historical processes.

Among the peculiarities of the battle for women's suffrage is the emergence of a group of female opponents, whose story has sometimes been neglected for the more tangible targets of the liquor lobby and bosses of machine politics. Woman suffrage is the only nationwide movement in American history to include some of its intended beneficiaries among its opponents. The latter's objections to suffrage provide useful cues toward understanding the successful inculcation of a dominant culture among women who argued (as some do today) that women did not need voting and office holding to exert influence. Threatened by the possibility of change at the turn of the century, some wealthy women argued that a woman's place was in the home and that fathers, brothers, and husbands were their proper legal and political representatives.

Thomas Jablonsky tells the story of this group of conservative women who founded the National Association Opposed to Woman Suffrage (NAOWS) in 1911. At first, these women had operated in the states, but when the suffrage battle concentrated on a federal amendment, they moved to Washington. Having left the local arena where they might influence their friends and neighbors, members of the NAOWS were less effective. Especially active in the South, anti-suffrage women used the traditional political vocabulary of that region, arguing that any constitutional amendment enfranchising women violated the privileges and powers of states under whose control the United States Constitution had rendered voting. They also effectively played the race card, arguing that woman suffrage in the South would increase the number of black voters proportionately to whites. In the end, the influence of the southern remonstrants (as opponents were called) is uncertain. But certainly their arguments held salience at a time in which virulent racism was endemic in the South. Of the eleven former Confederate states, only Tennessee ratified the amendment in 1920.

There is a special irony in the activities of these female opponents of suffrage. For while they made their crusade in the name of keeping the traditional place of women, they used the same tactics as their opponents. They lobbied, wrote letters to legislators, addressed legislatures, published a newspaper, tore down their opponents' posters and in all their tactics, moved beyond the home and hearth whose sanctity they intended to defend. Even to their use of red as a symbol (the suffragists used yellow), they mimicked their enemies and became the public women they did not want to be, in ironic testimony to the changing circumstances of all American women.

Still their objections raise other concerns such as the degree to which some American women had absorbed the passive, home-based domesticity inculcated by the dominant society. Stepping beyond their doorsteps was improper and unusual, and for the most part the women who were members of NAOWS were the wives of wealthy men who intended to protect their vested interest in a leisured, affluent life style. As is always the case in historical arguments, understanding the antithesis or opposition to suffrage improves an understanding of the thesis.

Among the important leaders of the final thirty years' offensive was Carrie Chapman Catt, the president of NAWSA, first from 1900 to 1904 and then again from 1916 to 1920. In their essay on Catt, Robert Booth Fowler and Spencer Jones tell the story of both her private and public life. Viewed from a larger perspective, Catt's life personifies that of other American heroes who, from childhood, absorbed the injustices against women and, rather than accepting such torments, devoted their lives to reform. The explanation for this sensitivity is often speculative. It lies in the home, perhaps some early childhood experience, or some configuration of genes, or even placement among siblings.

A college graduate despite her parents' objections, Catt also represents a new generation of women born two decades after the pioneers of the movement. Twentieth-century women were more likely to go to the increasing number of colleges that accepted women, in Catt's case, Iowa State University. Like Catt, they were more likely to work outside their homes. By 1910, 140,000 American women attended colleges and universities, representing 40 percent of those in college. By that same date, women were 20 percent of the American labor force. These women represented a pool of capable supporters and workers, who considered suffrage an obvious and tardy entitlement in a democratic society. Catt, for example, had learned to debate at college, and her skill as a speaker was only one of the talents she brought to the final suffrage offensive. Certainly the differences between her personal life and those of the pioneers reveal external transformations in American society that influenced all women.

Other personal experiences in Catt's life were familiar to American women of every generation, especially widowhood. Catt was widowed twice and had to support herself after her first husband's death; she was sexually harassed when she worked on a newspaper, and certainly this experience made her more sensitive to women's issues. Indicative of her growing independence was the arrangement with her second husband that she was to have time to pursue public endeavors, a commitment that soon focused on votes for women. Moreover, like other women who juggled commitments because of family responsibilities, her suffrage work was episodic. Obligations to her relatives forced her to retire periodically to take care of sick relatives.

While Catt's biography introduces themes well known to other white middle-class women in the late nineteenth and early twentieth centuries, it is her leadership of NAWSA that makes her a memorable subject for *Votes for Women*. Almost single-handedly she modernized NAWSA, shifting its tactics to what she predicted would be a "Winning Plan." She insisted that the organization give up its state-based strategy and concentrate instead on the passage of a federal amendment in Congress; she employed

advertising techniques and negotiated the purchase of a newspaper, succeeding through these tactics in turning the association into an efficient
publicity machine. Unlike her predecessors, she spent as much time ad-
ministering an organization of over one million members as traveling,
although she did a lot of that as well.

Throughout, Catt's unwavering commitment to a federal amendment
as the winning strategy defined the last stages of the struggle for suffrage.
Indeed, she became as single-minded as Susan B. Anthony in her focus
on suffrage, refusing to compromise NAWSA through any controversial
endorsements of the international peace movement or reforming the divorce laws. As a tactician and strategist, Catt stands as one of the new
women of the twentieth century, but her leadership also returns us to the
presidential model of suffrage history—from Stanton and Anthony to
Anna Howard Shaw to Catt.

Of all the leaders of the suffrage movement, Catt was the most engaged
in global suffrage work because she was briefly the president of the International Suffrage Association. But there were other American women who
saw the vote as a universal claim and sensed the power that solidarity
across national boundaries could provide in an age of rapidly improving
transportation and communication. Investigating the cross-fertilization
of the Anglo-American movements, Christine Bolt in her essay on "America
and the Pankhursts" probes the connections between the legendary
Pankhurst family of Great Britain and the Americans. The visits of mother
Emmeline and her daughters Sylvia and Christabel to the United States
reveal both the similarities and the differences between English and
American suffragists.

Both groups benefited from the contact. The English women spoke to
larger audiences at enthusiastic meetings in New York, Boston, and Chicago and earned more money than was possible at home. Representing
the most radical wing of the English movement, the Pankhursts enjoyed
a respite from their harassment by the authorities. Introducing themselves
as "freedom fighters and patriots," the Pankhursts, who thought the
American movement in a "curious state of quiescence," instructed women
in the uses of militancy. They taught Americans about the importance of
holding the party in power, no matter which party it was, responsible for
failure to achieve suffrage. They informed American women about the
importance of the spectacle, a highly developed British propaganda tool
involving the use of parades and pageants. It was not so much that activists had not known about such methods and occasionally used them; it
was rather that the Pankhursts emphasized their importance.

Still one export—that of militancy and specifically acts of violence against public property—reminded Americans of their differences with their English cousins. While Alice Paul, who had joined the Pankhurst organization while she was in England, did adopt picketing, obstruction, and hunger striking, the mainstream members of NAWSA did not. Somewhere in the behavioral gap between setting fires to property and picketing the White House rests an understanding of how comparing transnational suffrage movements sharpens a national subject.

In her article on a blood descendant of the suffrage movement, Harriot Stanton Blatch, who was the daughter of Elizabeth Cady Stanton, Ellen DuBois offers an intriguing perspective on changes in strategy through a case study of the suffrage campaign in New York State from 1913 to 1915. This campaign also reveals the difficulty imposed by the separation of powers within state governments, as suffragists in this instance first had to persuade both houses of the state legislature to pass a law authorizing a referendum on woman suffrage. Then they had to spend months campaigning through a large state with sixty-two counties in order to persuade male voters to support the referendum. Still, given its size and location, Blatch reasoned that victory in New York would be worth the effort and expense.

Like Catt, Blatch represented a new American woman. She went to college, traveled, and had international contacts—eventually in her case, even an English husband. Blatch also understood the importance of the new advertising techniques in a mass consumer culture, and her application of them in an in-your-face-style suggested transformations in gender relationships, at least on the part of some American women, by the twentieth century.

Blatch's commitment to working women introduces us to the issue of class in the suffrage movement. She attempted to organize self-supporting women into suffrage groups, insisting on holding events during lunch breaks for those who worked. Sometimes the campaign for votes for women is dismissed as an effort by upper-class women, who want the vote in order to clean up American politics. Such a perspective misinterprets the efforts of suffragists like Blatch, who intended to make the suffrage movement the arm of all American women. Certainly Blatch, her mother, and Susan B. Anthony were initially committed to encouraging working women to join the suffrage movement. In the latter's newspaper, *The Revolution*, they argued for an activist state that would intervene on behalf of labor, male and female. Forty years later, Blatch organized parades with tradeswomen and garment workers marching in special units carrying banners proclaiming "Women Need Votes to End Sweat Shops." While she harbored irritations about the fact that an ignorant German male who could not speak English and knew nothing about the United States would have the vote before she did, she nevertheless fought for the inclusion of immigrant women in her suffrage association. Nor was she willing, like Catt, to focus entirely on suffrage.

The larger issue here is Blatch's understanding of the meaning of the vote. In what she appreciated as the last of the state campaigns before leaders turned their efforts to the passage of a federal amendment, the right to vote was a political entitlement, but its ends were to effect social and economic change. To dissever what suffrage women considered their natural right from the use of the vote for social and economic change, as is sometimes done today in women's history, is to mistake the true synthesis that is the essential meaning of votes for women.

In the final essay in *Votes for Women*, Linda Ford focuses on Alice Paul and the tactics of nonviolent protest used by her National Woman's Party. Ford argues that such militancy was critical for the last step in the final offensive for suffrage. Only because suffragists took to the streets and picketed in front of the White House and in turn were assaulted, harassed, jailed, and tortured through force feedings was public opinion stimulated to support suffrage. Especially during World War I, the contradictions within a supposedly democratic government that denied half its people the right to vote became embarrassingly obvious. Paul's actions, as well as her strategy of holding the party in power responsible for the delay in suffrage, publicized an injustice made especially ironic during a war against an autocratic government. Finally, in January 1918, President Wilson, who had long argued that suffrage was a state matter, endorsed the national amendment and began to use his influence on Democrats in Congress. But, according to Ford, presidential support came only after the deeds of women were employed as propaganda, and only after the authorities used violence as a form of punishment against women.

Ford's article summarizes some of the themes of this volume. Among them are the connections of American suffragists to an international movement, specifically in this case to the Pankhursts, whose radical Women's Social and Political Union was in turn influenced by Susan B. Anthony's visit to London in 1900. The personal links of the suffrage leaders and their power within their organizations are also on display in this article. For example, Alice Paul and Lucy Burns, during their years in London, had been members of the Pankhursts' organization. Paul also admired

Susan B. Anthony because in 1872 she had taken the radical step of voting and being arrested.

The civil disobedience organized by Paul and Burns has, like the suffrage movement itself, become invisible to Americans who recall and
admire the nonviolent resistance of the civil rights movement of the 1960s.
Who remembers the Nights of Terror in January 1917, when the police
permitted crowds of men to beat up female picketers in front of the White
House, then arrested the women, hit them with sticks, and hurled them
into cells in the Occoquan jail? Who remembers the use of force-feeding
when American women engaged in hunger strikes after the authorities
refused their demand to be treated as political prisoners or that Paul was
confined to a mental ward? Throughout this state-sanctioned violence,
Paul, born a Quaker, insisted, as Martin Luther King would later, on nonviolence. Meanwhile, more and more Americans were shocked by the treatment of women, whose placards in front of the White House quoted
Wilson's own wartime injunction: "We shall fight for democracy and the
right for all to have a voice in their government." As is often the case, the
violence of government officials provided a backlash of support for the
suffrage movement.

Through the story of Alice Paul's National Woman's Party, Ford unrav-
els some of the ideological tensions forever present in the suffrage movement as to how to gain the support of the most men and antagonize the
fewest. Paul, like many suffragists, believed that women were like men—
part of the mythic "We the People." But women, according to Paul, were
also different from men and would bring to the ballot booth their love of
peace, their interest in social reform, and their commitment to issues
overlooked by men. In this essay, as throughout *Votes for Women*, women
see gaining the vote as an expression of their humanity, as well as a way
to utilize power in a different way from men. This tension between equality
and the maternalist impulse derived from women's agendas grew out of
the suffragist's success in forging women into a self-conscious group with
a shared demand. For Americans today, the unresolved legacy of the suffrage campaign is the application to public policy of the conviction that
women are equal to men as human beings, but different from them as
females are to males.

While these eleven essays develop new issues, they confirm the importance of the suffrage movement both as a historical topic and by im-
plication as an on-going, contemporary process with different layers of
meaning. From the vantage point of her own pioneering struggle to bring

women's history out of the shadows, Anne Firor Scott contemplates the difference the vote has made. She provides a useful overview of suffrage as a historical subject, as a practical empowerment, and as an effective instrument of policymaking.

Today some of the predictions of women who never had the right to vote have been enacted by those who do. More women than men go to the polls, and women reveal statistically significant voting patterns from men in their partisan choices and in their attention to various issues. The meaning of suffrage to our national history will forever be unfinished from the perspective of historians who continue to find new stories. The women of the suffrage movement knew they were making history and so kept their records carefully. On another level, the unflinching assertion of previous generations of American women that the vote is the fundamental transaction within a democratic society remains a constant political reenactment for our present and future.

NOTES

1. Carrie Catt and Nettie Shuler, *Woman Suffrage and Politics* (New York: Scribners, 1923), 107.

2. Bonnie Anderson, *Joyous Greetings: The First International Women's Movement, 1830–1860* (New York: Oxford University Press, 2000), ix.

3. Quoted in Julie Roy Jeffrey, *The Great Army of Abolitionism: Ordinary Women in the Antislavery Movement* (Chapel Hill: University of North Carolina Press, 1998), 1.

4. Joan Kelly-Gadol, "The Social Relations of the Sexes," *Signs* 1 (Summer, 1976), 809–23.

1

THE CASE FOR REFORM ANTECEDENTS FOR THE WOMAN'S RIGHTS MOVEMENT

Alison M. Parker

The woman's rights movement and the demand for woman suffrage emerged in the first half of the nineteenth century from a variety of other movements. Suffrage became the primary goal of the woman's rights movement during the 1850s and remained so until women finally achieved the right to vote in 1920. In the early 1800s, however, it was not necessarily clear that suffrage would become the preeminent issue. Radical intellectuals and working-class women articulated concerns over the roles and rights of women, but often did so without demanding woman suffrage.

The Industrial Revolution, the second Great Awakening, and changing ideas of women's role in society combined to inspire many Americans, particularly in the North and Midwest, to participate in reform movements. The evangelical revivals of the antebellum era brought more women into reform movements by emphasizing women's greater piety and moral rectitude. Middle-class white women, in particular, benefited from the increasingly mercantilist and capitalist economy, but unlike their fathers and husbands, were ostensibly protected from the crass and corrupt business world by their confinement in the domestic sphere. The ensuing Cult of True Womanhood, or the Cult of Domesticity, seemingly limited women's role to the home, wherein they would nurture their husbands and children by inculcating piety and good citizenship. Although conservative in its origins and expectations, the Cult of True Womanhood also led women into moral reform. Because male religious,

education, and business leaders agreed that women were naturally morally purer than men, some women concluded that they must be able to
apply their nurturing, protective instincts to society as a whole.

Women first organized themselves together for charity work such as
feeding hungry widows, protecting wage-earning women from vice, re-
habilitating ("saving") prostitutes, and reforming prisons and insane asy-
lums. All this work moved women from the domestic into the public,
political sphere. Under the rubric of True Womanhood, pious middle-class
women could be found in tenements, in front of houses of prostitution,
inspecting prisons, and entering legislators' offices to demand change.
Benevolent women were not intent on challenging their place in society,
but a few found themselves believing that they could never solve the
problems of an urbanizing and industrializing America without the right
to vote. Corrupt or impious politicians would be defeated, some believed,
if only women had the vote.

A wide variety of reform causes gained strength in the first several decades of the nineteenth century. Temperance, for instance, was a response
to dangerously high rates of alcohol consumption, growing public awareness of a link between alcohol and men's domestic violence, and an increasing need on the part of employers for dependable, efficient workers.
Some laborers decided to limit their use of alcohol in order to become more
dependable at work and more responsible at home. A temperance movement of middle-class evangelicals arose, while workers formed separate
temperance societies, calling themselves Washingtonians. Women participated in the temperance movement, claiming a right to public activism that was based less on concerns about women's equality or females
with drinking problems than on the consequences of male drinking on
women and children. At first, women simply appealed to men to stop
drinking for the sake of their families. By the 1850s, however, some female temperance activists argued that only when women joined together
to secure their equal rights would they be truly protected from the evils
of alcohol. In this way, temperance activism could lead a participant to a
woman's rights and pro-suffrage stance.

Some social reforms were meant to improve women's status. After the
American Revolution, arguments for a basic education for girls met with
comparatively little resistance. What became more difficult was to secure
for females the opportunity to have the equivalent of a high school and
especially a college education. Those who supported higher education for
women generally believed in women's equal natural rights and intellectual capabilities. Unlike some other moral reforms, demands for equal

education more directly challenged women's subordinate status. If women were able to receive college and university educations, they might also be able to pursue professional careers. This demand was a direct challenge to women's place in the home. For this reason, equal education was a radical reform that attracted the attention of Mary Wollstonecraft, Frances Wright, and Margaret Fuller, all of whom believed that equal education would do more to improve women's status in society than voting rights.

Similarly, wage-earning women articulated a set of grievances centering on women's inequality at work without explicitly demanding suffrage. From unequal wages to unsafe and unsanitary working conditions and limited job options, working women demanded change. Although the woman's rights conventions of the 1850s featured speeches on the concerns of and conditions facing wage-earning women and although each convention established or heard from a Committee on Industry, the agenda of working-class women was less prominent in the movement overall. Instead, married women's property rights and woman suffrage were the goals that were most assertively promoted by the middle-class women who dominated the movement for woman's rights.

Of all the reforms of the antebellum era, radical abolitionism had the most compelling message for those women who participated in it and then organized the woman's rights movement. Those women who were drawn to abolitionism found a radical movement that spoke of freedom from oppression, of natural inalienable rights, and of the possibility of immediate redemption from sin. These arguments were compelling to women who, moreover, observed parallels between the legal condition of slaves and women. Once they began participating in the antislavery movement, women developed the rhetorical and practical skills that enabled them to create a woman's rights movement. Some historians have suggested that woman's rights activists did not adequately separate themselves from the abolitionist movement and so were unable to develop a clear enough agenda, organizational structure, or separate membership.

By the time of the Civil War and certainly in the postbellum years, woman suffrage came to be seen as the best way to solve a variety of perceived social ills, including marital inequity, unfair divorce laws, wage inequality, and intemperance. Indeed, some historians suggest that after the Civil War, woman's rights activists forsook work on a broader range of reform concerns in order to concentrate on suffrage. Susan B. Anthony, in particular, argued that all other reform issues of concern to women should be given less attention. She and others believed that once women won the right to vote, they would instantly force the passage of laws that they had been demanding for decades. Other reforms may have been sacrificed by activists who focused on suffrage, but the vote also provided women with a clear common goal and an agenda that was compatible with both assertions of natural equal rights and equal citizenship in the American republic.

Dispersed calls for woman's rights coalesced into an organized movement in 1848 with the first woman's rights convention at Seneca Falls, New York. Yet the movement had not developed overnight. Among the important forerunners were two British intellectuals, Mary Wollstonecraft and Frances Wright. Wollstonecraft wrote *A Vindication of the Rights of Woman* (1792), in which she argued that women were rational beings who should be able to be educated, earn their own livings, and develop their characters "regardless of the distinction of sex."[1] Wollstonecraft was committed to women's free and equal education. Her book was distributed in America and later publicized by several important activists, including Frances Wright.

In the late 1820s, Frances Wright, founder of the antislavery communitarian experiment, Nashoba, became the first woman to speak to large audiences of men and women on secular and political topics in the United States. Wright's public speeches were the most significant source of her fame. Thousands of people came, in part for the novel and "sensational" phenomenon of hearing a woman speaker and in part because of the attraction of her utopian rhetoric and free thought. Wright was an early proponent of the notion that marriage was a form of coercive bondage for women, who were thereby denied the right to inheritances, wages, and joint guardianship of their children. Like many antebellum reformers, Wright focused on marriage because it was simultaneously a legal institution, a religious commitment, and a powerful site of human emotions. Wright favored replacing current laws on marriage and illegitimacy (also biased against women, in her opinion) with what she termed nonlegalized bonds of "generous attachments." Partnerships based on mutual respect as well as love, she insisted, need not be officially regulated or sanctioned by either legal or religious authorities. She advocated improving education and professional training for women while protecting them from the legal inequalities of marriage and the superstitions of the church. Wright lobbied hard for the Workingmen's Party. Frances Wright never explicitly applied her argument that women and men have equal and natural rights to the idea that women should be given the right to vote. Perhaps this is because she participated in party politics and political debates without hesitation and saw herself as a powerful public speaker who could mobilize large numbers of male voters to support her favored Workingmen's Party. Her silence on the subject of women's political equality through voting rights also suggests just how unthinkable woman suffrage was.

Frances Wright's name became an epithet for many social conservatives and was used to pressure women to confine themselves to the domestic sphere. By attacking organized religion and the revivalism sweeping the United States as irrational, as well as by attacking marriage and prescribed sex roles, Wright epitomized to her critics the dangerous instability of free thought and woman's rights. Because she was a woman, Wright's public speaking was considered improper and immodest. Her detractors not only called Wright a "Red Harlot" but also labeled any woman who dared to attend her lectures as impure. In spite of or because of her notoriety, some other women held on to the spirit of Wright as a daring activist woman. In the 1880s, when Elizabeth Cady Stanton, Susan B. Anthony, and Matilda J. Gage wrote the *History of Woman Suffrage*, the first volume featured a portrait of Frances Wright on the frontispiece. Lauding her as a pioneer, they explained that "her radical ideas of theology, slavery and the social degradation of woman, now generally accepted by the best minds of the age, were then denounced by both press and pulpit, and maintained by her at the risk of her life."[2]

Woman's rights ideas developed not only from radical women intellectuals like Wollstonecraft and Wright but also from the demands of working women. Women from rural farm families entered into wage-earning work in New England textile mills in the 1820s. Their experiences highlighted the unequal wages and restricted job openings available to women. By the 1830s, factory women were experiencing work speed-ups, longer hours, and wage cuts. In spite of the fact that women were stereotyped as unable to organize, female mill workers did go on strike, marching in processions through the streets. Pride in themselves as native-born "daughters of freemen" inspired them to form associations to fight for better working conditions and hours. At the Lowell textile mills in Massachusetts, women created a union in 1845—the Lowell Female Labor Reform Association. Women workers found that tactics such as signing pledges vowing not to work on an extra loom (which would increase their work load and cause more accidents) could pressure factory owners to cancel these work speed-ups. Hoping to improve working conditions, wage-earning women also testified before legislatures considering protective labor laws. Their concerns for the rights of working women found a place in the woman's rights movement.

For middle-class women interested in respectability and independence, who wanted or needed to earn a wage and did not want to work as a private governess, teaching was the only real option. As public education expanded for boys and girls in the North and Midwest during the antebellum era, women began to be hired as teachers—mostly as a cost-cutting measure. Thus, as more women received educations and entered the teaching profession, salaries fell. Male teachers continued to dominate the leadership of the professional organizations and sometimes questioned why teachers were not as respected as other professionals. Susan B. Anthony was a schoolteacher for over a decade and fought against women's unequal wages and status within the profession. As she explained at an 1853 teachers' meeting:

> Do you not see that so long as society says a woman is incompetent to be a lawyer, minister, or doctor, but has ample ability to be a teacher, that every man of you who chooses this profession tacitly acknowledges that he has no more brains than a woman? And this, too, is the reason that teaching is a less lucrative profession, as here men must compete with the cheap labor of woman.[3]

Unequal pay was clearly a problem facing women, but many woman's rights advocates argued that a more fundamental and persistent problem blocking women's full political citizenship and wage-earning opportunities was their inferior educational opportunities. Dr. Harriot K. Hunt of Boston, for instance, sent a formal protest along with her taxes every year, in which she pointed out that free higher educational opportunities were available for males but not for females, showing that "the rights and interests of the female part of the community are sometimes forgotten or disregarded in consequence of their deprivation of political rights.[4] Attempts to provide better educations for girls and young women began with Emma Willard's Troy Female Seminary, founded in 1821. Willard's school was praised by Stanton and Anthony as the first to include "higher mathematics" for girls.[5] Oberlin College in Ohio opened in 1835 and accepted women and blacks, but women were not able to take a full course of study until the 1840s. Abolitionist and woman's rights activist Lucy Stone was among the first to graduate from Oberlin with a regular (not a partial or "literary") degree in 1847.

Among the leading intellectuals who strongly supported women's access to classical higher education was Transcendentalist Margaret Fuller.

She herself had received a private classical training from her father at home. In order to encourage women's intellectual development, Fuller initiated a series of "conversations" where women would meet to discuss important philosophical, literary, cultural, and political issues. In her 1844 book, *Woman in the Nineteenth Century*, she argued for women being able to hold any job, including political office: "We would have every arbitrary barrier thrown down. We would have every path laid open to Woman as freely as to Man."[6] Fuller connected women's access to education and occupations to real freedom. She further observed that both white women and slaves were restricted by unjust laws, a parallel that would also be drawn by women in the abolitionist movement.

Arguably, slavery was the most significant moral and religious issue facing antebellum American society. Abolitionist William Lloyd Garrison's call for the immediate emancipation of slaves appealed to evangelical women already active in moral reform, who believed that through emancipation they could help redeem both oppressed slaves and sinful slave-owners. Empathy and pity for their "enslaved sisters" gave white and free black women a rationale for becoming involved in antislavery activism. Female abolitionists condemned slavery as inherently disruptive of family ties between parents and children as well as wives and husbands. It was women's moral duty, they reasoned, to fight against an institution that denied slave women their rightful roles of wife and mother. Attending church in greater numbers than men and prizing their religious and moral sanctity, antebellum women justified their fight against slavery as a fight against sin.

Abolitionist women embraced the ideals of freedom and liberty represented by the American Revolution and its founding documents, arguing that the legal institution of slavery challenged these ideals and so needed to be abolished. In spite of the fact that male abolitionists first recommended that women simply engage in antislavery arguments with family and friends, women who put a priority on efficiency soon sought to organize for collective action. Women joined the American Anti-Slavery Society (established in 1833), for instance, in separate local female auxiliaries, of which there were more than one hundred by 1838. Two of the foremost women's abolitionist associations were the Boston Female Anti-Slavery Society (1832), founded by Maria Weston Chapman, and the Philadelphia Female Anti-Slavery Society (1833), led by the Quaker minister Lucretia Mott.

Just as white and black women were excluded from membership in the American Anti-Slavery Society until 1840, free black men did not allow women to participate in their conventions until the 1850s; even then, their presence was strongly discouraged. These national conventions promoted abolition and discussed economic and social problems facing free blacks. In an early attempt to challenge the subordinate role of women within the African American community, Maria Stewart, a free black woman, dared to speak publicly in Boston in the early 1830s. Advocating abolition, economic and educational self-sufficiency, and better educations for girls, she boldly urged blacks to "boycott white business . . . and [sue] for your rights."[7] In her speeches, Stewart asked:

> What if I am a woman; is not the God of ancient times the God of these modern days? Did he not raise up Deborah to be a mother and a judge in Israel? Did not Queen Esther save the lives of the Jews? . . . If such women . . . once existed, be no longer astonished then, my brethren and friends, that God at this eventful period should raise up your own females to strive by their example, both in public and in private, to assist those who are endeavoring to stop the strong current of prejudice that flows so profusely against us at the present.[8]

Her speaking career was short, however. Stewart gave it up in 1833, dismayed that her audiences proved unwilling to accept women's equality or political leadership.

Because of contemptuous treatment from both black men and white women, black women generally formed their own organizations. Free black women organized the first female antislavery society in the nation in 1832. They also provided support for their families and each other through antiracism initiatives and self-help programs, such as insurance and charity work, within their communities. Beneficial societies helped them pay for funeral expenses or the loss of a husband's wages. Free black women held fairs and bazaars to meet fundraising needs for antislavery and Underground Railroad efforts. They also supported the Colored Free Produce Society and boycotted slave-produced goods.

Women organized antislavery fairs to raise money, working together in each others' homes to produce goods to sell at the fairs. These activities were controversial, especially when black and white women worked together. Abolitionist women distributed tracts and newspapers and engaged in debates with other citizens, including the clergy, about the rightful place of women in the abolitionist movement. Those women who worked in the Underground Railroad learned to take serious risks in work that was physically hazardous and emotionally trying. Grassroots activism led to national Anti-Slavery Conventions of American Women, which took place in the late 1830s. These conventions drew together hundreds of women from many states, inspiring them to engage in more antislavery work. Women's antislavery activities led to charges that they were engaging in an unwomanly meddling in politics. Criticism often focused on the right of women to speak in public.

Generating much controversy in and out of the movement, a few women who became nationally prominent abolitionists came to view the inequalities of slaves and women (white and black) as interrelated. As Susan B. Anthony and Elizabeth Cady Stanton later observed: "Sarah and Angelina Grimké and Abby Kelley, in advocating liberty for the black race, were early compelled to defend the right of free speech for themselves. They had the double battle to fight against tyranny of sex and color at the same time."[9] Sarah and Angelina Grimké were sisters from a wealthy South Carolinian slaveholding family who became ardent abolitionists. In 1836, Angelina Grimké wrote *An Appeal to the Christian Women of the Southern States*, arguing that "I know that you do not make the laws, but I also know that you are the wives and mothers, the sisters and daughters of those who do. . . . You can speak on this subject. . . . You can act on this subject. . . . Try to persuade your husband, father, brothers and sons that *slavery is a crime against God and man*."[10] The Grimké sisters argued for equality within a religious context, pointing out that women and men were equally the children of God, who had endowed them with the same moral duties and also the right to carry out those duties.[11] Calls to activism that came out of a concern for morality, for the oppressed slaves, and for religious duty were generally more appealing to women than the natural rights approach of radicals like Frances Wright. But as they found themselves thwarted by prejudice against women's public activism, some female abolitionists moved toward the fight for woman's rights.

In 1837, Sarah and Angelina Grimké went on an extended antislavery lecture tour, daring to be the first women to speak widely to mixed audiences of women and men since Frances Wright. The Grimkés' position as respectable ladies did not spare them from sustained attack. The Council of Congregationalist Ministers of Massachusetts issued two Pastoral Letters in 1837 that condemned women's participation in public, political issues: "The power of woman is her dependence. . . . But when she assumes the place and tone of man as a public reformer . . . she yields the power which God has given her for her protection, and her character becomes unnatural."[12] Sarah and Angelina Grimké learned from this attack that "we are placed very unexpectedly in a very trying situation, in the fore-front of an entirely new contest—a contest for the *rights of woman* as a moral, intelligent and responsible being."[13] Angelina Grimké in 1838 argued that "it is a woman's right to have a voice in all the laws and regu-lations by which she is to be governed."[14] At the grassroots level, white and black abolitionist women's most important work was conducting door-to-door petition drives. Petitions were a form of political action that confronted politicians in the state or federal legislatures with abolitionist demands; petitioning thus involved women in mass democratic politics. Clarifying the links between white women's oppression and the oppres-sion of the slaves, Angelina Grimké spoke before the Massachusetts State Legislature in 1838 in support of women's antislavery petitions, arguing that they were an important way for women who did not have the right to vote to make political claims on the government.[15]

The Grimkés' assertions of women's rightful place in politics and aboli-tionism generated a debate within the American Anti-Slavery Society about whether or not women should be able to serve on committees. The con-troversy focused on Abby Kelley, a Quaker who in the mid-1830s became the corresponding secretary of the Female Anti-Slavery Society in Lynn, Massachusetts, and a fundraiser for the "Band of Seventy," a group of male agents (and the Grimké sisters) hired by the American Anti-Slavery Society to promote abolition. Kelley gave her first public speech to a mixed audi-ence at an 1838 convention of antislavery women in Philadelphia. As she spoke, rioters screamed, threw rocks at the windows, and before the con-ference ended, destroyed the building. Angry mobs frequently tried to dis-rupt abolitionist women's meetings, especially those composed of whites and blacks together. Speaking not only against slavery but against racial prejudice as well, Kelley became the target of a battle over the place of women and women's rights within the antislavery movement. When the New England Anti-Slavery Society allowed women to be members and par-ticipants at conventions, Kelley spoke at its convention and was appointed to a prominent committee. Now very visible, she attracted the wrath of conservative ministers within the abolitionist movement. During the American Anti-Slavery Convention of 1840, the chair nominated Kelley to the business committee. Consequently, about 300 men walked out in pro-test and formed the new American and Foreign Anti-Slavery Society, which forbade women from holding office and also refused office to Garrisonian radicals who rejected party politics. Radical Garrisonian women moved furthest into the public sphere by speaking to audiences of men and women and by holding office in mixed (male and female) abolitionist societies.[16]

By the 1850s, abolitionist women's activism and political commitments led many of them to participate in political party rallies and attend propaganda lectures, particularly of the Free Soil, Liberty, and Republican Parties. They made banners supporting the parties, "acted" in *tableaux vivants*, and published articles, songs, and poetry in support of political parties and candidates. Also by the 1850s, antislavery women publicly confronted those religious authorities who lacked commitment to or even opposed antislavery, sometimes breaking with their ministers and churches to form antislavery churches. Ironically, deeply religious abolitionist women doing work that they considered to be just and holy found themselves attacked and condemned by male ministers for stepping outside their domestic sphere. Those ministers and some male abolitionists who rejected women's participation inadvertently fueled women's demands for equal participation within the antislavery movement and ultimately within American society as a whole.

In many ways, woman's rights activism derived from the antislavery movement. Looking back, Stanton and Anthony argued that

> above all other causes of the "Woman Suffrage Movement," was the Anti-Slavery struggle. . . . In the early Anti-Slavery conventions, the broad principles of human rights were so exhaustively discussed, justice, liberty, and equality, so clearly taught, that the women who crowded to listen, readily learned the lesson of freedom for themselves, and early began to take part in the debates and business affairs of all associations.[17]

Abolitionist women went from empathizing with the plight of female slaves to connecting the oppression of slaves to a growing awareness of their own oppression. The controversy over their full participation in the antislavery movement further highlighted to women activists their marginalized and unequal status in a movement that was ostensibly fighting for freedom. Historian Ellen DuBois suggests that many women entered the antislavery movement already aware of their oppression as women, expecting the movement to acknowledge and resist women's inferior social and political status. As a New York activist, Emily Collins, explained:

> All through the Anti-Slavery struggle, every word of denunciation of the wrongs of the Southern slave, was, I felt, equally applicable to the wrongs of my own sex. Every argument for the emancipation of the colored man, was equally one for that of woman; and

I was surprised that all Abolitionists did not see the similarity in
the condition of the two classes.[18]

Abolitionist women, who later formed the core of woman's rights activists, brought to the woman's rights movement an ability to organize
and express their discontent in political and public ways. Although women
from other moral reform causes such as temperance also moved into
woman's rights activism, antislavery women were more prepared to join
an unpopular cause and to anticipate and handle the hostility they received from the general public. Radical abolitionism arguably took more
courage—more of a break from convention—to join. This was necessary
for those who would argue publicly for woman's rights.

As white and black women participated in abolitionism and other reform
causes, they became increasingly aware of the legal inequalities facing
women. During the antebellum era, married women, in particular, were
treated unequally and unfairly by state laws that kept their property and
their earnings from them and that penalized women far more heavily in
divorce cases by refusing to allow women to be the primary custodians of
their own children. Historian Michael Grossberg points out that in the
nineteenth century, although the American judiciary gradually began to
grant more women custody of their children in divorce cases, women
reformers' attempts formally to change legal statutes met with public resistance. The judiciary, he suggests, could assess the character of the parents in each case without admitting a broad assault on the normative
patriarchal family.[19]

Married women's legal status as "femme couverts," which meant that
married women's legal independence was erased and subsumed under their
husbands, was publicly challenged by Ernestine Rose, a Polish Jewish
immigrant and woman's rights activist. In 1836, Rose presented the first
petition to the New York Legislature in support of a Married Woman's
Property Act that had been introduced by radical lawyer and legislator
Thomas Hertell. With great effort, she found five women willing to sign
the petition with her. The bill was reintroduced each year, and each year
Rose submitted more petitions in support of it. Soon, she was aided by
Paulina Wright (Davis) and Elizabeth Cady Stanton. From 1840 on, Rose,
Stanton, and Wright appeared before legislative committees to argue in
favor of the Married Woman's Property Act. The New York legislature finally passed a limited bill in 1848 that protected the property that women
brought into their marriages and inherited after. It most impacted rich
women and was considered a limited victory because it did not allow

women to keep any wages they might earn while married. However modest this seemed to activists, who would initiate another campaign to strengthen it, this type of legislative reform was also threatening and radical because it was based on the notion that mothers and fathers, wives and husbands, were equal.

A preeminent leader of the woman's rights movement had been aware even as a child of women's inferior legal and social status. Elizabeth Cady Stanton was raised in upstate New York and was allowed by her father, a judge, to be tutored in a classical education. He also allowed her to sit in his law office and listen to him discuss cases with his clients. It was there that she first realized that married women did not have legal rights to their earnings, their property, or their children. Elizabeth Cady Stanton attended Emma Willard's Female Seminary, yet her desire to attend college remained unfulfilled since none at the time admitted women. Her early introduction to the problems facing women was magnified when she attended the World Anti-Slavery Convention in 1840 as the new wife of abolitionist delegate Henry Stanton. She observed as the convention decided not to seat the women delegates sent from the United States and then sat in solidarity with them where they had been relegated—behind a curtain in the gallery. There, Stanton met and was influenced by Lucretia Mott, the abolitionist and Quaker minister. Disturbed by women's inequitable treatment, even within a radical movement, they talked of one day holding a woman's rights convention in the United States.

Over the next eight years, Stanton had several children and moved with her husband to the small manufacturing town of Seneca Falls, New York. Isolated and burdened by child bearing, child care, and housework, Stanton grew discontent. When she and Lucretia Mott met again in July 1848, they found themselves ready to organize a convention on "the social, civil, and religious rights of woman." Eager to explore the status of women and urge progressive change, several hundred attended the Seneca Falls Woman's Rights Convention. Ironically, although both Lucretia Mott and Elizabeth Cady Stanton spoke, out of prevailing notions of propriety, men conducted most of the meeting.

To provide a focus for the Seneca Falls convention, Stanton wrote a Declaration of Sentiments that was modeled on the Declaration of Independence. In it, she argued that

the history of mankind is a history of repeated injuries and usurpations on the part of man toward woman, having in direct object the establishment of an absolute tyrany over her. . . . He has never permitted her to exercise her inalienable right to the elective franchise. He has compelled her to submit to laws, in the formation of which she has no voice. . . .

Having deprived her of this first right of a citizen, the elective franchise, thereby leaving her without representation in the halls of legislation, he has oppressed her on all sides. He has made her, if married, in the eye of the law, civilly dead.[20]

Critiquing the legal status of antebellum women, the Declaration of Sentiments asserted women's equality as citizens and then listed the grievances that women had with their current status in the republic. The Declaration of Sentiments included a list of resolutions, each of which was proposed separately to the convention for debate. The resolutions called on women to question laws that restricted their rights, educations, earnings, abilities, and civil status. Women, it asserted, must be able to speak publicly and act freely in religious work and in their churches. One resolution criticized the double standard of sexual morality that existed for men and women. More specifically challenging women's place in society, another demanded that women have equal access to "the various trades, professions, and commerce." The most controversial resolution stated that "it is the duty of the women of this country to secure to themselves their sacred right to the elective franchise." Women's lack of the right to vote was given a causal value—other complaints followed from this denial of a basic right of citizenship.

The Declaration of Sentiments was not only in keeping with the language of the Declaration of Independence but also with the Constitution, which empowered states to set voting requirements in gender-neutral language that could grant women the right to vote and hold public office. The flexibility of the Constitution was ignored by all states except New Jersey. Propertied New Jersey women were able to vote from 1776 to 1807, but were then forbidden from voting because of fears that they had provided the margin of victory (for the Federalist party) in a close election. Historian Linda Kerber argues that women could have become voting citizens without a constitutional amendment if the states had consistently extended those rights soon after the American Revolution. Instead, after the Civil War, the Fourteenth Amendment to the Constitution added the word "male" to its definition of eligible voters, thereby limiting the possibility of women's voting without another amendment to explicitly grant women the suffrage. Arguments against woman suffrage generally suggested that women would mindlessly vote as directed by husbands, brothers, and fathers, and that by appearing at the polls they were forsaking their femininity.[21]

Not surprisingly, therefore, the most controversial resolution in the 1848 Declaration of Sentiments was that for woman suffrage, which passed only after eloquent appeals were made on its behalf by Elizabeth Cady Stanton and Frederick Douglass. It was this resolution that was singled out for particular condemnation by the outraged press. Independence was considered a crucial prerequisite for voting rights; women's exclusion from suffrage was based on women's status as dependents of fathers and husbands. Historian Ellen DuBois argues that "the suffrage demand challenged the idea that women's interests were identical or even compatible with men's. As such, it embodied a vision of female self-determination that placed it at the center of the feminist movement."[22] Because the ballot represented positive, patriotic claims to citizenship and self-determination, it was central to Stanton's Declaration of Sentiments. The Seneca Falls convention is rightly described as the birthplace of the woman's rights movement. Although woman's rights activists faced certain and determined opprobrium, they were also pleased by the publicity, however negative, that the meeting at Seneca Falls had generated in the press.

From 1848 to 1860, activists held woman's rights conventions to organize reform campaigns, generate publicity for woman's rights issues, and inspire public debate. Interestingly, however, an official national organization did not emerge because many women felt embittered by their experiences within hierarchical antislavery organizations that had closed off options to women. Angelina Grimké wrote to the 1852 Woman's Rights Convention in Syracuse, New York, and urged women to keep an informal structure without a national organization: "The tendency of organization is to kill out the spirit which gave it birth. Organizations do not protect the sacredness of the individual; their tendency is to sink the individual in the mass, to sacrifice his rights, and to immolate him on the altar of some fancied good."[23] Grimké's distrust of organizations was in great part due to the 1840 split within the national antislavery organization over the issue of women's participation and rights.

New York, Massachusetts, Pennsylvania, Ohio, and Indiana all regularly held regional woman's rights conventions from 1850 to the Civil War. During that time, national conventions were held annually (with the exception of 1857) in a variety of locations, including Worcester (Massachusetts), Syracuse (New York), Philadelphia, Cincinnati, and New York City. In Illinois and other Midwestern states, support for the woman's rights movement began with women's antislavery work and paralleled the growth of female seminaries and academies there. Not only were more women being educated, but many also came from the East to teach, bringing woman's rights ideas with them. Southern women, in contrast, did not participate in the woman's rights movement before the Civil War. There were fewer benevolent and women's clubs, fewer colleges for women's advanced education, fewer missionary societies that encouraged women's activism, and fewer urban areas where middle-class activism might have developed. Most significantly, southern women had not had the training or consciousness raising that northern activists had had within the abolitionist movement.[24]

Those black women who participated in the woman's rights movement before the Civil War were mostly northern middle-class free blacks. These women, including the socially and politically prominent members of the Forten, Purvis, and Remond families, were well-educated activists who believed that voting rights would improve women's status in society. In spite of the fact that most black activists were literate and comparatively well-off, it was Sojourner Truth who became the symbol for black women's activism in the antebellum era. An illiterate former slave, she was celebrated by some white women for her straight-talking wisdom and was opposed by others who did not welcome black women's participation in the movement. Other voices emerged at woman's rights conventions, such as that of "Mrs. Prince, a colored woman, [who] invoked the blessing of God upon the noble women engaged in this enterprise, and said she understood woman's wrongs better than woman's rights, and gave some of her own experiences to illustrate the degradation of her sex in slavery."[25] For Mrs. Prince, racial and sexual oppression were inseparable.

The Woman's Rights Convention of 1850 held in Worcester, Massachusetts, drew thousands of people from nine states and featured well-known speakers like abolitionist and woman's rights advocate Lucy Stone. The number of participants grew at each annual convention, and women and men collaborated publicly as equals at these conventions. The organizers were ideologically committed to free speech, so anyone was allowed to talk at the conventions, including rabid opponents. Ironically, Abby Kelley was not invited to the Massachusetts Woman's Rights Convention of 1855 because some woman's rights activists, including organizer Paulina Wright Davis, wanted to bring greater respectability to woman's rights by avoiding association with such a famous radical abolitionist.

A major goal of the woman's rights movement was to change public opinion regarding women's capacities and rights. At the Syracuse, New York, National Woman's Rights Convention of 1852, Ernestine Rose offered a resolution explicitly rejecting duties without rights: "[I]t is in accordance with the principles of republicanism that, as a woman has to pay taxes to maintain government, she has a right to participate in the formation and administration of it."[26] To change public opinion regarding women acting in the public sphere, activists spoke publicly and wrote numerous articles, pamphlets, and books. Some women publicized the cause of woman's rights through small journals, but most of the publicity came from articles in major newspapers that covered (typically in a hostile, derogatory tone) local, state, and national woman's rights conventions. However slanted, this coverage provided a public forum for the issues raised by the movement.

Is having too much media today actually more harmful? And not having one central org. to supp for the mvt?

Equal wages, job opportunities, and shorter hours were goals of the woman's rights movement because of the influence of working women. Woman's rights conventions of the 1850s included reports on women in industry and speeches calling for equal wages and the opening of all job fields to women. One speaker suggested: "make woman equal before the law with man, and wages will adjust themselves." A Committee on Industry suggested that "the one great cause, therefore, of the inadequate compensation and inferior position of woman, is the unjust apportionment of avocation." Although the fight for economic rights was a part of the woman's rights movement, its middle-class leaders generally focused more on married women's property laws rather than on workplace conditions or the length of the work day.[27]

Organizing petition campaigns and lobbying legislators, the antebellum woman's rights movement focused most successfully on reforming laws that impacted married women. As an organizer for temperance and woman's rights causes, Susan B. Anthony had encountered a fundamental difficulty raising funds—married women were not in control of money. Anthony explained "as I passed from town to town was I made to feel the great evil of women's utter dependence on man. . . . I never before took in so fully the grand idea of pecuniary independence. Woman must have a purse of her own."[28] At New York State woman's rights conventions, Ernestine Rose, Susan B. Anthony, and Elizabeth Cady Stanton organized a campaign to strengthen the limited Married Woman's Property Act of 1848 so that women could be assured of joint custody of their children, make wills and inherit property, and keep their own earnings. These petition campaigns succeeded in getting the earlier Married Women's Property Act amended in 1860. Married women's property acts of varying strength also passed in Maryland, Mississippi, Michigan, Missouri, Ohio, Rhode Island, and Vermont.

Just as fights over woman's rights had taken place within the abolitionist movement, by the 1850s, some women became frustrated by their status in the temperance movement. As early as the 1830s, women had made up at least half of the members of local temperance organizations but remained unequal members; official decisions and strategies were made by the men. In 1852, Susan B. Anthony, a committed temperance activist, was chosen, along with Amelia Bloomer, to attend the Men's State Temperance Society Convention. They arrived (in bloomers and Anthony with short hair) only to find themselves the objects of ridicule and hatred from the male delegates, many of them members of the clergy. Ultimately, the men decided that although the female delegates had been invited to the meeting, they must remain silent. In response, Anthony organized the New York Woman's State Temperance Society with Elizabeth Cady Stanton as president. Susan B. Anthony, Elizabeth Cady Stanton, and Amelia Bloomer pointed to the vulnerable position of wives and children of drunken men. They advocated changes in divorce and child custody laws that would enable a woman to leave her husband without having to give up her children.

By situating demands for reform of divorce laws in terms of the victims of alcoholics, woman's rights advocates hoped to reshape the temperance movement and formulate an approach to divorce reform that might appeal to the sympathies of male legislators. This attempt was unsuccessful, for conservatives within the temperance movement itself could not accept divorce reform. Stanton persisted in linking temperance and woman's rights:

> Is it not legitimate in this to discuss the social degradation, the
> legal disabilities of the drunkard's wife? If in showing her wrongs,
> we prove the right of all womanhood to the elective franchise. . . .
> If in pointing out her social degradation we show you how the
> present laws outrage the sacredness of the marriage institution . . .
> the discussion of this question . . . lead[s] us legitimately into the
> consideration of the important subject of divorce?[29]

Within a year, conservatives rejected the idea of divorce reform and removed Stanton from the presidency and pushed Anthony and Stanton out of the temperance movement. Anthony, in particular, had begun as a temperance activist but now saw that she must fight for her rights as a woman before she could fully and freely engage in any other type of reform.

Meanwhile, as the years passed, the national woman's rights conventions inspired some women reformers to think about forming a national organization. Each year, convention attendees would hear the same types of speeches, pass approximately the same resolutions, and get the same press coverage. Even as more intensive campaigns to pass or reform married women's property laws were succeeding in several states and as national woman's rights leaders emerged from local campaigns, some began to call for more action. Although the conventions still rejected forming a permanent woman's rights organization, in 1859, a coordinating committee was formed to write one standard memorial for woman's legal and equal rights that was to be submitted simultaneously to every northern state legislature.[30] Ellen DuBois argues that this was not enough, that the antebellum woman's rights movement was ultimately constrained by its close association with the antislavery movement. She points out that by relying on the existing abolitionist organizations to provide a structure for lecture circuits, leaders, and members, the woman's rights movement was unable to flourish independently or develop its own constituency or issues.

Before the Civil War, other problems surfaced in the woman's rights movement. Just as she had tried to make it a part of the temperance movement, Elizabeth Cady Stanton tried to make divorce reform part of the national campaign for woman's rights. A liberalized divorce bill had passed in Indiana with the support of Senator Robert Dale Owen (who had been a freethinker and co-editor of the *Free Enquirer* with Frances Wright in the 1820s and early 1830s). At the 1860 National Woman's Rights Convention in New York City, Stanton proposed that "loveless unions" be dissolved, shocking most women at the convention who were much more comfortable campaigning for married woman's rights.[31] This sensitive issue was avoided in part by the intervention of the Civil War. The 1861 Woman's Rights Convention was canceled as activists put aside their campaign in favor of war work in the U.S. Sanitary Commission and abolitionism. Woman's rights activists and female abolitionists joined together in 1863 to form the Women's Loyal National League which, among other things, engaged in a massive petition drive in favor of a constitutional amendment to end slavery. Woman's rights was only able to become a mature movement after the Civil War, when it could separate itself from abolitionism. The woman's rights movement reached a wider audience, Ellen DuBois suggests, by turning away from more radical arguments about natural rights and women's individualization. Instead, by emphasizing "women's special, maternal-based vision," woman's rights activists were then able to bring together large numbers of women to fight for woman suffrage.[32]

NOTES

1. Mary Wollstonecraft, *Vindication of the Rights of Woman* (1792), quoted in Miriam Gurko, *The Ladies of Seneca Falls: The Birth of the Woman's Rights Movement* (New York: Schocken Books, 1974), 16.

2. Elizabeth Cady Stanton, Susan B. Anthony, and Matilda J. Gage, eds., *History of Woman Suffrage*, vol. 1 (1881; reprint, New York: Arno & The New York Times, 1969), 35 (hereafter cited as *HWS*).

3. Stanton, et al., *HWS*, 514.

4. Stanton, et al., *HWS*, 259.

5. Stanton, et al., *HWS*, 36.

6. Margaret Fuller, *Woman in the Nineteenth Century* (1844), quoted in Eleanor Flexner, *Century of Struggle: The Woman's Rights Movement in the United States* (Cambridge, Mass.: Belknap Press, 1975), 67.

7. Maria Stewart, quoted in Ann D. Gordon, ed., *African American Women and the Vote, 1837–1965* (Amherst: University of Massachusetts Press, 1997), 27.

8. Maria Stewart, quoted in Flexner, *Century of Struggle*, 45.

9. Stanton, et al., *HWS*, 52–53.

10. Angelina E. Grimké, *An Appeal to the Christian Women of the Southern States* (1836), cited in Larry Ceplair, ed., *The Public Years of Sarah and Angelina Grimké: Selected Writings, 1835–1839* (New York: Columbia University Press, 1989), 55–56.

11. Jean V. Matthews, *Women's Struggle for Equality: The First Phase, 1828–1876* (Chicago: Ivan R. Dee, 1997), 33.

12. "Pastoral Letter: The General Association of Massachusetts to the Churches Under Their Care" (1837), in Ceplair, ed., *The Public Years*, 211.

13. Angelina E. Grimké to Theodore Dwight Weld, Aug. 12, 1837, in Ceplair, ed., *The Public Years*, 277.

14. Angelina E. Grimké, *Letters to Catherine [sic] E. Beecher, in reply to An Essay on Slavery and Abolitionism, addressed to A. E. Grimké* (1837), in Ceplair, ed., *The Public Years*, 197.

15. Angelina E. Grimké to Theodore Dwight Weld and John Greenleaf Whittier, August 20, 1837, in Ceplair, ed., *The Public Years*, 284. Gerda Lerner, *The Grimké Sisters from South Carolina: Pioneers for Woman's Rights and Abolition* (New York: Schocken Books, 1967).

16. Dorothy Sterling, *Ahead of her Time: Abby Kelley and the Politics of Anti-Slavery* (New York: W.W. Norton, 1991), 38, 105.

17. Stanton, et al., *HWS*, 52–53.

18. Stanton, et al., *HWS*, 89.

19. Michael Grossberg, *Governing the Hearth: Law and Family in Nineteenth-Century America* (Chapel Hill: University of North Carolina Press, 1985), 246–47.

20. Stanton, et al., *HWS*, 70–73.

21. Linda Kerber, "'Ourselves and Our Daughters Forever': Women and the Constitution, 1787–1876," in Marjorie Spruill Wheeler, ed., *One Woman, One Vote: Rediscovering the Woman Suffrage Movement* (Troutdale, Ore.: NewSage Press, 1995), 27.

22. Ellen Carol DuBois, *Feminism and Suffrage: The Emergence of an Independent Women's Movement in America, 1848–1869* (Ithaca, N.Y.: Cornell University Press, 1978), 46.

23. Lerner, *The Grimké Sisters*, 333.

24. Elna C. Green, *Southern Strategies: Southern Women and the Woman Suffrage Question* (Chapel Hill: University of North Carolina Press, 1997), introduction.

25. Stanton, et al., *HWS*, 384.

26. Stanton, et al., *HWS*, 132.

27. Stanton, et al., *HWS*, 265, 590.

28. Susan B. Anthony, quoted in Gurko, *The Ladies of Seneca Falls*, 174.

29. Stanton, et al., *HWS*, 494.

30. Matthews, *Women's Struggle for Equality*, 81.

31. Stanton, et al., *HWS*, 716–35.

32. Ellen Carol DuBois, *Woman Suffrage and Women's Rights* (New York: New York University Press, 1998), 289; and DuBois, *Feminism and Suffrage*, 52.

2

VOICES OF SUFFRAGE

Sojourner Truth, Frances Watkins Harper, and the Struggle for Woman Suffrage

Nell Irvin Painter

After the Civil War, in the midst of debates over black and woman suffrage, Sojourner Truth, a former slave and committed abolitionist, addressed the American Equal Rights Association: "If colored men get their rights, and not colored women theirs, you see the colored men will be masters over the women, and it will be just as bad as it was before." It was a typically courageous stand for this important supporter of woman suffrage. Before the Civil War, black and white men and women, including Truth, Frederick Douglass, Elizabeth Cady Stanton, Susan B. Anthony, and other reformers, had worked together against slavery and for woman's rights without seeing these causes as conflicting. In fact, Douglass had been a staunch supporter of woman's rights, demanding the vote as one of woman's essential rights as early as 1848, while Anthony had been a paid agent of the American Anti-Slavery Society as well as a suffragist.[1]

During the Civil War, the woman's rights–abolitionist community held together seamlessly. In 1863, Stanton and Anthony formed the Women's Loyal National League, the first organization to petition Congress to make emancipation permanent and universal in a Thirteenth Amendment to the U.S. Constitution.[2] But Reconstruction tore abolitionists apart. Republican politics demanded black male suffrage, abandoning any lobbying for universal voting for all adults—at a time when feminists glimpsed a victory of their own in the wings. As an African American activist, Truth's position was a significant one.

Throughout her life, Truth combined pleas for the abolition of slavery, black voting, and woman suffrage into a commitment to human rights. Her speeches reminded listeners of a preacher whose biblical imagery softened what was a radical message of equality. But when the woman's movement split between those who favored black male voting over universal suffrage for all adults, Truth made clear that women, black and white, needed the ballot. Given her consistently radical stand, many Americans wondered about the origins of this preacher of human values.

Truth had been born a slave in the late 1790s in Ulster County, New York. She had escaped from slavery and in the 1820s belonged to communities of radically egalitarian evangelicals. Her legal freedom from slavery came when she was liberated under a New York statute of 1817 that freed slaves under forty in 1827. Like many former slaves, she found sanctuary in a city—in this case New York. Here she met reformers such as Arthur Tappan, and in 1843, she changed her slave name Isabella to the resonant name of her future—Sojourner Truth. By 1850, she had published her famous autobiography *Narrative of Sojourner Truth—A Northern Slave*, which told the story of her abusive early years as the property of New York owners. Some gaps exist in the biography of Sojourner Truth, but by the 1840s, she was living in a utopian commune in western Massachusetts. With the encouragement of William Lloyd Garrison and his family, she had become part of a network of reformers, attending and speaking at meetings of antislavery reformers. In 1850, she attended the first annual woman's rights convention in Worcester, Massachusetts.

Throughout this decade, she supported herself as a live-in domestic. She also sold her *Narrative* and gave dramatic speeches on woman's rights. Having no permanent home, she often stayed with leaders of the woman's movement including Susan B. Anthony and Elizabeth Cady Stanton. Thus, Truth became part of an informal association of female reformers. Other black women including free-born Nancy Prince and Charlotte Forten were part of the prewar woman's movement, but as was the case with white women, commitments were made on an individual basis because there was no permanent sustaining organization devoted to woman suffrage. Still, women learned how to begin the process of changing American opinion on voting for women by circulating petitions and giving speeches. Newspapers began to cover their conventions and often expressly noted "colored people scattered through the audience."[3]

By the late 1850s, Truth was a big enough draw to convene a series of meetings on her own in Indiana. There is no record of what Truth said, but in an effort to challenge her credibility, proslavery and antifeminist sympathizers, of whom there were many in Indiana, interrupted her meeting, claiming that her voice was so deep she was a man. To prove she was a woman, Truth responded that as a slave she had suckled many a white babe to the exclusion of her own children. According to the report in the *Liberator*, she quietly asked the audience as she disrobed, if they too wished to suck. "It was not to her shame that she uncovered her breast before them, but to their Shame."[4]

During the Civil War, Sojourner Truth spoke at prounion rallies in the North, sometimes wearing a red, white, and blue uniform. At one point, she was arrested for entering Indiana because a law forbade any black from entering the state. Like other northern abolitionist women she volunteered for the cause, collecting food for the First Michigan Regiment of colored soldiers stationed near Detroit. And she was proud that her grandson, like 174,000 other blacks, fought in the Union Army.

In the Reconstruction period, when it was obvious that freed blacks needed the protection of the ballot in the South, Truth insisted that women should get the vote along with black men. Most of the activists who clamored for woman suffrage after the Civil War had been energetic abolitionists. They were black and white, male and female, and they included Stanton, Anthony, Douglass, Lucy Stone and her husband Henry Blackwell, Truth, Parker Pillsbury, Josephine Griffing, Charles Lenox Remond, Frances Dana Gage, Gerrit Smith, Frances Ellen Watkins Harper, William Lloyd Garrison, and Robert Purvis.[5] Douglass, Truth, Remond, Harper, and Purvis were black, but not of one mind about the suffrage issue as it evolved out of the older demand for woman's rights.

The broad agenda of woman's rights—securing women rights to their wages, their inheritances, and the custody of their children; admitting women to institutions of higher learning and the professions; and permitting women to vote, hold office, and serve on juries—dovetailed with the needs of black people, who also lacked a wide range of civil rights.

For as long as anyone could remember, black men and all women had been powerless together. Now that black men were advancing, why not women? Julia Wilbur of Rochester, Sojourner Truth's co-worker in humanitarian aid for freed people, who had been emancipated but who had few resources to support herself, discovered personal implications in black men's voting. Watching freedmen, whom she considered ignorant and superstitious, voting for the first time in the District of Columbia, Wilbur confessed she felt "a little jealous—the least bit humiliated." In the mid-1860s, words like "humiliation" and "degradation" became common in one strand of woman suffrage rhetoric.[6] Suffrage priorities—whether or not to support the Fifteenth Amendment giving black males the right to vote without any mention of women—split reformers. From the breach emerged two competing woman suffrage communities—the National Woman Suffrage Association headed by Stanton and Anthony, which supported universal voting, and the American Woman Suffrage Association led by Lucy Stone and Henry Blackwell, which supported black voting first. Each sought the blessing of Sojourner Truth.

After the ratification of the Thirteenth Amendment that gave constitutional status to the emancipation of all slaves, the organized movement of abolitionism broke up. For William Lloyd Garrison, longtime president of the American Anti-Slavery Society and Truth's previous ally, Confederate defeat and the Thirteenth Amendment closed the work of abolition. Many others, including Truth and Wendell Phillips, who then became president of the society, saw black suffrage as necessary to sustain emancipation. The passage of black codes by southern legislatures virtually reinstalled slavery, and the rape and murder of black Republicans by white supremacists demonstrated that by itself emancipation would not bring freedom to blacks.

In this climate of violent reaction, the American Anti-Slavery Society under Phillips concentrated on the radical Republican goal of enfranchising black men. Blacks were the strongest supporters of the Union and the Republican party in the South, but black women could not be enfranchised without giving the vote to much larger numbers of southern white women, who would probably vote Democratic. Soon Congress with its heavy Republican majorities wrote and passed further constitutional amendments, the Fourteenth and Fifteenth, which the states ratified between 1865 and 1870.

In this setting of political progress, universal suffrage supporters formed the Equal Rights Association, an organization important to Sojourner Truth. While she and many other abolitionists agreed with Douglass and Phillips that "this hour belongs to the Negro," she also supported woman suffrage in tandem with black male suffrage.[7] Attending meetings in 1866 in Boston and New York, Truth and the poet Frances Ellen Watkins Harper, who spoke at both meetings, championed rights for blacks and for women in the name of black women.

These two important black activists—Harper and Truth—were a contrasting pair. Harper was born free in Baltimore in 1825 and was educated by her schoolmaster uncle, William J. Watkins, who was an abolitionist and a woman suffragist.[8] Moving to Philadelphia, she worked on the Underground Railroad with blacks like William Still and published in the African Methodist Episcopal Church's newspaper, the *Christian Recorder*. In the 1850s, she honed her speaking skills as an agent of the Maine Anti-Slavery Society and published two volumes of poetry. After the death of her husband and the end of the Civil War, she toured the South as an advocate of black civil rights, temperance, education, and high moral standards.[9]

In contrast to the outspoken, uneducated, and very dark-skinned Sojourner Truth, Frances Ellen Watkins Harper was ladylike, "slender and graceful," with a speaking voice that was "soft" and "musical," even as it could be assertive.[10] She was too educated, too polished, and too respectable to be taken for an exotic or a foreign work of art. She was not a picturesque character who provoked laughter and affection as Truth did.

In the 1866 meetings both attended, there are no records of Truth's position. But Harper sounded vexing themes—themes of race and gender that are still with us. Except on the ideal of women's enfranchisement, she disagreed with Stanton and Anthony. Harper questioned whether formal emancipation in 1865 had given black men an advantage over white women. Harper said no; Stanton and Anthony said yes. Would the vote, of itself, satisfy the needs of all women? Stanton and Anthony said yes. Harper, pointing to the persistence of class discrimination and discrimination in the lives of poor black women, said no.[11] With Truth and other abolitionists, Harper saw the necessity for continuing the work of emancipation in the South.

Like Truth, Harper refused to separate her sex from her race. Black women were women, she insisted; their concerns were *women's* issues, just as the concerns of white women were women's issues. Most abolitionists were content to pretend that woman suffrage meant the same thing to women of all races whether black, white, or red. Harper shredded the pretense. She could hear white women silently appending "white" and "middle-class" to their definition of "woman," and at the meeting she took them on:

> You white women speak here of rights. I speak of wrongs. I, as a colored woman, have had in this country an education which has made me feel as if I were in the situation of Ishmael, my hand against every man, and every man's hand against me. Let me go tomorrow morning and take my seat in one of your street cars . . . and the conductor will put up his hand and stop the car rather than let me ride.

This was black women's reality, Harper said, but white suffragists turned their backs. Until white women acknowledged black women's predicament, she would dismiss woman suffrage as a whites-only affair. Anger threaded through her taunt to white women: " . . . if there is a class of people who need to be lifted out of their airy nothings and selfishness, it is the white women of America."[12] This kind of talk was too strong for those soon to be the country's leading woman suffragists, and Harper's speeches do not appear in Stanton and Anthony's *History of Woman Suffrage*. A different black woman was needed, and she proved to be Sojourner Truth.

Who better than a celebrity ex-slave to dilute Harper's argument and refute her standing as a representative black woman? In May 1867, Anthony invited Sojourner Truth to a meeting of the Equal Rights Association in New York, and Stanton welcomed Truth as her houseguest. Meanwhile, Harper remained in South Carolina, lecturing among the freedpeople. Throughout the convention, Stanton and Anthony referred to Truth as "Mrs. Stowe's 'Lybian Sybil,' " a reference to Harriet Beecher Stowe's popular 1863 article about Sojourner Truth.

Truth's style was not barbed like Harper's; she disagreed with white suffragist's rhetoric, without attacking white women directly. Instead of opposing Stanton and Anthony, she differed from them. When Truth came to the podium she acknowledged the cheers that greeted her, warning an overwhelmingly white, Stanton-adoring audience that "I come from another field—the country of the slave." While Stanton and Anthony concluded that emancipation was over and done with, Truth justified the Fourteenth Amendment, which introduced the word "male" into the United States Constitution for the first time, but gave blacks some protections as citizens of the nation. In her mind, slavery had only partially been destroyed, she said, and liberty had not yet been achieved. Truth defended the political rights of black men, but she also spoke of the rights of black women. Although she shared with Stanton the long-standing assumption that women owned themselves and were autonomous persons, Truth made the women in question black. Black women appeared rarely in Stanton's rhetoric. In contrast to the position of middle-class wellborne white women, Truth noted, "[t]here is a great stir about colored men getting their rights, but not a word about the colored women."

When the leaders of the National Woman Suffrage Association spoke of black women, they usually demeaned black men. In the 1860s—as in later times—black women occasionally found white champions, but often at the expense of black men. Paulina Wright Davis, for instance, claimed that freedwomen did not want to marry freedmen out of fear of losing their children and their earnings. Black women were smarter than black men, Davis held, because they had learned from their mistresses. Black men, she said, had learned from their masters and wanted only to whip their wives.[13]

When Truth pointed to the weaknesses of black men as an argument for black women's legal and economic rights, she focused more on money than personal violence. Recalling the refugees in Washington and perhaps the husbands of her hardworking daughters in Battle Creek, Michigan, where she now lived, she depicted black men as strutting idlers: "when the women come home, they ask for their money and take it all, and then scold because there is no food." Money and its control by husbands was the context of her famous quote: "if colored men get their rights, and not colored women theirs, you see the colored men will be masters over the women, and it will be just as bad as it was before." Because the vote could be a means of passing legislation to protect wages, Truth argued that she wanted to keep agitating for woman suffrage before federal policy hardened.[14] White women needed the vote, but black women needed it even more, having less education and a more limited choice of jobs. "[W]ashing," she said, "is about as high as a colored woman gets." Such legal and economic suffrage arguments sprang from her personal experience.

Her view of women's need for legal rights contained another jab at men, but men of a different standing, who were well-educated white lawyers. In Ulster and Westchester counties, and Washington, D.C., she had been in court three times, and from this personal experience came her view that "in the courts women have no right, no voice; nobody speaks for them. I wish woman to have her voice there among the pettifoggers."

As a poor working woman, Truth knew life at the bottom of the economic ladder. Even as she acknowledged, like Harper and other leaders of the suffrage movement, political inferiority to poor men, Truth felt needs more economic than political. She returned repeatedly to a theme she had sounded as early as 1851: her right to equal remuneration because she worked like a man. This time she included immigrant women who labored:

> I have done a great deal of work; as much as a man, but did not
> get so much pay. I used to work in the field and bind grain,
> keeping up with the cradler; but men doing no more, got twice as
> much pay; so with the German women. They work in the field

and so as much work, but do not get the pay. We do as much, we eat as much, we want as much.

Truth wanted the independence that comes from having one's own money. "When we get our rights," she concluded, "we shall not have to come to you for money, for then we shall have money enough in our own pockets; and may be you will ask us for money."[15] Truth's ideas ranged far from the vote but stayed within the prevailing ideology of woman suffrage, equating women's voting with a recasting of the entire political economy.

In a famous confrontation at the Equal Rights Association meeting, George T. Downing took the floor. He asked Stanton if she opposed the enfranchisement of black men if women did not get the vote at the same time. Downing's question and Stanton's response went to the heart of the problem of Reconstruction for woman suffragists on all sides. Stanton first said she would not trust the black man to make laws for her, because "degraded, oppressed himself, he would be more despotic with the governing power than even our Saxon rulers are." If truly universal suffrage were not feasible, she preferred to enfranchise educated people first, for "this incoming tide of ignorance, poverty, and vice" must not be empowered. Without woman suffrage, only the "highest type of manhood" should vote and hold office.

Another white suffragist, Abby Kelley Foster, took strenuous exception to Stanton's position. So too did Josephine Griffing, the most active woman suffragist in Washington, D.C. In deep distress at the choice demanded, Charles Remond refused to discriminate between a vote for black men or black women. He claimed for his wife and sister all that he claimed for himself.[16] After such heated exchanges, a chasm divided the meeting.

Susan B. Anthony brought Truth back to the floor as an ex-slave, exaggerating the injury to Truth's right hand and turning it into a drama of slavery: "one of her fingers was chopped off by her cruel master in a moment of anger."[17] Truth became a symbol of slavery rather than of Reconstruction, just as, aligned with the no-compromise faction of the suffrage movement, she continued to focus on the necessity of votes for women.

In her speech Truth tried to bridge the gulf widening between the political claims of race and sex: "We are now trying for liberty that requires no blood—that women shall have their rights—not rights from you. Give them what belongs to them; they ask it kindly too. (Laughter). I ask it kindly."[18] In her characteristically disarming rhetoric, she concluded with a story about Battle Creek taxes, noting that she was a nonvoting woman property owner subject to road taxes.

After the furious Downing-Stanton exchange on competing suffrages, Truth still occupied an intermediate position, as did Charles Remond. Others in the meeting, notably Henry Ward Beecher, the nation's most famous preacher and brother of Harriet Beecher Stowe, also tried not to choose. At this meeting, neither Truth nor Remond acknowledged the increasing distance in 1867 between black male suffrage, now obtainable, and woman suffrage, still chimerical. Remond closed the meeting with a tribute to black men's service in the Revolutionary and Civil wars, and Truth welcomed the day when the "colored people might own their soul and body." At this moment—when straddling was still possible in woman suffrage circles before the emergence of two separate organizations—Truth stood for both blacks and women without stating priorities.

Truth's presence in their company served the Stanton and Anthony camp, even though her comments, in this extremely contentious meeting, set her gently on the side of the abolitionists, who would soon repudiate Stanton and Anthony's position. The issues were the Fourteenth Amendment, allegiance to the Republican party, and whether black male suffrage should be held hostage to woman suffrage. On every issue, Truth disagreed with Stanton and Anthony. As the largely illiterate Truth said:

> You know, children, I don't read such small stuff as letters, I read men and nations. I can see through a millstone, though I can't see through a spelling book. What a narrow idea a reading qualification is for a voter! I know and do what is right better than many big men who read. And what's that property qualification! just as bad! As if men and women themselves, who made money, were not of more value than the thing they made. If I were a delegate to the [New York] Constitutional Convention I could make suffrage as clear as daylight.[19]

In 1867 and 1868, Stanton and Anthony increasingly set themselves at odds with their former comrades in reform such as Lucy Stone and Frances Harper, who refused to make woman suffrage their first priority. In suffrage campaigns in Kansas and New York, Stanton and Anthony allied themselves with Democrats willing to back woman suffrage in order to stymie black male enfranchisement. In Kansas, where unsuccessful referenda on the separate issues of black male and universal female voting were held in the fall of 1867, differences among supporters of suffrage expansion intensified. Truth did not go to Kansas, as many suffragists did, nor did Harper. The principal ally of the Anthony and Stanton faction became the notorious negrophobe, George Francis Train, who underwrote their newspaper *The Revolution*. As they pulled farther away from the ideals of universal suffrage, their language grew increasingly nativist, racist, and classbound.

In the January 1869 meeting of the Equal Rights Association, hosted by Josephine Griffing in Washington, D.C., Stanton delivered a fiery keynote that disparaged the "dregs of China, Germany, England, Ireland, and Africa," who were polluting the American polity. As the United States Congress moved toward the Fifteenth Amendment that would enfranchise black men, Stanton thought it disgraceful that "Patrick and Sambo and Hans and Yung Tung" should make laws for women like herself. How could American politicians fall so low as to "make their wives and mothers the political inferiors of unlettered and unwashed ditch-diggers, bootblacks, butchers, and barbers, fresh from the slave plantations of the South, and the effete civilizations of the Old World?" She called universal manhood suffrage an "appalling question."[20]

Truth missed this meeting, but Harper, Douglass, and Stephen S. Foster, a veteran abolitionist and the husband of Abby Kelley Foster, did not. The men denounced Stanton for bigotry and disregard for the Reconstruction amendments so crucial in the South. For Douglass, this was a tragic moment. His beloved abolitionist community lay in a pile of smoking ashes.[21] Harper, too, rushed to defend the morals and rights of freedmen. She had concluded that if the United States could handle only one question [at a time], she "would not have black women put a single straw in the way, if only the men of the race could obtain what they wanted."[22] As black women so often have done when black men come under attack, Harper fell silent on the rights of black women. Concluding that she must now choose between her identity as a woman and her identity as a Negro, she abandoned black women and rallied to the side of black men: "[w]hen it was a question of race, she let the lesser question of sex go."[23] In the conflict between black men and white women, black women disappeared.

Torn apart in 1869, the Equal Rights Association gave way to two new organizations dedicated to woman suffrage. Stanton, Anthony, some old abolitionists (Josephine Griffing, for example), and many women new to the cause founded the all-female National Woman Suffrage Association (NWSA). The NWSA turned its back on black male suffrage and the issues of race and Reconstruction that as early as 1868 Anthony had declared the "dead questions of the past."[24]

Unable to stomach Stanton's rhetoric and Anthony's Democrats, supporters of black male suffrage and the Republican party in turn founded the American Woman Suffrage Association (AWSA). Its leaders, Lucy Stone and Henry Blackwell, had waged the Kansas campaign with Anthony but had no use for George Francis Train. Harper, also a founder, addressed AWSA meetings in 1873 and 1875, where she spoke of her disillusionment with the priorities set by white women. According to a recent student of blacks in the suffrage movement, Harper argued that "when it was a question of race [I] let the question of race go. But the white women all go for sex, letting race occupy a minor position."[25]

Truth still sought a middle road, avoiding NWSA-AWSA politics while speaking for women's political rights in general terms and focusing on justice and fairness. In western New York from August to October 1868, she convened meetings nearly every day, speaking sometimes more than once a day. Though seventy at the time, she kept a strenuous schedule and addressed crowds that numbered in the thousands. Reports of this tour omit the content of her speeches, noting only that she spoke for more than an hour at a time "in her usually impressive and sarcastic manner, much to the satisfaction of the majority present."[26]

In the 1870s, Truth chose to ally herself with the AWSA. She attended their meetings in New York in May 1870 and in Boston in January 1871.[27] Truth spoke briefly at the Boston meeting, presenting a maternalist argument based on her view of women as the moral guardians of American society. As the mother of five children, she argued that women ought to have their rights not only for themselves, as others had contended, but also "for the benefit of the whole creation, not only the women, but all the men on the face of the earth, for they were the mothers of them." Woman deserved her "God-given right, and be the equal of men, for she was the resurrection of them."[28]

Even after finding her place in the AWSA, Truth sought to heal divisions in her community. In Battle Creek in 1872, she took a heroic step in concert with Susan B. Anthony and other friends in Rochester, including Amy Post. After the ratification of the Fourteenth Amendment, suffrage women had seized on a suffrage strategy called the "New Departure" to argue that the first clause of that amendment—that all persons born or naturalized in the United States were citizens—effectively granted suffrage to women. As a citizen born in the United States, Truth voted—or at least tried to—in the 1872 presidential contest that reelected Ulysses S. Grant, for whom she had campaigned.[29] Anthony's arrest in Rochester made the vote a milestone in the history of woman suffrage. Truth's 1872 action embedded her deeper in the Stanton-Anthony version of that history, and so it was her story, not Frances Harper's, that appeared in the history of the woman's suffrage movement.

The passions that rent woman suffrage in 1869 kept its two branches at loggerheads for the next twenty years. Stanton and Anthony's radicalism drew in a new generation of wealthy, young adherents, who turned their back on race and defined women as white, middle, and upper class. The less militant AWSA limped along under Lucy Stone. When the two groups reunited in 1890, the new National American Woman Suffrage Association carried Stanton and Anthony's stamp. By this time Truth, although she retained a lifetime commitment to woman suffrage, had turned to other causes, particularly the movement to encourage blacks to settle in the West.

The politics of woman suffrage, which was largely controlled by Stanton and Anthony and preserved historically in their monumental six-volume *History of Woman Suffrage*, produced a new symbolic Truth—the Stanton-Anthony suffragist. The Stanton-Anthony Truth tended first and last toward women. For her, the Fourteenth Amendment portended worry, not triumph, if "colored men get their rights" before women are enfranchised. Since the black woman Frances Ellen Watkins Harper would not separate the woman in her identity from the black, she disappeared from the Stanton-Anthony history. She nonetheless represents a significant approach to suffrage. Indeed, the story of African American women in this first generation of the suffrage struggle reveals not only the commitment for human justice undertaken by remarkable black women such as Truth and Harper, but it also demonstrates the double jeopardy of black women.

NOTES

1. The Declaration of Sentiments of the first woman's rights convention at Seneca Falls, New York, in 1848 had included a demand for suffrage only as its ninth resolution, which was the only one not to pass unanimously. With Frederick Douglass's support, Stanton was able to muster a bare majority. Elizabeth Cady Stanton, Susan B. Anthony, and Matilda Joslyn Gage, eds., *History of Woman Suffrage*, vol. 1 (New York: Fowler &Wells, 1881), pp. 72–73; Ellen Carol DuBois, *Feminism and Suffrage: The Emergence of an Independent Women's Movement in America, 1848–1869* (Ithaca, N.Y.: Cornell University Press, 1978), pp. 39, 41. For more information on Truth, see Nell Irvin Painter, *Sojourner Truth: A Life, A Symbol* (New York: W.W. Norton, 1996).

2. Truth's friend, Amy Post, was prominent in the Rochester branch of the Women's Loyal National League. Nancy Hewitt, *Women's Activism and*

Social Change: Rochester, New York, 1822–1872 (Ithaca, N.Y.: Cornell University Press, 1984), p. 196.

3. Rosalyn Terborg-Penn, *African American Women in the Struggle for the Vote, 1850–1920* (Bloomington: Indiana University Press, 1998), p. 17.

4. *Boston Liberator*, October 15, 1858.

5. Rosalyn Terborg-Penn finds ten black men and six black women identifiable as suffragists before the Civil War. Rosalyn M. Terborg-Penn, "Afro-Americans in the Struggle for Woman Suffrage" (Ph.D. diss., Howard University, 1977), p. 33. Although William Lloyd Garrison, the most prominent abolitionist of the antebellum era, did not attend woman suffrage meetings after the Civil War, he was an advocate for votes for women. Like many others, including Truth, he sided with the American Woman Suffrage Association when the woman suffrage movement split over black male suffrage in 1869. Walter M. Merrill and Louis Ruchames, eds., *The Letters of William Lloyd Garrison*, vol. 6, *To Rouse the Slumbering Land, 1868–1879* (Cambridge: Harvard University Press, 1981), pp. 1–2.

6. Hewitt, *Women's Activism and Social Change*, pp. 199, 207. The theme of comparative degradation had figured in woman's rights rhetoric since the 1848 Seneca Falls Declaration of Sentiments, which included this indictment of man's power over woman: "He has withheld from her rights which are given to the most ignorant and degraded men—both natives and foreigners." Stanton, Anthony, and Gage, eds., *History of Woman Suffrage*, vol. 1, p. 70.

7. DuBois, *Feminism and Suffrage*, p. 54; Hewitt, *Women's Activism and Social Change*, p. 207.

8. Terborg-Penn, "Afro-Americans in the Struggle for Woman Suffrage," p. 35.

9. Frances Smith Foster, "Frances Ellen Watkins Harper (1825–1911)," in Darlene Clark Hine, ed., *Black Women in America: An Historical Encyclopedia* (Brooklyn, N.Y.: Carlson Publishing, 1993), pp. 532–37.

10. Frances Smith Foster, ed., *A Brighter Coming Day: A Frances Ellen Watkins Harper Reader* (New York: Feminist Press, 1990), p. 15.

11. In 1868, the white women typesetters associated with Stanton and Anthony in the Working Women's Association practically echoed Harper: One of the typesetters doubted that the vote, of itself, was "the greatest panacea for the correction of all existing evils." DuBois, *Feminism and Suffrage*, pp. 134–35.

12. Foster, ed., *A Brighter Coming Day*, p. 219. In 1897, Frances Watkins Harper spoke at a reception for Harriet Tubman that one of William Lloyd Garrison's sons planned and the AWSA hosted in the offices of its organ, the Boston *Woman's Journal*. Earl Conrad, *Harriet Tubman* (Washington, D.C.: Associated Publishers, 1943), p. 215.

13. Stanton, Anthony, and Gage, eds., *History of Woman Suffrage*, vol. 2, p. 391.

14. On Truth's biblical imagery in this speech, see Erlene Stetson and Linda David, *Glorying in Tribulation: The Lifework of Sojourner Truth* (East Lansing: Michigan State University Press, 1994), pp. 178–80.

15. Stanton, Anthony, and Gage, eds., *History of Woman Suffrage*, vol. 2, p. 193.

16. Ibid., vol. 2, pp. 214–16, 220–21.

17. Ibid., vol. 2, p. 224.

18. Ibid., vol. 2, pp. 224–25.

19. Ibid., vol. 2, pp. 926–27. The New York Constitutional Convention that Truth was referring to ended the forty-six-year-old property qualification for black male suffrage without enacting woman suffrage, further antagonizing the Stanton-Anthony faction.

20. Ibid., vol. 2, pp. 353–55.

21. Ibid., vol. 2, p. 383.

22. Ibid, vol. 2, pp. 391–92.

23. Ibid., vol. 2, p. 391.

24. Ibid., vol. 2, p. 342.

25. Foster, "Frances Ellen Watkins Harper," p. 533; Terborg-Penn, *African American Women*, p. 32. Stanton, Anthony, and Gage, eds., *History of Woman Suffrage*, vol. 2, pp. 347, 383–85, 391.

26. [Olive Gilbert and Frances Titus], *Narrative of Sojourner Truth; A Bondswoman of Olden Time, Emancipated by the New York Legislature in the Early Part of the Present Century; with a History of her Labors and Correspondence Drawn from her "Book of Life"* (1878; reprint, Salem, N.H.: Ayer Company, 1990), pp. 299–302.

27. Ibid., pp. 217–20; *New York Herald*, 12 May 1870, p. 10; Stanton, Anthony, and Gage, eds., *History of Woman Suffrage*, vol. 2, p. 766. According to the *Herald* report, working women's issues took up a great deal of time at both the AWSA and the NWSA, which were both meeting in New York at the same time.

28. *Narrative of Sojourner Truth*, p. 218.

29. Ibid., pp. 231–32.

3

NEW YORK STRATEGY

The New York Woman's Movement and the Civil War

Faye Dudden

The traditional story of woman suffrage has been shaped by the assumption that women had to win the vote *before* they could hope to exercise political power or influence. In this account, the Civil War figured as a mere hiatus in women's activism or at best a prelude to the flurry of suffrage agitation that marked the Reconstruction era. During the war, it was argued, women's rights activists, who had hitherto shunned formal organization, learned its value through an organization called the Women's Loyal National League (WLNL) through which they mounted a massive petition campaign for the final abolition of slavery in the Thirteenth Amendment. At the end of the war, emancipation accomplished, these abolitionist women sought recompense for their patriotic labors in the form of woman suffrage. But the women were, in Eleanor Flexner's words, "so inexperienced in politics" that they failed to realize that in the 1860s woman suffrage was "far ahead of practical political possibilities."[1]

The New York woman's movement during the Civil War provides a case study that challenges this traditional account: it reveals that prominent women's rights activists in fact entered politics before suffrage. Elizabeth Cady Stanton and Susan B. Anthony and their coworkers in New York State were anything but naïve about politics, and the war years were not really a hiatus. Their political activities before and during the war, which were organized around what I will term a "New York strategy," gave them an advanced education in legislative maneuver and partisan politics. They emerged from the war convinced that insider politics worked, and believing that women could be inside "players," even without the vote in hand.

Such a reinterpretation is prompted in part by recent scholarship that reveals a range of women's political activities in the antebellum era. According to this new scholarship, female "politicos" were insiders who strategized, spoke up behind closed doors, and helped determine patronage choices. Later they went further by conveying their views to the public at large—through lobbying, being present on public occasions, writing for publication, and even making public speeches.[2] Women were especially influential among the Whigs and their successors, the Republicans, but also in third parties like the Know-Nothings and in issue-oriented agitation like the campaign against Indian removal.[3] Often they were political wives like Jessie Benton Fremont, who furnished her husband with invaluable political connections, acted as his chief adviser and secretary, and was hailed during the 1856 campaign by Republican banners for "Fremont and Our Jessie."[4]

Of course, women's antebellum political actions prompted mixed feelings, even among political women themselves. The campaign of 1860, for example, revealed Mary Todd Lincoln to be a highly political wife—knowledgeable about politics, ready to talk to reporters, an aggressive campaigner with pen and ink, and, once the election was won, full of strong opinions about patronage appointments. Yet Mary Lincoln, captive to conventional beliefs about women's sphere, also tried to disavow her political activities and claim that she was a "wholly domestic" woman. During Lincoln's presidency, press coverage would notice her ambition and influence, and Mary Lincoln's ambivalence would lead her to conceal much from both the public and her own husband.[5] Antebellum women who wielded political influence did so by informal methods and within limits defined by their own hesitancy and the sufferance of men.

As the Civil War approached, the limits of women's informal political power were still to be tested, and no one had more reason to engage in such testing than the women's rights leaders of New York State. They had been functioning for over twenty years within an abolitionist movement that fiercely debated the wisdom and the uses of political action. Even though women's full participation in the antislavery movement had been championed by William Lloyd Garrison, who condemned political participation as a compromise with sin, the Garrisonian women who had formed the woman's rights movement had never abjured politics. On the contrary, suffrage was a key demand at Seneca Falls in 1848. Political abolitionists—the men who constructed the Liberty Party in

1840, participated in the Free Soil coalition in 1848, and threw their energies into the Republican Party in 1856—did not usually welcome women's participation.

However, Garrisonians practiced a kind of "anti-politics" that involved petitioning, holding conventions, circulating speakers and tracts, mounting test cases in the courts, and lobbying for legislation.[6] Moreover, the events of the 1850s pressed all abolitionists to take up politics, as the Fugitive Slave Act, the Kansas Nebraska Act, and the Dred Scott decision served to demonstrate that "moral suasion is moral balderdash." This 1850s turn toward politics drew some antislavery women into active partisanship, while prompting others to shift their focus or to withdraw.[7]

In New York State during the 1850s, activist women learned ways of working with politicians and within politics on behalf of women's rights. The Tenth National Woman's Rights Convention, held in New York City in May 1860, was largely devoted to celebrating the accomplishments of the New York woman's movement. Just two months earlier the New York State legislature had passed a pair of landmark laws, one allowing married women title to their own earnings, and the other giving wives joint custody of their children. The bills passed after a prolonged grassroots campaign of over six years, climaxing in 1859–1860, when six lecturers circulated through the state, conventions were held in forty counties, and lectures were delivered in 150 towns and villages. But there was also ceaseless political work in Albany, where Susan B. Anthony's campaign to persuade legislators caused her to refer to herself as a "member of the lobby."

The activist women worked closely with two key politician allies—Anson Bingham, a Republican member of the Assembly Judiciary Committee, and Andrew J. Colvin, a Democratic member of the Senate Judiciary Committee. To cap these efforts, Elizabeth Cady Stanton delivered a brilliant address to the legislature at a session in which women crowded the galleries. The new laws were not just the product of petition signatures and eloquent arguments: they also represented the fruits of coalition-building inside the state legislature, where advocates of the women's cause joined forces with legislators interested in legal code revision and debtor protection.[8] Speech after speech at the 1860 convention gave special emphasis to this pathbreaking New York legislation. The convention participants even approved a resolution declaring, "The geographical position and political power of New York make her example supreme; hence we feel assured that when she is right on this question, our work is done."[9]

Mastering the complexities of New York State politics came naturally to Elizabeth Cady Stanton. She was a political daughter. Her father was a distinguished judge, a state legislator, and a member of Congress, as well as state elector for Republican candidate John C. Fremont in 1856—and—she was a political wife, or would have been, if Henry B. Stanton had been more successful as candidate or appointee. Her husband played a prominent role among antislavery Democrats, including the Barnburners and Free-Soilers, before he joined the new Republican Party. Stanton's cousin Gerrit Smith was the mainstay of the Liberty Party, further cementing her links to the political wing of the abolitionist movement. Stanton's article "A Woman's View of our Late Elections," which she wrote for the New York *Tribune* in November 1854, demonstrated her easy grasp of the political landscape, as she shrewdly ran down the outlook for the *eight* distinct political factions then active in New York.[10]

Susan B. Anthony was a less likely political recruit, for, as a confirmed Garrisonian from a Quaker background, she often condemned participation in regular politics. But like her father, Daniel Anthony, who voted for the first time in 1860, she was also being drawn toward political action by the end of the 1850s. As a New York State agent for the American Anti-Slavery Society since 1856, Anthony lobbied for legislative measures such as a new personal liberty law to forestall the capture of fugitive slaves. Anthony may have had an unlikely tutor in politics: as early as 1852, she had developed a personal relationship with Thurlow Weed—the leader of the Whigs and later Republicans, whose power as editor of the *Albany Evening Journal* earned him the nickname "the Dictator." While she was in Albany to lobby the legislature for six weeks in early 1859, she often called on Weed. In the summer of 1860, when Stanton asked Anthony's advice about attending an abolitionist political convention, Anthony came down in favor of practical (and even prioritized) political action: "If you see your way clear to help both woman and the Negro, or only the Negro, then go by all means." Anthony's skepticism about politicians should probably be understood as an instance of "antipartyism," a common phenomenon among insurgent political factions and third parties in that period.[11]

New York State was a superb school in which to learn the art of politics. The antislavery politicians of upstate's "burned over district" won occasional victories for progressive measures by taking advantage of New York's strong intraparty rivalries and fierce factional feuds within major parties, which left openings for independent efforts and third parties. It was worth mastering this complex web of patronage, personality, and policy, for this state had great national influence, boasting the largest congressional delegation and bloc of electoral votes. In addition, the press magnified New York's influence, for New York City was home to national magazines and powerful major newspapers whose weekly editions circulated around the nation. The woman's rights movement had already acknowledged New York's media preeminence. Although the national woman's rights conventions had rotated among different cities since 1850, in 1858, they decided to meet every year in New York, for the sake of coverage in the New York press.[12]

Anthony and Stanton were joined in New York State by many activist women whose names pepper the first volume of the *History of Woman Suffrage*. Three were particularly prominent and politically savvy. Ernestine Rose had begun the process of petitioning the state legislature for women's rights in 1837. Lydia Mott hosted lobbying activities and monitored legislative action from her home near the capital in Albany. And Martha C. Wright, Lucretia Mott's sister, lived in Auburn, New York, and shared inside political gossip with William Henry Seward's wife, Frances.[13]

As the audience at the 1860 convention learned, the New York women developed a strategy based on insider lobbying, general public agitation, and flexibility about goals. On the inside, they had learned to assess what was "gettable" and who was a potential ally—which meant taking imperfect politicians as they came. The new laws had passed despite the fact that the 1860 New York legislative session was notoriously corrupt, having devoted much of the session to handing over New York City street railway franchises in exchange for bribes. The woman's rights leaders were aware of the character of many of the politicians who had voted for their bill, for as Ernestine Rose joked at the 1860 convention, "We 'Woman's Rights women' have redeemed our last legislature, by inducing them to give us one good act, among so many corrupt ones, and it strikes me that they owe us quite as many thanks as we owe them! (Laughter)."[14]

While lobbying inside the legislature, the women kept up enough general agitation on the outside to create the impression of widespread public interest. Outside agitation might even take its lead from inside possibilities: the Seneca Falls convention of 1848 may be seen as an early instance in which the woman's movement took a cue from the New York State legislature. After the state constitutional convention in 1846 raised questions of equal suffrage, and the legislature passed the first married women's property law in April 1848, networks of antislavery men and women came together in the Free Soil movement, which in turn provided the backdrop to the convention in Seneca Falls. Stanton noted at the time that the passage of the Married Women's Property Act in April 1848 "encouraged action on the part of the women, as the reflection naturally arose that, if the men who make the laws were ready for some onward step, surely the

women themselves should express interest in legislation."[15] Neither public
agitation nor insider lobbying could stand alone. In 1860, Ernestine Rose
felt compelled to warn against "some ladies who think a great deal can be
done in the Legislature without petitions, without conventions, without
lectures . . . without anything but a little lobbying."[16]

Finally, the New York strategy was preeminently flexible about goals.
As Ernestine Rose explained, the New York women asked the legislature
for the full range of women's rights, but as Rose noted, "We differ from
the [Garrisonians] . . . we are ready to take as much as we can get." Stanton
similarly observed that women made their case for the 1860 laws on the
basis of "expediency and precedent." Although it had been clear since
Seneca Falls, if not before, that the vote was "the right by which all others
could be secured," as Frederick Douglass put it, the New York strategy
discouraged theoretical prioritizing and instead emphasized seizing opportunities as they arose.[17]

The 1860 convention's showcasing of the "New York strategy" was
overshadowed when, midway into the second day of the proceedings,
Stanton introduced a set of resolutions in support of the right of divorce
and faced immediate opposition. The resulting debate caused a sensation
in the newspapers, and historians have tended to cite the divorce brou-
haha as an indicator of divisions within the movement or of Stanton's
native radicalism. Instead, it can be seen as the latest product of the New
York strategy. Stanton knew that a bill to liberalize New York divorce laws
had lost by the narrow margin of four votes; on this issue male political
allies were not only ready to act but also seemed close to victory. Stanton
therefore tried to rally the women's convention, hoping a persuasive
speech might sway the last few votes. The ensuing uproar scotched her
hopes but, undaunted, she would proceed as an individual to lobby the
legislature again for divorce reform in the 1861 session, enlisting Lucretia
Mott and Ernestine Rose to do the same.[18]

In the winter of 1860–1861, in the face of southern states' secession,
the activist women of New York confronted a drastically changed political landscape, and they swung into action in response. Anthony put together a group of abolitionists for a "No Compromise with Slaveholders"
speaking tour across upstate New York. The speakers, including both
Stanton and Anthony, urged disunion rather than compromise, and in
city after city from Buffalo to Albany, they were threatened and howled
down by hostile mobs. The "mob tour" can be seen as an early instance
of the civil war hiatus, in the sense that the activist women set aside the
woman's cause for that of antislavery. But it is better understood as re-

flecting the New York strategy's flexibility about goals. The "mob tour" had the specific purpose of intervening in Republican state and national politics by trying to check Thurlow Weed.

At the end of November 1860, Weed urged, in his influential *Albany Evening Journal*, that the South be placated with a fresh round of concessions. Weed called for restoration of the Missouri Compromise line— which would have violated the fundamental Republican principle of no further territorial expansion for slavery. Although William Henry Seward spoke more vaguely, it was widely assumed that Seward might fall into line with his political alter ego. Weed's apostasy created a virtual revolt in the ranks of antislavery Republicans in New York, and the "No Compromise with Slaveholders" tour was implicitly directed against the chief compromiser, Weed. Anthony revealed her understanding of her former mentor and current opponent when she commented on the inactivity of the local authorities, conservative Weed Republicans, who allowed the mobs to operate freely in hopes of discrediting the abolitionists as troublemakers. "Good stiff-backed Union Democrats," Anthony observed, would have broken up the mobs. Although his compromise efforts proved unavailing in 1861, Weed would continue to be a major headache, for this powerful Republican politician believed that reunion must come on the basis of reassuring southern unionists by guaranteeing slavery.[19]

In the months and years that followed, Stanton and Anthony saw old methods of antislavery political agitation given new force by the extraordinary events of the war. The two women, who had argued "let them go in peace" in January, decided in April to support a war to save the union, and like nearly all abolitionists, they made the switch in response to an extraordinary speech Wendell Phillips delivered at the Boston Music Hall shortly after the firing on Fort Sumter. Phillips electrified the abolitionist community and clinched the case for war with an argument from John Quincy Adams, who had affirmed the right of the nation to abolish slavery in time of war. The women saw that war gave traditional activist methods like speaking and publishing new power to persuade. Oratory, always an effective force in nineteenth-century politics, saw its impact redoubled by the war. According to the *New York Tribune*, five million people either heard or read Phillips's antislavery speeches in the winter and spring of 1861–1862.

Stanton and Anthony watched and encouraged the emergence of a powerful female political orator unrelated to any male politician. Twenty-year-old Anna Dickinson, who could not vote herself but could persuade male voters, quickly became a person of influence within the national

Republican Party. Eventually, the Democrats were so hard-pressed, they began fielding woman speakers of their own. With the public hungry for war news and analysis of the nation's ordeal, newspaper circulation shot up. Antislavery journalism's impact was also amplified, as Garrison's Boston-based *Liberator* and the New York-based *National Anti-Slavery Standard*, edited by Anthony's old friend Oliver Johnson, gained new respectability and wider audiences. Abolitionists found new allies in mainstream journalism by 1862, as Horace Greeley was joined by Sidney Howard Gay— an old antislavery colleague of Stanton's husband—at the *Tribune* and Henry Ward Beecher and Theodore Tilton took over at the *Independent*. Finally, the war made antislavery agitation more effective than ever by providing a new argument: as slavery was the cause of the war, only emancipation could bring lasting peace. Veteran speakers like Stanton and Anthony, who had been mobbed in 1861, found themselves respected, even popular by the summer of 1862. Anthony undertook a speaking tour in which she was "entirely off old anti-slavery grounds and on the new ones thrown up by the war."[20]

The women also found their inside political influence more potent than ever, after the Stantons moved to New York City in the spring of 1862, and Anthony joined or visited them there for most of the balance of the war. Stanton saw Wendell Phillips often, dined with Horace Greeley, and picked all the latest inside political news from her brother-in-law Samuel Wilkeson, who served as chief Washington correspondent for the *Tribune*. Anthony could see her old friends at the *Anti-Slavery Standard* office. These insider connections to opinion leaders, like newspaper editors and leading orators, probably translated into real, if undocumented, influence on national political issues for Stanton and Anthony. However, they paid a price for suspending their insider efforts in Albany on women's behalf: the 1862 legislative session in Albany repealed some key provisions of the 1860 laws, much to Anthony's disgust.[21]

In the spring and early summer of 1862, abolitionists began to win the argument at the national level, and Congress passed a succession of antislavery measures, abolishing slavery in the District of Columbia and in the territories, and in July 1862, passing the Second Confiscation Act, which allowed for the seizure and freeing of the slaves of traitors. But Lincoln, who had enraged abolitionists when he overruled local emancipation proclamations by Generals John C. Fremont and David Hunter, showed no indication of willingness to enforce the Confiscation Act. Finally, in the aftermath of the battle of Antietam, on September 22, 1862, Lincoln issued his preliminary Emancipation Proclamation. Abolitionists were quick to see, however, that this legalistic document only promised future action on January 1, 1863, and in New York State, the Democratic opponents of emancipation opened up a fierce campaign to stop the emancipation process by defeating the Republicans in the fall elections.[22]

In the New York State gubernatorial campaign of 1862, Susan B. Anthony took to the stump, arguing not only for policy but also for a major party candidate. The radical faction of the state Republican party, realizing that Weed opposed emancipation almost as much as the Democrats, managed to dominate the state convention and nominate James S. Wadsworth who endorsed the Emancipation Proclamation. Wadsworth supporters included the women's old ally, Andrew J. Colvin; perhaps Anthony was repaying Colvin for his support of women's issues in the 1860 session. Certainly, she understood that a Wadsworth victory would not only cut Weed out of power but also ally the Union's largest state with the emancipation policy. Anthony made five speeches in Schuyler County before the election.[23]

When the votes were counted, however, Wadsworth lost to the Democrat Horatio Seymour, who had denounced emancipation as "a proposal for butchery of women and children, for scenes of lust and rapine, and of arson and murder." Worse yet, Seymour's triumph was evidently due to the fact that the Weed faction chose to sit out the election, preferring to lose the governorship rather than lose control over the Republican organization and its patronage. Weed's sabotage could not be proven, but charges began to fly as soon as the election was over. Stanton's husband Henry, who also had taken the stump for Wadsworth, believed Weed and Seward were behind the loss. In the Wadsworth campaign, the New York women took a vivid lesson in the insider, hardball politics practiced by a cynical pro like Weed.[24]

Though Lincoln did issue the Emancipation Proclamation on January 1, 1863, abolitionists could scarcely allow themselves to celebrate. Slavery remained legal in loyal areas, and they feared that emancipation based on executive order would not be enforceable or sustained by the courts. Stung by Republican reverses in the fall elections, abolitionists returned in 1863 to a strategy they had experimented with in the fall of 1861—forming broad coalition groups or what would in the twentieth century be called "popular front" organizations. Known as the Loyal Leagues or Union Leagues, they enrolled 600,000 to 800,000 members by the year's end. The leagues were private membership organizations, many of them complete with initiation fees, ceremonies, and secret passwords, but their aim was to influence public policy, specifically the Republican policy of emancipation and war. In this context and as part of this larger effort, Stanton and Anthony launched their Women's Loyal National League, which collected over 400,000 signatures and thus facilitated passage of the Thirteenth Amendment.

The Union Leagues were organized on a broad basis of loyalty to the Union, while their ruling assumption—that saving the Union required destroying slavery—was deliberately muted. The leagues helped to shift the North's war aims in midstream, expanding them from union to emancipation, and they steeled the northern population against war weariness. By publishing pamphlets and broadsides and holding mass meetings, the leagues molded public opinion, mobilized their base, and got out the vote at election time. Union Leagues were able to claim credit for notably better results at the polls across the North in 1863 for Republican or "Union" candidates. The leaders of the leagues played insider politics, expecting to influence policy, appointments, and nominations—including the upcoming 1864 presidential contest, about which many in the leagues felt they would "*make the sentiment* [emphasis original] which at least define[s] the character of the nominee."[25]

In New York State, rival leagues reflected the ongoing struggle inside the Republican Party between the Weed/Seward conservatives and the radicals. The Weed machine moved first, organizing the Loyal League of Union Citizens, whose members pledged to support "the Government in all its constitutional efforts to suppress the rebellion"—a revealing adjective, since opponents of the Emancipation Proclamation denounced it as unconstitutional. The radicals, including both Henry B. Stanton and Gerrit Smith, hastened to create a rival Loyal National League, which embraced ending slavery as a war necessity.[26] Stanton and Anthony signaled their inspiration by adopting the name of the men's radical organization in New York for their *Women's* Loyal National League. Abolitionist men encouraged the women to form the organization, and the Union Leagues offered a model for Stanton and Anthony in part because their male relatives were heavily involved (Anthony's brother was one of the founders of the Kansas Union League.) Yet, because women lacked the vote, their organizational activities could only partly mimic the men. Petitioning seemed an obvious possibility. Abolitionists had been circulating emancipation petitions for years, and women were long accustomed to doing a large part of the work of petition-carrying. The WLNL could organize, promote, and claim credit for the petitioning, yet they clearly intended to do more since they made it a membership organization.[27] Decades of experience had taught them that gathering signatures did not necessitate enrolling members.

They wanted to create a permanent political pressure group of women—looking ahead, as many men of the leagues did, to the presidential contest of 1864.

Through the league the women could pursue their New York strategy of seizing available opportunities, wielding a new and promising organizational tool. At the initial meeting of the WLNL, held on May 14, 1863 in New York City, the leaders presented a pledge "to give support to the government in so far as it makes the war for freedom." They endorsed emancipation through the president's proclamation, but also called for additional measures to secure freedom for all slaves. And they called for the "civil and political equality of every subject of the government"—a carefully chosen phrase that would, of course, extend equal citizenship to black men and to white and black women. Insisting on emancipation but also looking past it, the women hoped to see the next political opportunity organized around the question of equal rights, which could extend logically to women as to black men. It was an opportunity they were eager to seize after the 1862 setback in the New York legislature.[28]

There were, however, drawbacks to front groups. Predictably, an abolitionist "ultra" like Abby Kelley Foster detected "something equivocal in the call" and asked whether it implied loyalty to the present administration, which she thought criminally slow to move against slavery and hence not deserving of support. On the other hand, and equally predictably, patriotic ladies who responded to the call for the initial meeting objected to the league's program as too radical. At the first meeting a Mrs. Hoyt of Wisconsin complained from the floor that antislavery and women's rights were being "dragged into this meeting." The leaders fended off such complaints with practical activities on which extremes could agree. The emancipation petition was one specific political goal, and presidential politics was, they hoped, another. In a typically frank speech, Ernestine Rose observed that just eighteen months remained before the next presidential election and predicted that if present policies were continued, the Democrats would win and strike a compromise to welcome back the South with slavery intact. Rose called upon women to prevent such a catastrophe. Her point was clear: the Lincoln administration was a failure, and women should see to its replacement.[29]

Thus, the WLNL was from the outset interested in presidential politics. Stanton invited Jessie Benton Fremont to preside at the May 23 WLNL meeting. Given her husband's status as the chief hope of the anti-Lincoln radicals, this appearance could have converted the League meeting into an early platform for an 1864 Fremont candidacy. Jessie Benton Fremont declined, but in November 1863, the WLNL invited another radical presidential hopeful, Ben Butler of Massachusetts, to address the group. Although Butler too had to decline, the WLNL's intention not only to petition but also to have a hand in encouraging an alternative to Lincoln in the coming presidential election was abundantly clear. Stanton adroitly linked the two goals in her 1863 speech, "The Future of the Republic": "Let us with the only political rights we have under the Constitution, the right of petition, build the platform for the next presidential campaign in universal emancipation."[30]

Busily engaged in building a political membership organization of women, Stanton was blindsided in October 1863, when two major New York papers broke the story of a corruption scandal at the New York Custom House, making accusations against her husband. Henry B. Stanton had to resign his position and then withstand a lengthy congressional investigation. He found it difficult to defend himself because it soon emerged that his son, Neil, acting as his clerk, had indeed taken small bribes seven or eight times. Although she described it as "the deepest sorrow of my life," Elizabeth Cady Stanton never mentioned the scandal in her autobiography, and later scholars have tended to focus on what it says about Stanton as a mother, who blamed others when her eldest and favorite son turned out to be a bad apple. But whatever Neil Stanton's failings, his mother was right to characterize the episode as part of a "Custom House raid" by Thurlow Weed.[31]

Lincoln's election had made Elizabeth Cady Stanton a political wife, since Henry Stanton, who had campaigned energetically for the Republicans, was rewarded with a patronage appointment as Deputy Collector of the Port of New York, a prominent position within the largest bastion of federal patronage, the New York Custom House. Lincoln, determined to divide the Republican patronage between the two New York State factions, gave the top customs house positions to radicals like Stanton and his boss Hiram Barney. But Weed looked enviously at the New York Custom House, since it had 1,200 employees on whose salaries the customary assessment for political purposes was 2 percent. Perhaps without fully realizing it, Henry Stanton, who was temperamentally inclined to be a "pacificator," placed himself in the cockpit of a fierce struggle for New York patronage control.[32]

The scandal involved bonds that shippers were required to post. The risk of a hefty forfeiture was designed to prevent their running the blockage into the Confederacy. Henry Stanton, placed in charge of the bonding, was enforcing a new procedure based on jerry-rigged documentation, a procedure that might or might not turn out to be enforceable. As it turned out, among the 4,000 to 5,000 bonds handled by Stanton's office, about 150 were found to have been subject to irregularities of various kinds. Neil Stanton had accepted small bribes to return a handful of bonds to the parties that had given them, but the investigators were not satisfied by Neil's admission of misconduct. Following rumors and finding that some other bonds turned up missing or with inaccurate paperwork, they embarked on a major fishing expedition in Custom House waters. Far from being able to help his patron, Salmon P. Chase, at a moment when Chase's presidential aspirations were flowering, Henry Stanton was rendered an embarrassment. The whole scandal was suspiciously advantageous for the Seward/Weed faction in its efforts to undermine the radicals and take over the Custom House. Indeed, it would later be revealed that A. M. Palmer, a clerk of Barney's who was sharing an office with Stanton, was secretly acting on Weed's behalf.[33]

After several months of taking testimony, the House investigating committee issued its final report on June 15, 1864. Elizabeth Cady Stanton was stunned to find her husband condemned for "no uncommon carelessness, if not culpable complicity." The committee had actually turned up no evidence of indictable crimes, but the author of the report was determined to cast the most unfavorable light on its findings. The House committee thus trained its guns on picayune misdeeds in an era rife with major misconduct; Weed himself, for example, was meanwhile profiting handsomely from shady, albeit legal, trade in Confederate cotton through the lines in the South. Stanton's brother-in-law Samuel Wilkeson, who looked into the discrepancy between the inconclusive testimony about Custom House practices and the report's harsh conclusions, declared flatly that the author, Representative Calvin T. Hulburd, had been bribed. Stanton told her cousin Gerrit Smith that it had actually been proposed by "a man in high position" that Henry should "buy his peace"—that is, pay a counterbribe to be cleared. Elizabeth Cady Stanton was profoundly embittered against Weed but even more against Lincoln, whom she considered ultimately responsible for Weed's ability to get his way. In July 1864, Stanton told Wendell Phillips that she would like to give him a history of the last eight months, to convince him of "the utter rottenness of the present administration." She offered a recitation of "deeds, facts, names" proving the Lincoln administration's corruption, but Phillips, in turn, assured her that he needed no such convincing.[34]

As the presidential contest of 1864 neared, the women were understandably skeptical about Lincoln's renomination. The president's Reconstruction policy, which he announced in December 1863, provoked a serious split in abolitionist ranks. Surprisingly, Garrison emerged as Lincoln's chief apologist. Having thundered against compromise for decades, Garrison now argued that Lincoln was the best practical alternative. Such half-a-loaf reasoning appalled veteran abolitionists, and Wendell Phillips took the lead in condemning Lincoln, pointing to Lincoln's Reconstruction policy in Louisiana, where the new state government refused blacks the vote and bound them to labor contracts that, Phillips charged, effectively substituted serfdom for slavery. Phillips made a persuasive case, but the anti-Lincoln forces needed an alternative candidate. By February, the Chase candidacy had fizzled, and in March 1864, Garrison and his ally Oliver Johnson renewed the case for Lincoln with editorial endorsements in the *Liberator* and the *National Anti-Slavery Standard*. Abolitionist support was important to Lincoln in this election, especially in New York, where anti-Lincoln sentiment was strong. Thus, control of the abolitionist press was significant: Phillips jeered that a million dollars would have been a cheap price for the *Liberator*'s endorsement of the administration.[35]

Anthony and Stanton were among the radicals who, like Phillips, turned to John C. Fremont as an alternate candidate. Anthony gave the use of the WLNL rooms in the Cooper Union for the first meetings of the Freedom and Fremont Club. As she wrote Charles Sumner, "I rejoice in any movement that asserts the right to examine and pronounce upon the administration." Clearly, she was reacting to a sense of being muzzled by Garrison and Johnson's control of the antislavery press on behalf of Lincoln. In April 1864, Anthony and Stanton strategized with Jessie Benton Fremont about her husband's candidacy. Stanton also signed a public statement calling for a special convention at Cleveland designed to nominate Fremont. As Stanton pointed out in a public letter, it was the only call ever issued for a political convention "demanding the right of suffrage for the black man—that safeguard of civil liberty, without which emancipation is a mockery." Stanton and Anthony actually wanted to use the anniversary meeting of the WLNL in mid-May to nominate Fremont themselves, but refrained at Wendell Phillips's urging.[36]

Elizabeth Cady Stanton still hoped to use the WLNL anniversary meeting scheduled in mid-May 1864 to endorse Fremont and publicize his cause. In the call for the meeting, she urged women to make themselves "a power for freedom in the coming presidential campaign." Boston feminist Caroline Dall responded to Stanton in the *Liberator* in an open letter dated May 1. Dall opposed making the WLNL meeting an "electioneering caucus" and warned that while "woman should interest herself in all national questions," she must not expect to "dictate." Women should be above ordinary politics, Dall claimed. Yet she revealed her own political stance when she declared that four years earlier, "God safely led an honest and humble man" to the presidency. Stanton responded in an open letter of her own, reminding the readers of the abolitionist press that the WLNL was already political; indeed, it was "the first and only organization of women for the declared purpose of influencing politics." Her effective rebuttal scoffed at the premise of dictation and probed the notion that God interested Himself in American presidential elections.

The significance of this public debate about which candidate women should endorse in 1864 may be judged by two responses to it. First, William Lloyd Garrison helped Dall's case by refusing to print Stanton's reply until after the WLNL meeting was safely over.[37] Second, Lincoln congratulated Dall, who subsequently boasted that she had "two messages of thanks from the President for my letter to the Loyal League." And third, Lincoln himself apparently attempted to woo Elizabeth Cady Stanton with a personal interview just prior to the 1864 WLNL meeting. According to Stanton's letters, she and her husband traveled to Washington, where they "had a long talk with Abraham" at the White House. Stanton found Lincoln a "stronger and better man than I had from his official acts supposed him to be, but," she concluded significantly, "I am not in favor of his reelection." Because Henry B. Stanton was in political limbo at this point (owing to the Custom House scandal), the invitation to the Stantons surely reflected Lincoln's desire to talk with the wife and not the husband—he wanted to win Stanton and the WLNL women away from Fremont.[38]

The women paid a price for their independence: the antislavery press imposed a near-blackout on the WLNL anniversary meeting that convened in New York City on May 12, 1864. Garrison's *Liberator* refused to mention the meeting at all, while Johnson's *Anti-Slavery Standard* and Gay's *Tribune* merely printed the text of the executive committee report. The report included resolutions, one of which called for the elective franchise for all citizens who were taxed or bore arms—a formula that embraced at least some blacks and women. Another resolution explicitly endorsed the right of suffrage for black men. Yet we know nothing more about what transpired at the meeting, though it was said to have included "soul-stirring speeches" by Wendell Phillips as well as Stanton, Anthony, Rose, and Mott. Stanton and Anthony thus learned the price of being unable to control the press coverage of their political efforts. So infuriating was the press blackout to Anthony that she described the "spirit of the Lincoln press on Fremont and the abolitionists" as "diabolical." Only the New

York *Herald*, traditionally hostile to both women and abolition and delighted to detect dissension in the ranks of its enemies, ran coverage. The *Herald* reporter, noting that when an unnamed participant on the floor tried to defend Lincoln by declaring, "The intention of the President is to emancipate," Anthony in the chair responded that she "didn't care a fig for his intentions. It was an old saying that Hell is paved with good intentions."[39]

Of course, Lincoln went on to reelection. Fremont proved disappointing as a candidate, reverting in his letter of acceptance to bland "front" tactics, which lost him the chance to galvanize abolitionists. Anthony and Stanton fretted about these blunders, but after the Democrats nominated McClellan on a peace platform, Fremont's candidacy became virtually a dead letter and most abolitionists swung behind Lincoln. Holdouts like Stanton and Anthony and Wendell Phillips were left to take consolation in the idea that they had influenced Lincoln by forcing him to ask for a constitutional amendment to end slavery in the 1864 Republican platform. On the eve of the election, Stanton could only declare, "It will be a satisfaction to us in the future to feel that we did what we could." On the contrary, the women later preferred to forget their opposition to a martyred president and to claim instead their petition campaign—which finally bore fruit when the Thirteenth Amendment cleared Congress in January 1865—as if it had been the only point of the WLNL.[40]

The New York activist women thus engaged in intense political activity before they possessed the vote or had even defined their movement around winning it. The 1860 woman's rights convention revealed them as flexible and pragmatic about goals and intent on what was "gettable"— which explains their quick shift in priorities, from women's rights to antislavery, and from state to national issues, in response to secession and war. In both the mob tour and the Wadsworth campaign, they were speakers for the antislavery cause, but the difference between the two episodes reveals their movement, along with other abolitionists, toward a more "inside" political position, in which they could endorse a major party candidate in a contest of national import. In the Loyal League, they learned the uses of membership or "front" organizations. But they also confronted the limitations of a female mass constituency, for unlike the men's leagues, they could marshal only petition signatures, not votes. Adept at defining ideological goals in political terms, they perceived that emancipation would open up the question of equal rights and hence in turn women's rights. Yet in the Custom House scandal, they were reminded that ordinary politics was often not about ideology at all, but rather just a game of greed and gain. Responding to the politics of the moment prompted them in 1864 to insist on the vote for black men, even while lacking suffrage rights themselves. In their effort to stop Lincoln, the women saw evidence that they had indeed achieved a measure of national political influence when they were recognized by the president himself. Yet in the same episode, shut out of the abolitionist press, they were reminded of their dependence on resources they did not control. At the war's end, faced with Lincoln's reelection and Weed's ascendancy, the women could hardly consider themselves as political winners, but they were political players, with the insights, connections, and bruises to prove it.

NOTES

1. Eleanor Flexner, *Century of Struggle: The Woman's Rights Movement in the United States*, ed. Ellen Fitzpatrick, enlarged edition (Cambridge and London: Harvard University Press, 1996), 136–37, 139, 141. "Hiatus" in Ellen DuBois, *Feminism and Suffrage: The Emergence of an Independent Women's Movement in America, 1848–1869* (Ithaca: Cornell University Press, 1978), 52. Wendy Hamand Venet, *Neither Ballots Nor Bullets: Women Abolitionists and the Civil War* (Charlottesville and London: University Press of Virginia, 1991) begins the work of revision with valuable chapters on the Women's Loyal National League and the election of 1864, although she views these episodes as steps toward politics rather than accomplished political practice (p. 148).

2. Janet L. Coryell, "Superseding Gender: The Role of the Woman Politico in Antebellum Partisan Politics," in *Political Identities: American Women and the Emergence of a Secular State*, ed. Stephanie Cole and Alison Parker (Arlington: University of Texas Press, 2000).

3. Elizabeth R. Varon, "Tippecanoe and the Ladies Too: White Women and Party Politics in Antebellum Virginia," *Journal of American History* 82 (Sept. 1995): 494–521; Rebecca Edwards, *Angels in the Machinery: Gender and Party Politics from the Civil War to the Progressive Era* (New York: Oxford University Press, 1997); Jean Gould Hales, "'Co-Laborers in the Cause': Women in the Ante-bellum Nativist Movement," *Civil War History* 25 (June 1979): 119–38; Mary Hershberger, "Mobilizing Women, Anticipating Abolition: The Struggle against Indian Removal in the 1830s," *Journal of American History* 86 (June 1999): 15–40; and the summary of scholarship in Ronald P. Formisano, "The 'Party Period' Revisited," *Journal of American History* 86 (June 1999): 112–19.

4. Pamela Herr, *Jessie Benton Fremont: A Biography* (New York: Franklin Watts, 1987), 262–63, and chaps. 17–18; Edwards, *Angels in the Machinery*,

28; *The Letters of Jessie Benton Fremont*, ed. Pamela Herr and Mary Lee Spence (Urbana and Chicago: University of Illinois Press, 1993).

5. Jean H. Baker, *Mary Todd Lincoln; a Biography* (New York: W.W. Norton, 1987), 160–62, 180–81.

6. Richard H. Sewell, *Ballots for Freedom: Antislavery Politics in the United States, 1837–1860* (New York: Oxford University Press, 1976); Henry Mayer, *All on Fire: William Lloyd Garrison and the Abolition of Slavery* (New York: St. Martin's Press, 1998). Political abolitionists did sometimes welcome women, see Nancy Isenberg, *Sex and Citizenship in Antebellum America* (Chapel Hill and London: University of North Carolina Press, 1998), 19–20.

7. Lori Ginsburg, *Women and the Work of Benevolence: Morality, Politics, and Class in the 19th Century United States* (New Haven and London: Yale University Press, 1990), chap. 4, "Moral Suasion is Moral Balderdash;" Formisano, "'Party Period' Revisited" 113–17.

8. Norma Basch, *In the Eyes of the Law: Women, Marriage, and Property in Nineteenth-Century New York* (Ithaca and London: Cornell University Press, 1982), esp. chap. 6; *Selected Papers of Elizabeth Cady Stanton and Susan B. Anthony*, ed. Ann D. Gordon (New Brunswick, N.J.: Rutgers University Press, 1997), 1:304, 405–7.

9. SBA as a member of the lobby, in SBA to Unknown, [25 Feb. 1859], Patricia G. Holland and Ann D. Gordon, eds., *Papers of Elizabeth Cady Stanton and Susan B. Anthony* (hereafter *Papers*) (Wilmington, Del., 1991, microfilm), reel 9. On the New York State efforts, see *Proceedings of the Tenth National Woman's Rights Convention, Held at the Cooper Institute, New York City, May 10th and 11th, 1860* (Boston: Yerrinton & Garrison, 1860), 6–7. On ECS's speech, see ECS to Isaac Fuller, 19 Mar. 1860, *Papers*, reel 9.

10. ECS, "A Woman's View of our Late Elections, *New York Semi-Weekly Tribune*, 8 Dec. 1854, in *Papers*, reel 8.

11. SBA to ECS, 25 Aug. 1860, *Papers*, reel 9: ECS, "A Woman's View." Sidney David Brummer, *Political History of New York State During the Period of the Civil War* (New York: AMS Press, 1967), 70; Sylvia Hoffert, *When the Hens Crow: The Woman's Rights Movement in Antebellum America* (Bloomington: University of Indiana Press, 1995), chap. 5; Gordon, *Selected Papers*, vol. 1, p. 440.

12. Carol Kolmerton, *The American Life of Ernestine Rose* (Syracuse: Syracuse University Press, 1999); Harper, 1:199; *Selected Papers*, 1:75n, 432–33, 473–75, 433n.

13. *Proceedings of the Tenth National Woman's Rights Convention*, 47; Mark Wahlgren Summers, "'A Band Of Brigands': Albany Lawmakers and Republican National Politics, 1860," *Civil War History* 30 (June 1984): 101–19.

14. Judith Wellman, "The Seneca Falls Women's Rights Convention: A Study of Social Networks," *Journal of Women's History* 3 (Spring 1991): 22.

15. *Proceedings of the Tenth National Woman's Rights Convention*, 11.

16. *Proceedings of the Tenth National Woman's Rights Convention*, 54, 11, 36.

17. Douglass in *History of Woman Suffrage*, 1:170–73.

18. Elizabeth Cady Stanton, *Eighty Years and More: Reminiscences, 1815–1897* (Boston: Northeastern University Press, 1993), 215, 217; Lydia Mott to ECS, 1861, *Papers*, reel 9.

19. The mob tour in clippings, Jan.–Feb. 1861, in *Papers*, reel 9; Harper, 1:207–13; Stanton, *Eighty Years*, 210–13. Albany *Evening Journal*, 24, 27 Nov. 1860; *NASS*, 8, 15 Dec. 1860; Brummer, *Political History*, 99–101; Glynden Van Deusen, *Thurlow Weed: Wizard of the Lobby* (Boston: Little, Brown, 1947), 299, 300, 310. Reaction to Weed in Lydia Mott to ECS, 28 Nov. 1860, *Selected Papers*, 1:450. SBA quote re Democrats in Harper, 1:216.

20. James M. McPherson, *The Struggle for Equality: Abolitionists and the Negro in the Civil War and Reconstruction* (Princeton, N.J.: Princeton University Press, 1964), 49–51, 82, 86; Giraud Chester, *Embattled Maiden: The Life of Anna Dickinson* (New York: G.P. Putnam's, 1951); Venet, *Neither Ballets Nor Bullets*, chap. 3; Louis Starr, *Bohemian Brigade: Civil War Newsmen in Action* (New York: Knopf, 1954), 203; SBA to Lydia Mott, in Harper, 1:222.

21. Toasts at Christmas Dinner, 25 Dec. [1862?], Wendell Phillips to ECS, 7 Apr. [1863?], *Papers*, reel 10; Wilkeson in Starr, *Bohemian Brigade*, 66–68; SBA to Lydia Mott, [after 10 Apr. 1862], in *Selected Papers*, 1:475–76.

22. On the 1862 campaign, see Brummer, *Political History*, chap. 8; De Alva Alexander, *Political History of New York* (New York: Henry Holt, 1906) vol. 3, chap. 3.

23. A speech, marked in Anthony's handwriting years later, "SBA—during the Gen. Wadsworth campaign—1862," in *Papers*, 10:339, is probably the speech mentioned in Harper, 1:222, as delivered at Mecklenburg in Schuyler County in the fall of 1862 on "Emancipation the Duty of the Government." Anthony spoke in five different locations in Schuyler County in the last week before the election. *The Havana (N.Y.) Journal*, 25 Oct. and 1 Nov. 1862.

24. Seymour as quoted in Alexander, 3:40; Brummer, *Political History*, 250–51, 290; Van Deusen, *Thurlow Weed*, 301–2; Henry B. Stanton, *Random Recollections* (New York: Harper, 1887), 216.

25. The 1861 strategy in McPherson, *Struggle for Equality*, 75–79. Guy James Gibson, "Lincoln's League: The Union League Movement during the Civil War" (Ph.D. diss., University of Illinois, 1957); Clement Silvestro, "None But Patriots: The Union Leagues in Civil War and Reconstruction" (Ph.D. diss., University of Wisconsin, 1959).

26. Gibson, "Lincoln's League," chaps. 10–12; Brummer, *Political History*, chap. 10; Henry W. Bellows, *Historical Sketch of the Union League Club of New York* (New York: G.P. Putnam's, 1879). Henry B. Stanton and Gerrit Smith in Gibson, 229, 240–45.

27. Daniel Read Anthony in Gibson, 111, 335. Male encouragement in Harper, 1:226; Stanton, *Eighty Years*, 236; SBA to Charles Sumner, 1 Mar. 1864, *Papers*, reel 10.

28. *Proceedings of the Meeting of the Loyal Women of the Republic, held in New York, May 14, 1863* (New York: Phair, 1863), 32, 15.

29. Abby Kelley Foster to SBA, 20 Apr. 1863, in *History of Woman Suffrage*, 2:877; *Proceedings of the Meeting of the Loyal Women*, 19, 23–24, 46.

30. *Proceedings of the Meeting of the Loyal Women*, 15; JBF to ECS, 4 May 1863, in Herr and Spence, eds., *Letters of Jessie Benton Fremont*, 351; Benjamin F. Butler to ECS, SBA, et. al., [1863 before Nov. 28], *Papers*, reel 10; ECS, "The Future of the Republic," *Papers*, 10:639.

31. Arthur Harry Rice, "Henry B. Stanton as a Political Abolitionist" (Ph.D. diss., Columbia University, 1968), 422–62; ECS to Horace Greeley, 18 Jan. 1864, *Papers*, reel 10; Elizabeth Griffith, *In Her Own Right: The Life of Elizabeth Cady Stanton* (New York: Oxford University Press, 1984), 114–15; ECS to Horace Greeley, 18 Jan. 1864, *Papers*, reel 10.

32. Brummer, *Political History*, 137n. HBS as a "pacificator" in HBS to Charles L. Woodbury, 12 Nov. 1852, Henry B. Stanton Papers, Library of Congress.

33. Rice, "Henry B. Stanton," 422–62; 38th Congress, First Session, United States House of Representatives, Reports of Committees, Report No. 111, "New York Custom-House," generally and 43–4 (Palmer's office location). John Niven, *Salmon P. Chase* (New York: Oxford University Press, 1995), 351–52; Frederick J. Blue, *Salmon P. Chase: A Life in Politics* (Kent, Ohio and London: Kent State University Press, 1987), 233–35.

34. 38th Congress, Report No. 111, "New York Custom-House," 3; Van Deusen, *Thurlow Weed*, 285–94; Samuel Wilkeson to Sidney Howard Gay, [1 Jul 1864], Sidney Howard Gay Papers, Columbia University; ECS to Wendell Phillips, 3 July [1864]; Wendell Phillips to ECS, 20 July 1864, ECS to Gerrit Smith, 3 July 1864, all in *Papers*, reel 10.

35. McPherson, *Struggle for Equality*, 242–45, chap. 12; William Frank Zornow, *Lincoln and the Party Divided* (Norman: University of Oklahoma Press, 1954); Mayer, *All on Fire*, 563–67; *Liberator*, 18 Mar. 1864, 20 May 1864; *National Anti-Slavery Standard* (hereafter *NASS*), 26 Mar. 1864.

36. SBA to Charles Sumner, 6 Mar. 1864; ECS to Jessie Benton Fremont, [Apr. 1864]; *Principia*, 26 May 1864; Wendell Phillips to ECS, 25 Apr. 1864; ECS to Wendell Phillips, 26 Apr. 1864, all in *Papers*, reel 10.

37. ECS to Caroline Dall, 14 Apr. 1864 in *Papers*, reel 10; "Letter from Mrs. C.H. Dall," *Liberator*, 6 May 1864, *NASS*, 7 May 1864; Stanton's reply in *Liberator*, 3 June 1864, and *NASS*, 11 June 1864. Caroline Healey Dall to Elizabeth Neall Gay, 23 June 1864, Sidney Howard Gay Papers.

38. ECS to Gerrit Smith, 6 May [1864] and ECS to Wendell Phillips, 6 May [1864], *Papers*, reel 10.

39. *NASS*, 28 May 1864; *New York Tribune*, 13 May 1864, 28 May 1864. "Soul-stirring" in Harper,1:237; one-paragraph notice of the meeting and the speakers in the *Independent*, 19 May 1864. SBA to ECS, 12 June 1864; and see also SBA to Anna Dickinson, 1 July 1864, "It seems to me that Liberator and Standard are gone *stark mad*" in *Papers*, reel 10. *New York Herald*, 15 May 1864, in *Papers*, 10:808.

40. SBA to ECS, 12 June 1864; ECS to Wendell Phillips, 6 Nov. 1864, *Papers*, reel 10.

4

WOMAN SUFFRAGE IN CONGRESS

American Expansion and the Politics of Federalism, 1870–1890

Allison Sneider

In the years between 1878, when Senator Aaron Sargent of California first proposed a woman suffrage amendment to the federal Constitution, and 1887, when the first Senate debate on Sargent's amendment took place, suffragists, like other Americans, had their eyes on the West.[1] Beginning soon after the Wyoming Territory enfranchised women voters in 1869— followed by Utah in 1870 and Washington in 1883—suffrage activists regularly petitioned Congress to establish the precedent that "no *more states shall* come into the Union, except on the basis of perfect *equality of rights* to women—civil & political."[2]

Where suffragists saw new political opportunities, legislators saw potential dangers. Territorial expansion refocused national attention on Indians and Mormons, whose "uncivilized habits" and "licentious practices" were perceived as equal threats to the health and vitality of American institutions. Widely understood to reflect the multiple possibilities of what America could become, territorial expansion therefore raised to the forefront of political debate the character of the Union.

The partisan battling that accompanied the admission of new states into the Union revived the pre-Civil War debate over states' rights and national power with an added, gendered dimension. Because women could vote in Wyoming, Utah, and Washington territories, legislators found themselves confronting the possibility that turning the territories into new states might inadvertently set national precedents authorizing women's ballots. Although woman suffrage was not nearly as divisive as the expansion of slavery into the territories three decades earlier, congressmen on both sides of the aisle considered the idea of votes for women "fraught with great danger to the free institutions under which we live, and to the harmony, welfare, and good order of society."[3]

One possibility open to legislators hostile to women's ballots was to disfranchise women voters by using Congress's authority to overturn territorial constitutions. To many, however, this idea appeared to be a potentially dangerous violation of the constitutional principle that voting rights were governed by state (not national) law. Women voters in western territories thus presented national legislators with a serious conundrum: a conundrum that put questions of woman suffrage, states' rights, national authority, and federal relations at the forefront of discussions over the admission of new states into the Union.

At first, congressional attention to these interrelated issues revolved around Indians and Mormons. In the 1880s, congressional efforts to resolve the political status of Indians and Mormons resulted in the passage of two federal laws that affected the voting rights of both groups. In February 1887, the Dawes Severalty, or General Allotment Act, in part provided the conditions for establishing Indian citizenship and guaranteed those Indians living on allotted lands, who willingly "adopted the habits of civilized life," the same rights, privileges, and immunities as other United States citizens.[4] One month later, the Edmunds-Tucker Act disfranchised the women of Utah Territory, as one of a series of punitive measures directed against the polygamous practices of the Mormon Church.[5]

Although historical accounts of the suffrage movement have given these subjects little scrutiny, suffragists (including Mormon suffragists in Utah Territory) paid careful attention to the decades-long national debates over Indians and Mormons that resulted in the passage of these two federal laws.[6] Using the Indian and Mormon questions as foils, suffragists attempted to make the case that any legislation which might enfranchise male Indians within the several states and disfranchise women voters in Utah Territory underscored the premise that suffrage generally, and woman suffrage particularly, was both a national concern and the proper object of federal legislation. Emboldened by the national approach to resolving the political problems posed by Indians and Mormons throughout the 1880s, many suffrage activists pushed for a national solution to their own question.

Bringing together questions of women's rights and states' rights, of domestic relations and federal relations, western expansion thus set the stage for the only congressional debate on a woman suffrage amendment to the federal Constitution to occur in the nineteenth century. The combined activities of turning some Indians into citizens and potential voters, barring Utah women from the polls, and turning territories into new states helped put the question of votes for women on both the national agenda and the congressional calendar at a time when many Americans continued to view woman suffrage as a dangerous and radical demand. In the context of an expansive Union, the congressional history of woman suffrage illustrates how the debate over women's rights was often as much about the limits of constitutional authority, national sovereignty, states' rights, and the character of the electorate, as it was about the political capabilities of women.

Beginning in 1868, soon after passage of the Fourteenth Amendment guaranteed all citizens equal protection under the law, individual women in cities and towns across the country attempted to register, and to vote, in local, state, and federal elections. In some cases they were successful. Susan B. Anthony's celebrated 1873 trial and conviction for illegal voting in Rochester was one in a series of ambitious legal battles begun after the Civil War, and reaching up to the Supreme Court, in which suffragists argued that the Fourteenth and Fifteenth Amendments should be interpreted to include women.[7] When suffragists read these amendments, they viewed the Fourteenth Amendment's guarantee of equal protection under the law, and the Fifteenth Amendment's prohibition against abridging a United States citizen's right to vote on the basis of race, color, or previous condition of servitude as a baseline for the continued expansion of the franchise. In fact, many argued that, however inadvertently, the Fourteenth and Fifteenth Amendments had already enfranchised women. This strategy, the New Departure, was a hallmark of Reconstruction-era suffragism.[8]

The only New Departure case to reach the Supreme Court involved a Missouri suffragist, Virginia Louisa Minor. The case of *Minor v. Happersett* (1875)—one of the single most important Supreme Court rulings on women's rights in the nineteenth century—came about when Minor sued Reese Happersett, an election inspector who refused to allow her to vote.[9] In her brief submitted to the Court, Minor and her lawyer husband argued that the Missouri constitution, which limited the franchise to male citizens of the state, was in direct conflict with the Constitution of the United States and in violation of the Fifteenth Amendment. As a citizen of the United States, Virginia Minor demanded the right to vote.

The Supreme Court ruled against Minor. Interpreting the Fifteenth Amendment narrowly, as a particular solution designed solely to enfranchise freedmen, the Court's 1875 decision in *Minor v. Happersett* shut the door on suffragists' constructions that the Fourteenth and Fifteenth Amendments had already enfranchised women, and that national citizenship carried with it an inherent right to vote. The language of the Court's decision is striking. Declaring that the "United States has no voters of its own creation," Chief Justice Morrison Waite affirmed the authority of individual states to grant or withhold the ballot, except in the specific instances described in the Fifteenth Amendment.[10] The Court's decision theoretically sent women back to the states to pursue their struggle for the vote and made clear the principle that citizens and voters were not one and the same.

In the years after losing *Minor*, members of the National Woman Suffrage Association consistently referred to this decision as the moment when the Supreme Court conceded that "the old doctrine of State sovereignty is the true one and there is no nation."[11] Many believed that far more was lost than simply votes for women; they charged that they had also been deprived of one of the central gains of Reconstruction, the transformation of America from a confederacy of states to a centralized nation. As Elizabeth Cady Stanton told the Senate Committee on Privileges and Elections in 1878, "Such is the imperfect development of our own nationality that we really have no right as yet to call ourselves a nation . . . as the Supreme Court decision is in direct conflict with the idea of national unity."[12]

Despite their failure to win adherents to the New Departure in the courts, many members of the National Woman Suffrage Association remained intent on demonstrating to Congress the connection between their own claims to voting rights and the principle that voting rights were inherent in the condition of national citizenship. Toward this end, Matilda Joslyn Gage, chairman of the National Woman Suffrage Association's executive committee, began publishing a series of articles for her widely read monthly newspaper, the *National Citizen and Ballot Box*, that connected voting rights with national citizenship. This was a subject dear to Gage's heart and an underlying premise of many of her editorial endeavors. In addition to being "a general criticism of men and things," Gage's *National Citizen* was devoted to popularizing the position that "Suffrage is the Citizen's right, and should be protected by National Law."[13] Choosing to ignore the cultural opposition to women as voters, Gage focused instead on the thorny constitutional problem of American federalism. She hoped to make the case that "although, theoretically, the power over the suffrage is held to be in the hands of the States alone . . . the United States has endowed whatever class it pleased with the suffrage."[14] Chief Justice Morrison Waite's declaration in *Minor* that the United States has no voters, Gage opined, was "false upon the face of it."[15]

In an 1878 article entitled "United States Rights and State Rights," Gage produced a list of classes of voters whom she believed had been enfranchised by national law. First, Gage noted that "every enfranchised male slave has the ballot secured him under United States law, a law that overrode all State provisions against color." Along with ex-slaves, Gage included on her list "every Southern man disfranchised because of having taken part in the war, and who was afterwards granted amnesty." Gage then turned to the "naturalized foreigner [who] secures his right to vote under United States law, and cannot vote unless he first becomes a United States citizen."[16] Here Gage emphasized how the process of naturalization, a process subject to national (not state) law, turned foreigners into voters through the vehicle of citizenship.

In a subsequent article, "Indian Citizenship," Gage turned her attention to recent developments in United States' Indian policy as another way to explore how national legislation could create new voters in the states.[17] A resident of western New York, where a council of the Iroquois tribes had gathered for discussion of a Senate bill designed to grant Indian men citizenship, Gage noted with some satisfaction the Iroquois council's reluctance to see the passage of any American law that "should either allow or compel them to become citizens."[18] Comparing the meeting of the Indian council in New York, where the Iroquois "protest[ed] against citizenship about to be forced upon them," with the January 1878 meeting of the National Woman Suffrage Association in Washington, D.C., where white women "demand[ed] citizenship denied them," Gage sought to highlight the special irony she saw in congressional efforts to turn Indian men into citizens and voters before white women.[19]

Harnessing white racial prejudice to the suffragist cause, Gage complained that the "black man had the right of suffrage conferred upon him without his asking for it, and now an attempt is made to force it upon the red man in direct opposition to his wishes, while women citizens, already members of the nation . . . are denied its exercise."[20] Gage's writings made clear to her readers that she perceived U.S. efforts to incorporate Indians into the national political community as an insult to white women. References to Indian "savagery" and Indian "barbarism" throughout her text underscored the point: "Can women's political degradation reach much lower depth?",

Gage asked. "She, educated, enlightened, Christian, in vain begs for the crumbs cast contemptuously aside by savages."[21]

In 1878, when Gage wrote her article on Indian citizenship many Americans held divided and conflicted opinions about how best to deal with Indian populations they considered "foreign powers though living among us."[22] Throughout the nineteenth century, the legal understanding of Indians' relationship to government loosely paralleled women's own. The language used to describe the political status of both groups included references to "domestic dependency" and the problem of primary allegiance—in one case to tribes, in the other to husbands and families.[23] Although a shared status as political dependents sometimes caused white suffragists to look sympathetically on the plight of Indians, congressional efforts to turn some Indians into citizens (and voters) before white women did not encourage an equally sympathetic reaction. Susan B. Anthony, Isabella Beecher Hooker, and Sara Andrews Spencer, among others, believed that Indian voters would make woman suffrage that much harder to achieve because Indians, in their words, "have always made of their women beasts of burden."[24]

Gage shared many of the negative sentiments toward Indians expressed by Anthony and others. Yet, she also emphasized how national discussions of the Indian question could create new possibilities for suffragists. A subtle yet important part of her presentation of the Indian question was the assumption that Indian voting rights would inevitably flow from their new status as citizens. In Gage's view, national legislation granting citizenship to Indians should be viewed as simply another instance where the national government created voters and imposed them on the states.

In the years leading up to the 1887 passage of the Dawes Act, the Indian question repeatedly surfaced in suffragists' writings as an example of national efforts to create new voters within the states. Writing for the *Women's Tribune* in 1887, Clara Colby revisited the constitutional questions Gage had raised ten years earlier, and invited her readers to ponder "what happens to the claim that 'the question of suffrage belongs exclusively to the states' now that Nebraska for example, by no act of its own, has voters, in the Omahas, the Winnebagoes, and the Santees?"[25] Colby's question, like Gage's before her, however, went largely unanswered. Yet, Gage's argument that U.S. Indian policy violated the principle set forth in *Minor*, that the United States had no voters, continued the arguments behind the New Departure even after its defeat in the courts.

National discussions of the Mormon problem during this same period intensified suffragists' convictions of the national nature of the vote.

Careful attention to the Indian question led Gage and others to note how congressional anti-polygamy legislation also seemingly violated the principle that "the United States has not voters." Utah women had been granted the ballot in 1870 by the Mormon-dominated territorial legislature. In the 1880s, anti-polygamy legislation under discussion in both the House and Senate included a clause that would disfranchise all women voters in Utah Territory, Mormon and non-Mormon alike.[26] This legislation was premised, in part, on the belief that Mormonism so degraded women that they could not be trusted to vote independently of their husbands. Although early versions of this legislation did not pass the House, the 1886 congressional calendar included a new anti-polygamy bill sponsored by Vermont Republican George Edmunds that was a source of great dismay to suffrage activists in both the National Woman Suffrage Association and the American Woman Suffrage Association. Across the board, suffragists dismissed the argument that any situation, no matter how dire, could legitimize such a radical measure as the disfranchisement of women. As Lucy Stone, the eminent Boston suffragist wrote indignantly in the *Woman's Journal*, "If Senator Edmunds had undertaken to do the same thing to Irishmen or to colored men . . . the whole country would ring with it."[27] These sentiments were echoed in the West by Nebraska suffragist Clara Colby. Writing for the *Woman's Tribune*, Colby claimed that "the injustice and tyranny of that section [of the Edmunds bill] has no parallel in history." Here Colby drew attention to non-Mormon women who would also be disfranchised by the law. "Certainly no condition exists," she wrote, "which would warrant the de-citizening of the innocent thousands."[28]

Gage agreed with Colby and Stone. Protesting that the Utah question was not simply an issue of plural marriage, but a suffrage issue, she was incensed that "the government is continuously striving to touch the political rights of the women of this [Utah] territory." Claiming that since "the general government did not confer this right [to vote] . . . the United States according to its own theory, has no authority to interfere with this right, because according to that theory it has nothing at all to do with the suffrage question."[29] This was a somewhat ironic position. Although Gage opposed the Supreme Court's decision in *Minor*, here she argued that as long as *Minor* remained on the books it should at least be applied consistently.

In 1886, suffragists' opposition to the Edmunds bill entered the Senate with the help of Republican George Frisbee Hoar of Massachusetts. A long-time supporter of women's voting rights, Hoar sponsored an amendment

to the Edmunds anti-polygamy bill that would remove the clause disfranchising women voters. In the course of debate over his amendment, Hoar
reminded the Senate that suffrage was "a thing to be left to the people of
the Territories and the people of the States as a matter which comes within
the domain of local self-government."[30] Hoar's opposition to the Edmunds
bill shifted the debate away from the Mormon question to a discussion
of woman suffrage and states' rights.

Well known for his support of activist federal policies during Reconstruction, Hoar's arguments for the sanctity of state control over voting
rights might be expected to have had a hollow ring. Yet Hoar's arguments
against federal intervention into the political affairs of Utah Territory
resonated strongly with many of his Democratic colleagues, who protested
against the Edmunds bill because it interfered with local control over
voting rights.[31] This debate over anti-polygamy legislation for the Utah
Territory drew anti-woman suffragists, many of them white anti-woman
suffrage Democrats from the South, to a defense of the Utah Territory's
pro-woman suffrage policies. As one particularly vehement anti-woman
suffragist from Georgia told the Senate, "If the question [of woman suf-
frage] was up in his own state, he would vote against it; but, as the question before the Senate was one affecting the right already given to the
women of Utah by the laws of that Territory . . . he would vote to amend
the bill."[32] For a brief moment during the debate over the Edmunds anti-
polygamy bill, states' rights sentiments placed pro- and anti-woman suffrage legislators in a strange and uneasy alliance.

Given the widespread and pervasive hostility toward the Mormon practice of polygamy, this alliance—between legislators who favored woman
suffrage and those who opposed federal intervention into the political
affairs of Utah Territory—was not strong enough to amend the Edmunds'
bill. Hoar's amendment was defeated, clearing the way for Utah women's
eventual disfranchisement.[33] Yet, when the Senate took up the Washington statehood bill just three months later, in April 1886, the two questions of woman suffrage and national control over the ballot returned
full-blown and in a seemingly inseparable fashion.

In the case of Washington Territory, where women had also been enfranchised by an act of the territorial legislature, the Senate's primary concern
was an amendment to the Statehood bill offered by James Eustis, an anti-
woman suffrage, states' right Democrat from Louisiana. Eustis's amendment,
much like Edmunds's bill, was intended to disfranchise Washington women
by making it "a condition of admission of this State that the State constitution shall provide that the right of suffrage shall be limited to male citizens

of that Territory."[34] Because the presence of Mormons did not color this debate, the issue of states' rights, national authority, and woman suffrage emerged more clearly as divisive and contentious issues in congressional debates over Washington's admission into the Union.

Like the Edmunds bill, the Senate's discussion of Eustis's amendment illustrates how territorial expansion pushed some legislators toward an uncharacteristic defense of woman suffrage. One South Carolina Democrat, for example, promised to vote against any effort to disfranchise Washington women precisely because of his commitment to state control of the ballot, asserting "that the people of that Territory have the power to regulate those matters for themselves . . . it is their affair and not mine."[35] Although voting against Eustis's plans to disfranchise Washington women, he insisted that he did not wish to be understood as being in favor of woman suffrage. By opposing the Eustis anti-woman suffrage amendment, however, this was the effect if not the intent of his position.

Given women's enfranchisement within the territories, the question of how best to avoid national intervention into local political affairs while simultaneously opposing women's voting rights became a particular dilemma for many white southern Democrats hostile to increasing African-American political participation within their own states. One Kentucky Democrat summed it up this way: "Congress can not allow the most intelligent woman in any State in the Union to vote without allowing the most ignorant Negro woman in any State in the South to vote. . . . [Admitting Washington] is the entering wedge to universal female suffrage for white and black, refined and ignorant."[36] Unable to see how Congress could "deny the application of the principle of female suffrage everywhere if it establishes it in this case, over which it has absolute and unquestioned power to do as it pleases," this particular southern Democrat lent his support to the Eustis anti-woman suffrage amendment.[37] He did so even though this amendment intruded on states' ability to define for themselves who should vote. Eustis and his supporters viewed woman suffrage in Washington Territory as potentially more threatening to the practice of white supremacist politics within their own states than using national authority to intervene in local political affairs.

Suffragists followed the Senate's discussion of the Washington statehood bill closely and with a good deal of enjoyment. The *Woman's Journal* published the debates in their entirety. Over a span of several weeks, readers received a highly detailed lesson in how the woman question had become intertwined with territorial expansion, national power, and the contentious politics of black suffrage in the South. In all its complexity, the debate over Washington statehood made one point remarkably clear to all concerned. Despite the Supreme Court's efforts to send women back to the states to gain the ballot, expansionist politics had nationalized the suffrage issue. In this context, the question of a constitutional amendment to enfranchise women was harder to ignore if all future debates over territorial statehood were not to have the appearance of repeated national referenda on woman suffrage. Already a new battle over the admission of Wyoming Territory and the status of Wyoming's women voters loomed on the horizon, and women had exercised full voting rights in that territory for almost twenty years.

By the time the woman suffrage amendment came to the Senate floor in January 1887, suffragists were increasingly aware that the renewed attention to their question was due less to their own efforts, or to a sea change in popular opposition to women's voting rights, than the way western expansion was forcing the issue on an unwilling Senate. The suffrage amendment had acquired a momentum of its own. Legislators appeared eager to take up the question of woman suffrage if only to get it off the table. To many suffragists' dismay, this view seemed to characterize the position of even their staunchest allies. Elizabeth Cady Stanton, watching the progress of the debate from England, commented on this state of affairs in an open letter to the NWSA's January 1887 convention. Pointing out that the pro-woman suffrage Senator Henry Blair had urged the Senate to vote on the woman suffrage amendment "so that we may be relieved of the question, for at least this session, and perhaps for some Congresses to come, " Stanton took the opportunity to criticize "our champion."[38] "That sentiment rather grates on my heart strings," she explained. "If he had said I desire a vote, that women may be relieved from their crushing disabilities, that would have had a touch of magnanimity."[39] Not surprisingly, in this climate of divided opinion, the proposed woman suffrage amendment went down in defeat.

On June 27, 1890, Wyoming Territory entered the Union as a new state and women became full voters within the Union for the first time since the revolutionary period.[40] While certainly a victory for woman suffrage, and this is the way most historians have understood Wyoming's admission, it was also a defeat. In the context of the lost possibilities of the woman suffrage amendment to the national constitution, Wyoming's admission did not represent the ringing endorsement for woman suffrage that suffrage activists had hoped for. As one Senator explained to some of his more anxious colleagues, "the Republic will not go to pieces, the Union will not be dissolved," because women voters in Wyoming "[do] not determine the question of whether they shall vote anywhere else."[41]

In the 1870s, the twin premises of the New Departure—that suffrage was a right of citizenship and that this right was national in character— were rejected by legislators and jurists alike. In the 1880s, however, the task of bringing new states into the Union renewed legislative attention to the political status of Indians, Mormons, and enfranchised women within the territories, making voting rights a subject of national concern and debate. The legacy of expansionist politics on the woman suffrage movement was, however, mixed. While territorial expansion reopened the possibility of legislating voting rights at the national level for the first time since *Minor*, it also brought the woman question to a premature life and death in the Senate. Embroiled within the ongoing tensions of American federalism, suffrage politics in the 1880s points our attention toward some of the contradictions within a political consensus that treated the character of the electorate as an issue of national concern— increasingly policed through immigration and naturalization law into the twentieth century—but left control over voting rights in the hands of the states.

NOTES

1. See Chapter 5, Rebecca Edwards, "Pioneers at the Polls: Woman Suffrage in the West," in this volume.

2. Susan B. Anthony to George Frisbee Hoar, 21 Feb. 1882, George Frisbee Hoar Papers, Massachusetts Historical Society.

3. *Congressional Record*, 51st Cong., 1st sess., (26 Mar. 1890), p. 2671.

4. The United States government held allotted lands in trust for a period of twenty-five years. Although the law stated that "Indians to whom allotments have been made shall have the benefit of, and be subject to the laws, both civil and criminal, of the State or Territory in which they may reside," the twenty-five year patent kept Indian allotees in a condition of wardship. 8 Feb. 1887, *Statutes at Large of the United States*, 49th Cong., 2nd sess., chap. 119, sec. 6.

5. 3 Mar. 1887, *Statutes at Large of the United States*, 49th Cong., 2nd sess., chap. 397, sec. 20.

6. Sarah Barringer Gordon, "'The Liberty of Self-Degradation': Polygamy, Woman Suffrage and Consent in Nineteenth-Century America," *Journal of American History* 83 (Dec. 1996): 815–847.

7. *United States v. Anthony*, 24 F. 829 (U.S.C.C.N.D.N.Y., 1873).

8. Ellen Carol DuBois, "Taking the Law into Our Own Hands: *Bradwell, Minor,* and Suffrage Militance in the 1870s," in *Visible Women: New Essays on American Activism* ed. Nancy A. Hewitt and Suzanne Lebsock (Urbana: University of Illinois Press, 1993), pp. 19–40; Joan Hoff, *Law, Gender, and Injustice: A Legal History of U.S. Women* (New York: New York University Press, 1991); and Patricia Lucie, "On Being a Free Woman and a Citizen by Constitutional Amendment," *Journal of American Studies* 12 (1978): 343–358.

9. *Minor v. Happersett,* 88 U.S. 162 (1875).

10. Ibid.

11. Senator Henry W. Blair to the 21st Annual National Woman Suffrage Association Convention (1889), in Susan B. Anthony and Ida Husted Harper, eds., *History of Woman Suffrage, 1883–1900,* vol. 4 (Indianapolis: Hollenbeck Press, 1902), p. 144.

12. Elizabeth Cady Stanton, *Arguments Before the Senate Committee on Privileges and Elections of the United States Senate* (Washington, D.C.: Government Printing Office, 1878), 91–92.

13. *National Citizen and Ballot Box,* July 1878.

14. "United States Rights and State Rights," *National Citizen and Ballot Box,* May 1878.

15. Ibid.

16. Ibid.

17. "Indian Citizenship," *National Citizen and Ballot Box,* May 1878.

18. Ibid. The Senate bill to which Gage referred was mostly likely S. No. 107, "to enable Indians to become citizens of the United States," introduced on Oct. 23, 1877. *Congressional Record,* 45th Cong., 1st sess., pp. 135, 525–556; 2nd sess., pp. 1130–1131, 1361.

19. "Indian Citizenship," *National Citizen and Ballot Box,* May 1878.

20. Ibid.

21. Ibid.

22. Ibid.

23. *Cherokee Nation v. Georgia* 5 Pet. 1 (1831).

24. *Woman's Journal,* 22 Dec. 1877.

25. *Woman's Tribune,* 17 Dec. 1887.

26. "That it shall not be lawful for any female to vote at any election hereafter held in the Territory of Utah for any public purpose whatever, and no such vote shall be received or counted or given effect in any manner whatever; and any and every act of the legislative assembly of the Territory of Utah providing for or allowing the registration of voting by females is hereby annulled." 3 Mar. 1887, 49th Cong., 2nd sess., sec. 20, chap. 397.

27. *Woman's Journal*, 9 Jan. 1886.

28. *Woman's Tribune*, Feb. 1886.

29. *National Citizen and Ballot Box*, Feb. 1879.

30. *Congressional Record*, 49th Cong., 1st sess., (5 Jan. 1886), p. 406.

31. William Cohen, *At Freedom's Edge: Black Mobility and the Southern White Quest for Racial Control, 1861–1915* (Baton Rouge: Louisiana State University Press, 1991).

32. *Congressional Record*, 49th Cong., 1st sess. (6 Jan. 1886), p. 457.

33. In 1887, Utah women lost the vote.

34. *Congressional Record*, 49th Cong., 1st sess., (8 Apr. 1886), p. 3259.

35. "Admission of Washington Territory," *Woman's Journal*, 1 May 1866.

36. Ibid.

37. Ibid.

38. *Woman's Tribune*, Mar. 1887.

39. Ibid.

40. The 1776 state constitution of New Jersey enfranchised women as well as men. Women voted in New Jersey until 1807, when a new election law excluded women from the polls.

41. *Congressional Record*, 51st Cong., 1st sess., (25 June 1890), p. 6490.

5

PIONEERS AT THE POLLS

Woman Suffrage in the West

Rebecca Edwards

In the United States, the achievement of woman suffrage began on the frontier. The first territories and states to grant women full voting rights were Wyoming, Utah, Colorado, and Idaho. Seven of the next eight states that did so were also west of the Mississippi. Before the Nineteenth Amendment passed, giving all American women the ballot, most western states had already passed referenda or amendments, as had the territory of Alaska. The pattern was so marked that the editors of *Literary Digest*, commenting on rising pro-suffrage sentiment in 1912, reversed an old slogan, announcing, "Eastward the Star of Suffrage Takes Its Way."

Few leaders of the national suffrage movement had expected this regional pattern to emerge. Their organizations were based in the Northeast. The *Woman's Journal* hailed from Boston, and it carried ward-by-ward accounts of that city's suffrage campaigns beside shorter reports from the distant Plains, Rockies, and Pacific coast. Western suffragists often expressed a sense of isolation from the national movement. Though Susan B. Anthony traveled tirelessly in the West, the area was vast and the priorities of its women often unsettling to her. Meanwhile, other strategists lavished money and attention on New England or on lobbying Congress directly for a federal amendment. For many, the West was a low-stakes laboratory where suffragists could try out new tactics and, in case of victory, advertise the results to voters back east.

The striking regionalism of early suffrage victories has posed a problem for historians. Following the arguments of Frederick Jackson Turner, author of the "frontier thesis," some scholars have suggested that woman suffrage was a by-product of special frontier conditions. Pioneering, they argue, bred a democratic spirit, a strong sense of local community, and more respect (as well as higher wages) for female labor. There is some evidence to support this case, but it leaves important questions unanswered. If Oregon men voted for woman suffrage as a result of their pioneer spirit, why did referenda fail there in 1884, 1900, 1906, 1908, and 1910, before finally winning passage in 1912? After reviewing various possible explanations, historian Richard White calls the issue "perplexing." Noting the circumstances that led to suffrage in different states, he concludes that "the West's willingness to grant women the vote still ends up as something of a mystery."

Explaining how western women won the vote, in decades when most of their northeastern and southern sisters did not, requires careful attention to chronology. Wyoming and Utah territories demand attention first, as odd outliers that granted suffrage more than twenty years earlier than any other place, and a half-century before national suffrage was attained. The next set of victories—in Colorado and Idaho—were the result of specific political conditions in the 1890s. Then, a fourteen-year gap intervened before the next state gave women the ballot. This frustrating period for suffragists provides an important clue in explaining the subsequent blizzard of state-level successes between 1912 and 1919. For woman suffrage in the West, timing was the key.

William H. Bright, the legislator who sponsored woman suffrage in Wyoming, championed the cause for practical (perhaps even cynical) reasons. A southern Democrat, Bright moved to Wyoming to join a gold rush and later became president of the territory's legislature, made up of twenty men. Bright persuaded twelve of these legislators to vote for his bill. Noting the recent adoption of the Fifteenth Amendment to the Constitution, which enfranchised men irrespective of race or color, he argued that white women's votes would offset those of black men. Along with fellow Democrats, he also sought to twit the territory's governor, John Campbell, who had been appointed by Republicans in Washington. If Campbell vetoed the measure, members of his party might protest, since some radical Republicans favored woman suffrage. If Campbell signed the bill and the spectacle of women voting caused a scandal, blame was sure to fall on him.

Even more important, Bright seems to have borrowed an idea from a handful of congressmen who had recently tried to enfranchise women in the territories. These men sought publicity: they hoped woman suffrage was sensational enough to put remote areas on the map, leading to growth and prosperity. On a related theme, Bright expressed concern over a dearth of white women in the West, resulting from the rush of single men to the frontier. In territories like Wyoming—which had a 6–to-1 ratio of men to women—wives and mothers were in short supply. Yet in the East, as a result of deaths in the Civil War, it was men who were relatively scarce. Perhaps, Bright argued, suffrage would prompt more women to emigrate, balancing gender ratios and providing the best conditions for the growth of families.

For these reasons, the Wyoming legislature passed the suffrage bill. Governor Campbell signed it in 1869. A few Laramie suffragists had visited the governor to urge his support; otherwise, almost no women's mobilization had occurred. The result was nonetheless remarkable. Eastern reformers expressed their surprise and delight at this example of "advanced civilization" and innovation on the frontier. For a brief period, congratulatory telegrams poured in from as far away as Britain and Prussia. Though some Wyoming legislators changed their minds and sought to reverse the measure, Governor Campbell vetoed the repeal and suffrage stayed.

If these events had succeeded in attracting thousands of women to Wyoming, or had otherwise proved profitable or helped the territory grow, other western legislatures might have soon followed suit. But as a long-term strategy woman suffrage served none of the purposes set forth by its sponsors. Meanwhile, a second territory granted woman suffrage by a different logic. Utah, founded by Mormon pioneers in the late 1840s, had resisted incorporation into the American nation and fought to remain a haven for members of the Church of Jesus Christ of Latter-Day Saints. The founders of this movement had suffered persecution further east, culminating in the lynching of their leader Joseph Smith in Missouri. Trekking to the Salt Lake region, church members had relied on one another to build all the elements of a new society. After Utah became a U.S. territory, its leaders tried to shelter their church from the meddling of Congress and non-Mormon territorial governors who were appointed from Washington.

In these struggles, the most controversial issue was the Mormon practice of plural marriage. According to a doctrine set down by Joseph Smith, some men in the church took more than one wife. As a result, Mormon men were denounced in Congress and the national press as household tyrants whose wives were morally degraded. In December 1869, Congress began debate on a bill that would have disfranchised any man who expressed his support for polygamy. Mormons were shocked by the attack, and in January 1870, leading women in Salt Lake City organized two protest meetings. Speaking from the pulpit of the Mormon Tabernacle for the first time, women defended the political rights of their "fathers, husbands, and brothers" and their own right to marry whomever and however they pleased. Eliza Snow, a leading woman of the church, called upon Mormon women "to rise up in the dignity of our calling and speak for ourselves," and one of the meetings endorsed woman suffrage.

Male leaders of the church and Utah Territory had previously been lukewarm or hostile to the idea of women voting. (When asked about women's rights, church leader Brigham Young had joked that women had "the right to ask their husbands to fix up the front yard.") But facing congressional hostility, Mormon men now decided that women could be powerful allies. In February 1870, the territory's legislature extended the full franchise to the women of Utah. Pointing to the recent women's meetings in Salt Lake City, proponents argued that Mormon women would vote to defend the faith. The territory's non-Mormon governor signed the bill into law, apparently hoping the opposite—that Mormon women would use their new power to end polygamy. (Allison Sneider's essay, chapter 4 in this volume, takes a closer look at federal conflicts with Utah over polygamy and woman suffrage.)

The legislators' predictions proved far more accurate than those of the church's critics, and in the short term woman suffrage in Utah achieved the Mormons' political goals. It temporarily averted congressional measures to imprison polygamists and disfranchise Mormon men. It also strengthened the Mormons' voting majority in Utah, since the few non-Mormons were mainly single men in mining camps. For the next sixteen years, Utah women voted at all elections, demonstrating by overwhelming majorities their support for the policies and candidates selected by men in the church. Only a handful of non-Mormon suffragists in Utah tried to use the ballot to challenge plural marriage, and they did not come close to success.

In the following decade, the tangled history of Utah suffrage took several ironic turns. Mormon women's allegiance to their faith persuaded Republicans that female voting rights had strengthened the institution of polygamy, rather than undermining it. In 1887, on these grounds, Congress passed a measure disfranchising Utah women—over the combined protests of both Mormon and non-Mormon women in the territory, who had until recently been bitter opponents on the issue of plural marriage. Three years later, amid a barrage of legislation designed to punish polygamists, the church finally abolished plural marriage. Then, as Utah sought statehood in the 1890s, its leaders wrestled over whether or not its proposed state constitution should reinstate female suffrage. To ensure that it did, women mobilized a broad-based, highly visible suffrage movement throughout the territory, twenty-five years *after* they had first won the right to vote. Utah entered the union as a state in 1896 with its women reenfranchised.

In both Wyoming and Utah, the original passage of woman suffrage occurred during Reconstruction, in the wake of the Civil War. In this era of ferment, during which the nation enfranchised black men, various proposals for extending and strengthening citizenship rights appeared in legislatures and committee rooms around the nation. Political leaders in both Wyoming and Utah followed these debates and borrowed arguments from others who were working to advance political rights. The first wave of woman suffrage in the West, then, was linked to this era of constitutional creativity.

Yet the possibilities of Reconstruction must not be overstated, since they did not result in suffrage for women anywhere else. In Kansas, suffragists waged a bitter fight in 1867 that ended in defeat. Voters in Colorado Territory made the same decision ten years later. As the political energies of Reconstruction faded in the 1880s, referenda also failed in Nebraska, Oregon, South Dakota, and Washington Territory. In the meantime, the opportunities offered by Reconstruction were closed off by the courts. Having failed to secure women's federal voting rights explicitly in the Fifteenth Amendment, some suffragists argued that such rights were implied. They tried to vote and, when registrars rejected them, they sued. In *Minor v. Happersett* (1875), the U.S. Supreme Court ruled categorically that women had no federal voting rights.

The result of these developments was to link woman suffrage with Mormonism in the minds of many Americans. After all, Utah was the most populous and prominent place, where women had the vote. To the rest of the nation that experiment had brought dubious results. Non-Mormons, most of whom abhorred polygamy, argued that Mormon women were not using the vote wisely. Outside the territory, few suffrage leaders were willing to mount a defense of plural marriage. Only Elizabeth Cady Stanton traveled to Utah and defended Mormon women's right to practice polygamy if they believed it was right and good. (To the mortification of Susan B. Anthony and other colleagues, Stanton observed that husbands demanded a great deal of time and trouble, and she suggested that sharing one man among several women might be an improvement on conventional marriage arrangements.) Belva Lockwood, a lawyer who ran for U.S. president on the Equal Rights ticket in 1884, was among the

few other women's rights leaders who defended Mormonism, reminding
U.S. officials that the Constitution guaranteed freedom of religion.

Most other suffrage leaders felt that Mormons' adoption of suffrage—
which some believed was a convenient ploy for nefarious purposes—had
unfairly associated their movement with an immoral and unpopular religion. Mormon polygamy *was* unpopular. Newspapers and magazines circulated jokes about the inconvenience of having multiple wives, and
editors launched angry diatribes against western "harems" and Mormon
women's "enslavement." Furthermore, congressional deliberations over
policy in Utah were the most visible woman suffrage debates of the 1880s.
Persistent links between woman suffrage and Mormonism placed the
national suffrage movement in a difficult position. Movement leaders
tended to neglect Utah and heap praise on Wyoming as the model for
the nation to emulate. Even after the abolition of plural marriage, the
History of Woman Suffrage, compiled by leaders of the movement, down-
played the victory in Utah and focused on developments elsewhere.

The second wave of western suffrage victories took place in the 1890s
with the rise of a new political movement: Populism. Like Mormons,
members of the People's Party, or Populists, as they were called, cast themselves as outsiders and mistrusted the eastern political establishment. Like
Mormons, many western Populists believed women voters would defend
their cause. But Populists' key concerns were not religious but economic.
For these men and women, woman suffrage was part of a broader reform
agenda that included transforming the American economy and supporting farmers and industrial workers.

In some states the People's Party organized as early as 1890, the year in
which Kansas Populists swept to victory. The national party was created
on July 4, 1892, from the merger of two organizations: the Farmers' Alliance, dedicated to farmers' rights, and the Knights of Labor, a nationwide
labor union. Both these groups included women as organizers and lecturers, and female members participated in grassroots decision-making.
Most men in the southern wings of these movements, however, were
antagonistic to women's rights, and women there were reluctant to demand the ballot. Westerners were far more vocal in support of woman
suffrage, though many men in the movement—and even some women—
saw it as a side issue that distracted attention from the Populists' economic
program. The Populists' chief goals were a progressive federal income tax,
government ownership of railroads and telegraphs, and a looser money
supply to ease the burdens of debtors. As a result, and because of southern Populists' reluctance to support the measure, the party never included

woman suffrage in its national platform. At best, one of their conventions resolved "that the question of female suffrage be referred to the legislatures of the different States for favorable consideration."

This opened the way for state Populist coalitions to work for suffrage wherever support existed. By 1894, the *Woman's Journal* noted that Populists had put woman suffrage in their platforms in "nearly every northern State." On the basis of strong Populist endorsements of suffrage, Susan B. Anthony reluctantly began speaking on the party's rostrums in California and elsewhere, hoping the new movement would prove strong enough to give women in some states the right to vote. But in the Northeast and Midwest, the Populist movement was tiny and weak. Everywhere it was fragile, struggling with internal divisions, facing entrenched party loyalties among voters, and rocked by a massive economic depression that struck in 1893.

In only two states, Colorado and Idaho, did the rise of Populism coincide with full suffrage for women (though it is worth noting that a majority of the people of Utah, in the year they achieved statehood and readopted woman suffrage, also voted Populist). In Colorado, a Populist administration elected in 1892 put a suffrage referendum on the ballot the following year. Two other political parties promptly endorsed it. First were the Prohibitionists, who had long advocated "a temperance ballot," that is, women's right to vote on measures related to the sale of liquor. Second were the powerful Republicans, who had not previously offered much support but now found themselves pressured by the Populist initiative. Though the Colorado suffrage movement had faced earlier defeats, this time woman suffrage passed by the comfortable margin of 55 to 45 percent.

Because of Colorado's larger population, and especially the rapid growth of Denver, its victory was more significant for the national suffrage movement than was the passage of a similar referendum in Idaho in 1896, a year when Populists won power there. Yet the Idaho referendum passed by a much larger margin—almost two to one—with especially high support in the southeastern Mormon counties. As in Colorado, multiple parties endorsed the measure once it was presented, as did most of the state's newspapers. In both states, suffragists had been organized and visible for years before passage and played key roles in campaigning for the referenda and getting out the vote. In addition to the Colorado and Idaho Equal Suffrage Associations, those active in the campaigns included chapters of the Women's Christian Temperance Union, women in labor unions, and prominent female journalists, lawyers, lecturers, and leaders of reform and literary clubs.

Another similarity between the two states helps to explain why woman suffrage, once it was placed on the ballot, won the endorsement of the Republican and even Democratic parties, most of whose leaders in other states remained opposed to the idea of women voting. The recent, rapid growth of Colorado and Idaho's economies rested on their hardrock mines—in particular, by the 1890s, silver mines. That fact translated into overwhelming political support for "silver coinage," a proposal to increase the money supply by minting silver at a ratio of 16 to 1 to the value of gold (which would have increased silver's relative value). "Silver at a ratio of 16 to 1" was a key demand in almost every Populist platform at both state and national levels. Its popularity was so intense in the Rockies that many Republicans and Democrats also converted to the cause. In both Colorado and Idaho, political leaders urged voters to enfranchise women so they could help work for silver coinage. "A vote for equal suffrage is a vote for silver," proclaimed one Denver newspaper. "The silver states need all the votes they can get," added another Colorado editor. Though the political parties in both states argued over *how* to implement silver coinage, the linkage between that issue and woman suffrage helped ensure women's victory.

Populist leaders in Colorado rightly claimed credit for introducing their state's suffrage referendum, which pressured other parties to sign on. Yet the results of the initiative were a shock to the new party and especially to Populist Governor Davis Waite. Colorado voters blamed his administration for the devastating depression in 1893, which shut down many of the state's mines and brought the economy to a standstill. Looking for new leadership in 1894, like voters in many other states, Coloradans voted heavily Republican. These voters included a majority of the women whom Populists had worked to enfranchise and whom Waite and others had assumed would owe the party a debt of gratitude. After the election, Waite spoke with such bitterness that many Populists in other states backed off their pro-suffrage position. Western urban women, Waite warned, had Republican loyalties and should not be trusted with ballots. "The statements you have made," one Populist wrote to Waite from Minnesota, "have ended woman's suffrage in the People's party."[1]

If Populist leaders were disillusioned with the results of suffrage, leaders of the suffrage movement were equally frustrated with their political allies. Though some women sought the vote for specific purposes—for example, to pass anti-liquor legislation or Populist economic measures—others advocated it as a basic right of citizens rather than a way to advance such policy goals as silver coinage. Yet partisan alliances were crucial for suffrage victories. In the intense heat of political conflict, men enfranchised women with direct expectations about their future support. Afterward, women's votes brought one of two results. Either male party leaders were disappointed by women's independence, as in Colorado, or women's very loyalty, as in Utah, became a point of criticism for opponents. Men in other states concluded that female voters could do little good and much harm. "Oh I have been through the partisan battle," Anthony wrote wearily, "and I don't want to see it again." She began to advocate a strictly nonpartisan path.

As the depression ended and the Populist Party faded, it was not easy for suffrage advocates to implement either a partisan *or* a nonpartisan strategy. After 1896, prosperity began to return to most parts of the country and economic debates took on a more comfortable tone. Republicans held the White House as well as majorities in both houses of Congress and claimed credit for the end of hard times. By tacit agreement, Democrats were allowed to exercise "home rule" in southern states, but Republicans dominated the national political scene for over a decade. In these circumstances, the men who held power did not need women's aid, and new political movements had difficulty applying pressure on the dominant party.

Looking back at recent elections, conservative commentators in these years linked woman suffrage to Populism and radicalism in the West, rejecting both. It was widely noted that Colorado and Idaho, which had supported woman suffrage, were hotbeds of Populism, while California had stayed in the Republican column in 1896 and in the same election had defeated a woman suffrage referendum. One Oregon newspaper wrote that suffrage activism in Colorado and Idaho was "the outgrowth of the temporary socialistic spirit that prevails in those states." Between 1871 and 1890, the suffrage movement had suffered from the stigma of Mormon polygamy; in the years between 1897 and 1910, the stigma of radicalism was even worse, and suffragists later referred to this period as "the doldrums." In retrospect, the victories in Utah, Colorado, and Idaho seemed to have hampered the cause of suffrage in other states.

It is no accident that "the doldrums" ended when new issues and alliances reinvigorated party politics after 1910. Three parties, in fact, challenged Republicans: not only a rejuvenated, reformist Democratic Party, which captured the White House in 1912, but also the Progressive Party (active between 1912 and 1916) and the Socialist Party. Though these groups had different agendas, their followers cooperated in a number of states to work for the passage of woman suffrage and other legislative goals.

Socialists played especially key roles in a massive referendum campaign in California, where suffrage had been defeated in 1896 but won by a narrow margin in 1911. The California Women's Socialist Union ignored an international socialist directive forbidding coalitions with nonsocialists and instead cooperated with an array of women's clubs, labor unions, and other groups. They published materials in many languages, organized across class lines, and won enormous support for suffrage, especially among working-class men in Los Angeles.

There was not an absolute correlation in the early 1910s between the success of woman suffrage and states where men voted in large numbers for socialists or progressives. Some western states with powerful Socialist movements, such as Oklahoma, did not grant women the vote. Kansas adopted a constitutional amendment for suffrage in 1912, a year when its voters showed little support for new party movements. Nonetheless, as party competition sharpened there was a cascade of victories in the trans-Mississippi West between 1910 and 1914. In addition to California and Kansas, women won the full ballot in Washington (1910), Oregon (1912), Arizona (1912), Montana (1914), Nevada (1917), North Dakota (1917), and Nebraska (1917). Most of these states had strong Socialist or Progressive movements—in some cases both—and in most of them party competition was keen. After "the doldrums" between 1896 and 1910, the reinvigoration of electoral politics helped to bring renewed gains for women's political rights.

In the same years, more complex national patterns emerged and eastern states at last began to swing into the suffrage column. In 1913, Illinois became the first state east of the Mississippi to grant women suffrage and the first to do so by action of the state legislature, rather than by a constitutional amendment submitted to voters. In 1917, the United States entered World War I and members of the National American Woman Suffrage Association (NAWSA) threw themselves enthusiastically into war work, along with many other women's organizations across the United States. Women's patriotic efforts, they believed, would show national leaders that they deserved the vote, and indeed, support for suffrage grew rapidly in the late 1910s, with Democratic President Woodrow Wilson declaring himself in favor at the start of the 1916 campaign.

Meanwhile, the suffrage movement had modernized, taking up effective new tactics of lobbying, advertising, and grassroots organizing. Under the leadership of Carrie Chapman Catt, NAWSA focused its attention on a federal amendment rather than a state-by-state strategy, though Catt was able to formulate her "Winning Plan" partly because of the increasing momentum of state-level victories. In 1917, techniques similar to those used by Socialist women in California helped win full suffrage for women in New York, which controlled a whopping 45 electoral votes. As Rhode Island, Tennessee, Kentucky, and Maine fell into line, the pattern of western leadership began to break down. Yet victories in the West continued right up to the passage of the Nineteenth Amendment, which in that region was almost an afterthought: west of the Mississippi, only Texas, Arkansas, and New Mexico had not fully enfranchised women already. Montana Representative Jeanette Rankin, the nation's first woman in Congress, had already served her first full term.

Western leadership on the suffrage issue, then, had two overlapping causes. Suffrage emerged in the varied contexts of Wyoming, Utah, Colorado, and Idaho as part of citizens' perception that they held outsider status in the nation as a whole—what western historian Patricia Limerick has called a "pattern of dependence" on eastern financial and political institutions and resulting frustration with eastern control. For Wyoming legislators, woman suffrage promised to attract women, families, publicity, and economic growth to an arid and isolated locale. In Utah, it held out hope for protecting the rights of a besieged religious minority. In Colorado and Idaho, it emerged when the mining economy of the Rockies seemed threatened by fiscal conservatives in Washington, whose decisions the "silverites" sought to reverse.

In the last two cases these grievances had clear partisan dimensions, and the 1910s brought more suffrage victories as the Progressive and Socialist movements elaborated some of Populism's earlier themes and introduced new initiatives. Though neither of these movements existed exclusively in the trans-Mississippi West, they were strongest in that region. Socialism, in particular, was perceived by many in the East as another "western insurgency." Once again, a group of westerners described themselves as uniting against the unbridled power of eastern financiers and political interests and agitating for a variety of reforms, including votes for women. Not only energetic grassroots organizing, then, but also strong party competition—what political scientists call electoral competitiveness—was a crucial factor in suffragists' achievements in the West.

Because it resulted partly from a sense of western grievances and outsider status, as well as persistent challenges to the major political parties, western suffrage left an ironic legacy. On the one hand, western Americans can proudly claim a history of pioneering political justice for women, driven in part by the broader opportunities the frontier offered for remaking American society. Yet the very association of woman suffrage with

creative nineteenth-century movements that were nurtured in the West—
Mormonism and Populism—may have hampered the cause of suffrage in
the rest of the nation. National leaders like Susan B. Anthony and Lucy
Stone were keenly aware of the stigma attached to suffrage by those with
deep antipathies toward Mormonism and the political left. Yet they were
unable to break these links in the eastern public mind.

At the same time, western women's *choices* as voters immediately became part of the controversy over suffrage itself. When Utah enfranchised
women, those women who voted Republican risked being viewed as traitors to Mormonism, while the large majorities of Mormon women who
voted to support their church confirmed the belief, already held by many
Americans, that female voters would be easily manipulated or shamelessly
immoral. Helen Kendrick Johnson, conservative author of *Women and
the Republic* (1897), argued vehemently against woman suffrage on the
grounds that Colorado women had shown themselves to be Populists,
socialists, and anarchists—practitioners of a "strain of exalted fanaticism."
At the same time, the results of the 1894 campaign persuaded People's
Party leaders that the majority of Colorado women were Republicans and
traitors to the Populist cause.

The success of suffrage in the West was no mean achievement. It enabled thousands of American women to cast their ballots and participate
in campaigns—and a few to serve in elected office—before 1920. By the
1910s, western suffrage helped advance the national cause simply through
the rising number of states where women voted and these voters' growing visibility and clout. In granting women's political rights, the West
experienced early all the opportunities and dilemmas that would emerge
later nationwide. The West served notice to the nation, early on, that
women could be effective organizers in the political arena. Western women
showed that they cared deeply about politics and could be strong partisans in the midst of critical campaigns. They seldom united in one party;
diverse women had many different priorities and loyalties. And western
women showed that they could think for themselves, often straying from
the party-line paths that men wanted them to tread.

NOTE

1. All quotes in this chapter are from Rebecca Edwards, *Angels in the
Machinery: Gender in American Party Politics from the Civil War to the Progressive Era* (New York: Oxford University Press, 1997), 91–110.

6

RACE, REFORM, AND REACTION AT THE TURN OF THE CENTURY

Southern Suffragists, the NAWSA, and the "Southern Strategy" in Context

Marjorie Julian Spruill

As the end of the nineteenth century approached, American women were still struggling to gain their full rights as citizens—including the franchise. They sought this reform even as a wave of reaction swept the nation on the issue of who should vote—a wave of reaction particularly obvious in the American South. As a result, many white suffragists adopted arguments calculated to promote woman suffrage as consistent with, rather than opposed to, white supremacy.[1]

The accommodation of white suffragists to the racist politics of the turn-of-the-century South is one of the best-known and most frequently debated aspects of the southern suffrage movement. Historian Aileen Kraditor set the stage for this debate in 1965 when she wrote that the "principal argument" of the southern suffrage movement was that "the enfranchisement of women would insure the permanency of white supremacy in the South" and portrayed the National American Woman Suffrage Association (NAWSA) as reluctantly permitting the use of racist tactics in the suffrage movement as a concession to the racism of southern white women. Anne Firor Scott and many other scholars have challenged Kraditor on the centrality of race as a motive or tactic among white southern suffragists, insisting that these women—like suffragists in all parts of the nation—wanted the vote to advance the status of women and promote reform, and that the argument that woman suffrage would aid white supremacy was but a minor argument in their suffrage repertoire.[2]

Owing to Kraditor's work, southern white suffragists have been, in historian Suzanne Lebsock's words, "assigned primary responsibility for the movement's racist thought and policy" and the southern movement "has achieved its greatest fame as a purveyor of white supremacy." In her well-known case study of the Virginia suffrage movement between 1909 and 1920, Lebsock insisted that white suffragists in the state mentioned race only to defend their cause against the antisuffragists' "increasingly scurrilous" claims that enfranchising women would destroy white supremacy.[3] More recently, historian Elna Green also emphasized the racism of the antisuffragists and defended white southern suffragists as far more progressive on race than southern antisuffragists. Green also claimed that, throughout the thirty-year history of the woman suffrage movement in the South, the majority of white southern suffragists were not willing to exploit the race issue, instead choosing to follow the strategy of NAWSA which she implied was not racist.[4] Increasingly, however, scholars of the national suffrage movement have recognized racism as a major factor in suffrage ideology and strategy in all parts of the United States.[5]

Historians of the American woman suffrage movement have advanced many theories concerning the extent to which white suffragists used racist arguments and the relationship between national leaders and southern leaders in regard to developing and implementing a strategy that would aid their cause in turn-of-the-century America—an era widely regarded as the "nadir" of race relations in the United States. Yet it was inevitable that race would play a crucial role in the movement's history as late nineteenth-century NAWSA leaders struggled to build a truly national movement and southern white suffragists sought enfranchisement in the midst of a regional movement to restore white political supremacy. To understand this role, the southern suffragists, the NAWSA, and the "southern strategy" must be examined in the context of these national and regional developments, recognizing that the context—and thus the role of the race issue in the woman suffrage movement—changed over time.[6]

In fact, much of the disagreement about white suffragists' use of race-based arguments in the South depends on which time period is being discussed, particularly whether it is before or after the state-by-state disfranchisement of southern African Americans that occurred between 1890 and 1903. Working together, northern and southern leaders developed a "southern strategy" designed to exploit what the white South perceived as its "negro problem," a strategy these suffragists implemented during the first, predisfranchisement phase of the southern movement, and abandoned when it proved ineffective, as white male politicians in the region found other means of restoring white supremacy.[7]

It is important to understand that most southern white suffragists were reformers, eager to use women's vote to support improved public health and education measures and prohibition and to oppose child labor and corruption, but they were *radicals* only on the question of woman suffrage. On other crucial issues including race, their ideas were well within the "normal" range for the white South in the 1890s and early 1900s, and their strategy was clearly influenced by developments in southern and national politics. Though there was a range of opinions regarding race among the white suffragists in the South, few of them and none of the regional suffrage leaders strayed outside the bounds tolerated by white southerners of their era while their own enfranchisement was in doubt.[8]

Well aware of the regional antipathy toward the woman's movement as an offshoot of the antislavery movement and that the antis exploited for their own purposes any public support for woman suffrage by African Americans, white southern suffragists barred black women from participation in their organizations; only a few African-American women who remained in the South, such as those at Tuskegee Institute, worked openly for woman suffrage. In the final years of the movement's history, as the focus shifted to securing a federal amendment rather than state constitutional amendments, southern suffragists fought bitterly and openly with one another about states' rights, but even then maintained a public image of solidarity when it came to race relations.[9]

It is my argument that an organized southern suffrage movement with strong national support came into existence at the time that it did because many leading suffragists—southern and northern—believed the South's so-called negro problem might be the key to female enfranchisement. The organized woman suffrage movement began among white southern women at the very time that the most powerful white men of the region, alarmed by the specter of interracial cooperation in the Populist movement, sought to restrict rather than liberalize suffrage requirements. Though many black men had been prevented from voting through intimidation and violence or seen their ballots discounted through fraud, the 1890s witnessed a powerful movement to deprive black voters of the actual right to vote, disfranchising them "legally" through changes in state constitutions, including the adoption of literacy tests, "understanding clauses," poll taxes, etc. The politicians' efforts to restore white supremacy and establish the hegemony of the elite white men of the region through the Democratic Party was a crucial part of the context in which the southern suffrage movement must be analyzed.[10]

It is equally important to examine the second racially charged context: the efforts of national suffrage leaders to obtain a federal woman suffrage amendment. As Kentucky suffrage leader Laura Clay, a crucial link between northern and southern suffragists, warned NAWSA leaders in 1892, their goal could never be achieved "unless you bring in the South." In the late nineteenth century, many white leaders of the American suffrage movement, including Susan B. Anthony and Elizabeth Cady Stanton, remained angry and frustrated that former allies such as Frederick Douglass had failed to demand woman suffrage when African-American men were enfranchised through the Fourteenth and Fifteenth Amendments. As the suffragists, reunited in 1890 in the NAWSA, sought to build support state-by-state in all regions toward the eventual achievement of their own federal suffrage amendment, white suffrage leaders deliberately abandoned the historic association between black rights and women's rights. National leaders were influenced by the rising tide of immigration and the post-1898 "acquisition" of territories inhabited by people of color—factors that contributed to a decline of northern support for universal suffrage and facilitated sectional reconciliation between native-born whites from the North and South, who seemed united in the idea that only the "best people" should vote.[11]

Many southern and northern suffrage leaders came to believe that, as the elite white men of the South sought a means of countering the effects of black suffrage, they might be willing to resort to enfranchising white women—which could accomplish their goal without running the risks of disfranchising black men and being punished by Congress under the enforcement clause of the Fifteenth Amendment. The existence of this reactionary movement to disfranchise blacks (that the disfranchisers considered "reformist" as it would "clean up" southern politics by legally "improving" the quality of the electorate without their "having to" resort to fraud and violence) gave white southern suffragists—who wanted the vote for the same reasons as suffragists everywhere—grounds to argue that woman suffrage would be politically advantageous. Indeed, this infamous campaign of elite white southerners to regain hegemony in southern society encouraged white southern suffragists and their northern allies to believe that the South would actually lead the nation in the adoption of woman suffrage.[12]

Ironically, it was former abolitionist Henry Blackwell of Massachusetts, husband of suffrage leader Lucy Stone, who first proposed what historian

Aileen Kraditor later dubbed the "statistical argument," that the South could solve its "negro problem" by enfranchising women, increasing the numerical superiority of whites in the South. When it was later pointed out to him that the black population was not equally distributed county by county or state by state and might compound the "problem" in some areas, he tried to reassure white southerners by amending the proposal to include suffrage restrictions, particularly literacy tests, that would ensure that the majority of women voters would be white. Blackwell first advanced the original argument in 1867 and attempted to sell it to the judicious and influential Laura Clay in the 1880s, but she continued to use "justice" arguments until she heard the startling news that the 1890 Mississippi Constitutional Convention had taken Blackwell's suggestions to heart. After Blackwell lobbied Mississippi's congressional delegation in Washington and flooded convention delegates with literature advancing his scheme, the delegates seriously considered, though rejected, a proposal to enfranchise women who owned (or whose husbands owned) three hundred dollars worth of real estate.[13]

Impressed, Clay appealed to the NAWSA for a southern campaign. Eager to expand their base of support and indignant over exclusion from the Fourteenth and Fifteenth Amendments, national leaders responded enthusiastically. According to Carrie Chapman Catt, Anthony's right-hand woman in the 1890s and later president of the NAWSA, national leaders "could not believe that the nation would long allow its record of enfranchisement of illiterate men, fresh from slavery, and its denial of the same privilege to intelligent white women to stand unchallenged." In 1892, the NAWSA established a "Southern Committee" with Clay as chair, beginning a decade of commitment to the South.[14]

Clay's Southern Committee brought together the few southern white women already working for woman suffrage and brought national organizers into the region. Following Clay's advice, Anthony and Catt "launched their bark in the southern sea" in 1895, each sweeping through a portion of the region on a speaking tour. Significantly, NAWSA chose Atlanta for its 1895 convention—the first time in twenty-seven years that the convention was held outside Washington, D.C. To ingratiate themselves with their southern hosts and audience, Anthony asked Frederick Douglass, who was still a frequent participant in suffrage meetings in the North and in Washington, to stay away. White southerners, including General Robert Hemphill, a low-country conservative and ardent champion of woman suffrage, were featured speakers and flattered as "born orators"; after Hemphill's speech, Anthony asked the band to strike up

"Dixie" and he exited the podium to a chorus of rebel yells. Henry Blackwell and Carrie Chapman Catt gave speeches urging that southern states seek woman suffrage only with an educational qualification.[15]

Full of optimism, the northern and southern allies soon announced plans to seek enfranchisement for literate women at a constitutional convention to be held in South Carolina later that year—the second (after Mississippi) in a series of state conventions, in which southern states revised their constitutions to restrict or preclude black voting. When the South Carolina press suggested that an educational qualification would not be sufficient to disqualify black women, the suffragists amended the woman suffrage proposal to require property as well as literacy tests. The suffragists won the support of many men of their class, but the convention, dominated by the supporters of "Pitchfork" Ben Tillman—many of them illiterate and with limited property—defeated the suffrage proposal.[16]

Despite this defeat, the suffragists remained convinced that "the negro problem" would prove to be the key to victory in the South. Like many other Americans in the 1890s, they fully expected that restrictions of the type adopted by Mississippi and South Carolina (including poll taxes, literary tests, "understanding" the state constitution, etc.) to be challenged by Congress or overturned by the Supreme Court. Even Catt, encouraged by the support the South Carolina suffragists had received from leading conservatives in the state, saw in the experience proof "that Miss Clay is right when she demands more work in the South," and pledged to collect thousands more to be spent in the region. Five months later, she launched a major organizing drive in Mississippi, saying "in the fall, provided we have money sufficient, we desire to concentrate our forces upon the South. . . . While the South is not yet favorable to woman suffrage, it gives a very cordial hearing to it and I may also say that when interested at all they are invariably the very best people. A year or two of work there will change the sentiment and quite revolutionize."[17]

Southern suffragists and their northern supporters continued their southern strategy throughout the 1890s and into the early 1900s, appealing for enfranchisement at constitutional conventions in Louisiana in 1898, Alabama in 1901, and Virginia in 1902. In Alabama, the Huntsville *Republican* complained that "no matter how modest a constitutional convention is nowadays some female suffragist will find it out and insist on making a speech." Their only victory was the 1898 Louisiana measure giving taxpaying women the right to vote on tax questions. Kate Gordon, a genteel reformer from New Orleans who spearheaded the Louisiana campaign, rose quickly to national prominence; elected NAWSA corresponding secretary in 1901, she joined Clay as a second strong southern leader to the small national board. When leaving for New York to assume her new duties, she told a New Orleans newspaper:

> the question of white supremacy is one that will only be decided by giving the right of the ballot to the educated intelligent white women of the South. . . . The South, true to its traditions will trust its women, and thus placing in their hands the balance of power, the negro as a disturbing element in politics will disappear."[18]

The high watermark for the southern strategy based on exploitation of southern white determination to restore white supremacy was probably the 1903 NAWSA convention held in New Orleans. As in South Carolina, national leaders made an effort to appease southern hosts, excluding black women from the convention (though Anthony met privately with local black suffragists). And Dr. Anna Howard Shaw, later NAWSA president, publicly rebuked her audience, which included many curious New Orleans men and women as well as suffragists, for "putting the ballot into the hands of your black men, thus making them the political superiors of your white women." More significantly, the delegates adopted a statement officially recognizing "the principle of State rights, and leaving to each state the terms upon which the extension of suffrage to women shall be requested of the respective State Legislatures." Belle Kearney of Mississippi, a prominent orator for suffragists and the Woman's Christian Temperance Union (WCTU), gave a now infamous keynote address, celebrating the South for its Anglo-Saxon purity and political sagacity in devising means to counter the enfranchisement of "four million, five hundred thousand ex-slaves, illiterate and semi-barbarous." Yet she insisted that qualified woman suffrage was a better and more permanent solution to the "negro problem" than what these southern politicians had devised instead.[19]

By 1903, however, as Kearney's speech unwittingly acknowledged, the southern strategy had already failed. White conservative men preferred to restore white supremacy through the disfranchisement of black men without enfranchising *any* women. It was not always an easy task: in states such as North Carolina, the disfranchisers had to have the votes of poor white men to enact suffrage restrictions that actually disfranchised many poor whites along with blacks. To obtain this support they played the race card and the gender card at once, in a carefully orchestrated and violent campaign to convince white men that black political power encouraged black men to lust after social equality, including access to white women. Clearly, the elite white men who led this movement to restore their race and class to political supremacy in the South preferred to use white women as the indirect "inspiration" for white supremacy rather than the direct means of achieving it. Similar to black, middle-class men, who hoped that white men would accept them as fellow "Best Men," ruling over less educated men of both races—elite white women hoped that elite white men would accept them as equal partners whose votes would establish the hegemony of their race and class. But white conservative Democrats rejected both their offers, and despite the suffragists' expectations, the federal government proved willing to let the South get away with it.[20]

As it became clear that neither Congress nor the Supreme Court were going to prevent or punish the southern states for disfranchising African-American men, national leaders and most southern suffragists began to recognize what some southern leaders including Gordon, Clay, and Kearney were loathe to accept: that the southern strategy was moribund. In most southern states the fledgling suffrage societies grew inactive. The NAWSA did not experience similar "doldrums" during this period, but engaged in successful efforts to further deradicalize their image and broaden their base of support. But strong national support for the southern movement ceased: the NAWSA was not about to throw good money after bad in the South. In 1906, Harriet Taylor Upton, NAWSA treasurer and then president Shaw's right-hand woman, wrote: "I have often thought that the southern women might be enfranchised before the northern women because of the solution of the colored question, but we meet the indifference of southerners at every turn." The NAWSA's initiatives in the South ceased, and henceforth the South was regarded by national leaders as more of a problem than a promise.[21]

Kearney and Blackwell, and to a greater extent Gordon and Clay, were very reluctant to give up on the idea that they could win woman suffrage by exploiting the "negro problem" and became involved in still more blatantly racist campaigns in 1906 and 1907—even a formal campaign for a "white woman only" amendment in Mississippi. And Belle Kearney, acting on her own, issued a 1906 call for southern suffragists to join her in creating a southern suffrage organization, asking for suffrage "as a solution to the race problem," and requested NAWSA support. But the NAWSA refused to give its endorsement to either of these schemes, fearing that such an explicitly racist campaign would alienate supporters in the West and North.[22]

In a letter to Clay and Gordon, Alice Stone Blackwell, daughter of the late Lucy Stone and Henry Blackwell and editor of the *Woman's Journal*, beseeched them to call off the "whites only" campaign and made it clear that the NAWSA—after all—did have limits below which they would not stoop. She wrote:

> It is generally recognized through the North and West that the governments set up by the ignorant and newly enfranchised slaves were so intolerably bad and corrupt that the white people had to get rid of them and the setting up of qualifications of education, character, or property, so far as these are applied impartially to both races, is approved of by almost everybody in our part of the country except by a few ultra theorists who are absolutely wedded to the idea of a literally universal suffrage. But the application of these tests in such a way as to let in every white man, no matter how ignorant or bad in character, and to shut out every colored man, no matter how intelligent or how good, is regarded everywhere outside the South as an unmitigated iniquity.

Clay understood and accepted the NAWSA's decision, but Gordon was livid: "Alice Blackwell is certainly worked up over any efforts that may keep the black ladies out of their rights," she wrote to Clay. "We white ones can remain forever disfranchised so long as these ladies are not discriminated against."[23]

These events led to the decline of Clay's and Gordon's influence in the NAWSA, and never again would southern suffragists exercise the degree of influence in national affairs these two women enjoyed in the years before it became clear that the southern strategy of the 1890s had not borne fruit. The second stage of the movement, roughly 1910–1920, took place in a different context, especially regarding the race issue. For these last ten years, it was the Progressive movement that breathed new life into the movement in the South, as it had in the rest of the nation, and gave the regional suffragists a new expediency argument—but no one expected that southern Progressivism would cause the South to lead the nation in support of woman suffrage. During these years, the race issue was injected into the suffrage campaign not only by the suffragists but also by the antis, who depicted woman suffrage, especially by federal amendment, as a threat to states' rights, white supremacy, and southern civilization. Suffragists made few attempts to exploit the race issue strategically—because of this changed context.[24]

New leaders and far more numerous followers now appeared in the southern suffrage movement—many of them younger women who had come of age politically after disfranchisement and some who had moved to the South from elsewhere. Few of them displayed the antipathy toward the black vote of older suffrage leaders, particularly those from the Deep South states of Mississippi, Louisiana, and Alabama. Furthermore, "second generation" southern suffragists, women who became active in the last ten or twelve years of the movement, recognized that they had little to gain and a lot to lose by playing the race card, and most did not. A notable exception was Kate Gordon, still active, who had established a states' rights suffrage organization, rejecting NAWSA leadership and the federal amendment. She threatened to challenge formally the constitutionality of the "subterfuges" adopted by the southern states to solve the "negro problem," which would then open the way for a new campaign based on the old southern strategy; but she never took action and won scant support among southern suffragists. Another exception, but one that proves the rule, was one of the newer leaders, Madeline McDowell Breckinridge from Kentucky, who is considered one of the most liberal of the southern white suffrage leaders. In a speech before the NAWSA convention in Louisville in 1911, she proposed adoption of woman suffrage with an educational qualification as the first step toward "the intelligent limitation of the present unrestricted suffrage without fraud or violence." Significantly, Breckinridge's Kentucky was the one southern state that had not yet enacted any kind of suffrage restriction, and therefore the state's suffragists conceivably had something to gain by advancing this otherwise moribund argument.[25]

In this last decade, the white suffragists exhibited racist views and a willingness to seek their own political equality at the expense of African Americans, when they defended themselves against the antis' racist stratagems. For example, in North Carolina, suffragists issued a flyer "Woman Suffrage and White Supremacy in the South," which gave statistics showing that white women outnumbered blacks in the state and saying that "IF white domination is threatened in the South, it is, therefore, DOUBLY EXPEDIENT TO ENFRANCHISE THE WOMEN QUICKLY IN ORDER THAT IT BE PRESERVED." Such pamphlets signified that the suffragists regarded black suffrage as unthreatening because it was so thoroughly under control.[26] Reminding the public of this was exploiting the race issue, not "sidestepping" it, as one historian has claimed.[27] But it still demonstrates that the suffragists—even the second generation suffragists—were within the mainstream of southern white views on race in the early twentieth century and made it clear that catering to the race-related fears of white southerners was still an important element of their suffrage strategy.

Finally, in this last decade of the movement, most white southern suffragists did not publicly defend black women's voting rights—though many of them believed that "qualified" (educated) black women and men should be "allowed" to vote. They thought it appropriate that the same laws that excluded the "negro" would apply to the "negress" and insisted that even a federal woman suffrage amendment would not change this exclusion. Even Mary Johnston, a Virginia suffragist who privately objected to another suffragist's "assertion that we fear, hence inferentially will fight, the presence of the negro woman at the polls," publicly reassured fellow Virginians in a speech that the suffragists were asking for the enfranchisement of women on the same terms with men. "That means that just as you have closely restricted the negro male voter, so will the amended Constitution closely restrict the woman vote." Only "a few educated, property-owning, coloured women will vote, but not the mass of coloured women." And Pattie Ruffner Jacobs, an Alabama suffrage leader risen to national office, made this argument when she appeared before Congress as part of the NAWSA effort to sooth the fears of southern congressmen and gain support for the federal amendment: This amendment, she testified,

> does not inject any new problem into the franchise problems of the States. . . . It is a fallacy to contend that the prohibition of discrimination on account of sex would involve the race problem or any other complication. Both sexes will be obliged to meet all requirements of citizenship imposed by the State and each state can still protect the exercise of the franchise to the fullests [sic] extent of its power.[28]

In this last decade, the South was not the main hope of the NAWSA leaders. Indeed, part of Catt's "Winning Plan" was to avoid campaigns for state suffrage amendments in states she considered to be "hopeless," many of which were in the South. Focusing on key states like New York, Catt more or less conceded the South; the many state campaigns in the region had failed, and Catt wanted no further defeats that would embarrass suffragists and break the momentum of the movement. Southern suffragists were instructed not to launch campaigns for state amendments without NAWSA approval and to seek only partial enfranchisement, which state legislators could grant without holding referenda. Many southern suffrage leaders were disappointed, as they still entertained hopes of state victories, but most welcomed Catt's efforts to develop a coordinated national strategy and yielded to her on this point. Only Kate Gordon, resenting Catt's violation of the "states' rights" to determine their own strategies, launched a state campaign (in Louisiana), which went down in defeat.[29]

National leaders joined southern white suffragists in attempts to defend their movement against the idea that woman suffrage would endanger white supremacy. Two often-cited examples of this policy are the decision that African-American women must march in a segregated unit in the massive suffrage parade in Washington in 1913—a decision famously defied by the African-American suffrage leader Ida Wells-Barnett—and NAWSA's 1919 refusal to accept the application for membership of the Northeastern Federation of Women's Clubs, an organization of African-American women—begging the black women to understand that if NAWSA admitted "an organization of 6,000 colored women, the enemies [of the federal amendment] can cease from further effort—the defeat of the amendment will be assured."[30]

Even more telling is that, after the Nineteenth Amendment was ratified in 1920, so few southern white suffragists came out in support of southern black women, when southern states denied them the vote in the 1920s. Nor did national women's rights advocates, who were still working, it seemed, for "white women's rights" through the League of Women Voters led by Catt and the Woman's Party led by Alice Paul. This was the case even though black women appealed to these organizations for help: African-American women delegates to the Woman's Party convention declared: "Five million women in the United States cannot be denied their rights without all the women of the United States feeling the effect of that denial. No women are free until all are free."[31]

The role of race in the woman suffrage movement in the South and the nation is a crucial part of the suffrage story that historians will continue to study and debate. One of the greatest reforms in American history—woman suffrage—was achieved in the midst of a reactionary political climate, the so-called nadir of race relations in America. White suffragists—at once products of their culture and reformers trying to change it—adopted racist tactics in order to succeed. Clearly, in the late nineteenth and early twentieth centuries, white women of the South and the nation did not feel that their rights depended on advancing the political claims of black women—quite the contrary. The southern suffrage movement developed in the 1890s in the context of southern efforts to restore white supremacy *and* a national woman suffrage campaign focused on enfranchising white women. Therefore, white suffragists from the South—radical for their culture only on gender issues—and national suffrage leaders—in rapid retreat from their role as champions of African Americans—banded together to advance their own interests by exploiting what late nineteenth-century whites referred to as the South's "negro problem." Seen in context, it is not surprising that northern leaders pursued so vigorously this strategy—which complemented efforts elsewhere in the nation to counter the political influence of new immigrants and other "undesirable" voters. Nor is it surprising that some southern suffragists proved to be quite reluctant to acknowledge the defeat of this "southern strategy" that gained for them strong national support and once seemed so promising as a means of prying woman suffrage out of southern legislators, unmoved by arguments based on justice and equality. Not for many more decades—and not before the development of a very different context in the wake of the civil rights movement—did the majority of American feminists seem to agree that "no women are free until all are free."[32]

NOTES

1. See Marjorie Spruill Wheeler, *New Women of the New South: The Leaders of the Woman Suffrage Movement in the Southern States* (New York: Oxford University Press, 1993).

2. Aileen S. Kraditor, *The Ideas of the Woman Suffrage Movement in the United States, 1890–1920* (Garden City, N.Y.: Doubleday and Company, 1971), quotation p. 139; Anne Firor Scott, *The Southern Lady: From Pedestal to Politics, 1830–1930*, especially p. 182; Anastatia Sims, "Anne Firor Scott: Writing Women Into Southern History," in *Understanding Southern History: Essays on Notable Interpreters of the South*, ed. Glenn Feldman (Auburn: University of Alabama Press, 2001).

3. Suzanne Lebsock,"Woman Suffrage and White Supremacy: A Virginia Case Study," in *Visible Women: New Essays on American Activism*, ed. Nancy A. Hewitt and Suzanne Lebsock (Urbana: University of Illinois Press, 1993), pp. 63, 65, 66.

4. Elna C. Green, *Southern Strategies: Southern Women and the Woman Suffrage Question* (Chapel Hill: University of North Carolina Press, 1997).

5. The long-standing tendency to portray racism in the national movement as a pragmatic concession to southern racism rather than a reflection of the national leaders' own views is still evident but considerably diminished. Most scholars now recognize that by the early 1890s, in

the words of historian Ann Gordon, "white woman suffragists veered away from the sweeping democratic vision of universal suffrage that at times defined their movement and always attracted black women to the cause." Rosalyn Terborg-Penn has made it clear that while black women worked hard for woman suffrage from the beginning to the end of the campaign, by the late nineteenth century, "an anti-black woman suffrage strategy . . . reinforced differences among African-American and white woman suffragists, some of whom hoped to exclude black women from gaining the right to vote." Louise Newman in *White Women's Rights: The Racial Origins of Feminism in the United States* presents national leaders as working to develop self-serving ideas about the relationships between race, gender, and equality that would "establish the white woman as the primary defender and beneficiary of woman's rights at a time when the country was growing increasingly hostile toward attempts to redress the political, social, and economic injustices to which African Americans were subjected. Ann D. Gordon, "Woman Suffrage (Not Universal Suffrage) by Federal Amendment," in *Votes for Women! The Woman Suffrage Movement in Tennessee, the South, and the Nation*, ed. Marjorie Spruill Wheeler (Knoxville: University Press of Tennessee, 1995), p. 4; Rosalyn Terborg-Penn, "African American Women and the Woman Suffrage Movement," in *One Woman, One Vote: Rediscovering the Suffrage Movement*, ed. Wheeler (Troutdale, Ore.: NewSage Press, 1995), p. 137; Louise Michele Newman, *White Women's Rights: The Racial Origins of Feminism in the United States* (New York: Oxford University Press, 1999), pp. 4–5; Rosalyn Terborg-Penn, *African American Women in the Struggle for the Vote, 1850–1920* (Bloomington: Indiana University Press, 1998).

6. The concept of "nadir" in American race relations originates with Rayford W. Logan, introduced in his 1954 book *The Negro in American Life and Thought: The Nadir, 1877–1901* (New York: Collier Books).

7. On disfranchisement, see J. Morgan Kousser, *The Shaping of Southern Politics: Suffrage Restriction and the Establishment of the One-Party South, 1880–1910* (New Haven: Yale University Press, 1974); Glenda Elizabeth Gilmore, *Gender and Jim Crow: Women and the Politics of White Supremacy in North Carolina, 1896–1920* (Chapel Hill: University of North Carolina Press, 1996; and Edward L. Ayers, *The Promise of the New South: Life After Reconstruction* (New York: Oxford University Press, 1992).

8. Wheeler, *New Women of the New South*, especially chapters 3 and 4.

9. Ibid., chapters 4 and 5; Adele Logan Alexander, "Adella Hunt Logan, The Tuskegee Woman's Club, and African Americans in the Suffrage Movement," in *Votes for Women*, ed. Wheeler.

10. Wheeler, *New Women of the New South*, chapter 4; Kousser, *Shaping of Southern Politics*; Michael Perman, *Struggle for Mastery: Disfranchisement*

in the South, 1888–1908 (Chapel Hill: University of North Carolina Press, 2001).

11. Laura Clay to the editor, *Woman's Journal*, 10 March 1892, Laura Clay Scrapbook, Laura Clay Papers, Margaret King Library, University of Kentucky, Lexington; Ellen Carol DuBois, *Feminism and Suffrage: The Emergence of an Independent Women's Movement in America, 1848–1869* (Ithaca: Cornell University Press, 1978); Terborg-Penn, *African American Women in the Struggle for the Vote*; Lois W. Banner, *Elizabeth Cady Stanton: A Radical for Woman's Rights* (Boston: Little, Brown and Company, 1980), pp. 93–106; Andrea Moore Kerr, *Lucy Stone: Speaking out for Equality* (New Brunswick: Rutgers University Press, 1992); Kraditor, *Ideas of the Woman Suffrage Movement.*

12. Kousser, *Shaping of Southern Politics*; Gilmore, *Gender and Jim Crow*; Wheeler, *New Women of the New South.*

13. Wheeler, *New Women of the New South*, pp. 113–14; on Blackwell's proposal, see Aileen S. Kraditor, *Up from the Pedestal: Selected Writing in the History of American Feminism* (New York: Quandrangle, 1968), pp. 253–57; A. Elizabeth Taylor, "The Woman Suffrage Movement in Mississippi," *Journal of Mississippi History* 30 (Feb. 1968): 207–33; Paul E. Fuller, *Laura Clay and the Woman's Rights Movement* (Lexington: University of Kentucky Press, 1975), pp. 54–57.

14. Wheeler, *New Women of the New South*, pp. 115–16; Fuller, *Laura Clay*, pp. 44, 56–59; Taylor, "Woman Suffrage Movement in Mississippi," pp. 207–10; Carrie Chapman Catt and Nettie Rogers Shuler, *Woman Suffrage and Politics: The Inner Story of the Suffrage Movement* (Seattle: University of Washington Press, [reprint] 1970), pp. 227–31.

15. Wheeler, *New Women of the New South*, p. 116; A. Elizabeth Taylor, "Origin of the Woman Suffrage Movement in Georgia," *Georgia Historical Quarterly* 28 (June 1944): 63–79; Barbara Bellows (then Ulmer), "Virginia Durant Young: New South Suffragist" (Master's thesis, University of South Carolina, 1979), pp. 44–46; Fuller, *Laura Clay*, pp. 67–69.

16. Wheeler, *New Women of the New South*, pp. 116–17; Fuller, *Laura Clay*, 63–69; Bellows, "Virginia Durant Young," pp. 47–88.

17. Wheeler, *New Women of the New South*, p. 117.

18. Ibid., pp. 117–18.

19. Ibid., pp. 118–19.

20. Ibid., 118–19, 119–20; Taylor, "Woman Suffrage Movement in Mississippi," pp. 207–10; Bellows, "Virginia Durant Young," pp. 54–88; Anastatia Sims, *The Power of Femininity: Women's Organizations and Politics in North Carolina, 1880–1930* (Columbus: University of South Carolina Press, 1997), 34–43; Gilmore, *Gender and Jim Crow*, 61–89.

21. Wheeler, *New Women of the New South*, pp. 119–20; Sara Hunter Graham, "The Suffrage Renaissance: A New Image for a New Century, 1896–1910," in *One Woman, One Vote*, ed. Wheeler, pp. 157–78.

22. Wheeler, *New Women of the New South*, pp. 120–23.

23. Ibid., pp. 123–25.

24. Ibid., pp. 125–27.

25. On Minnie Fisher Cunningham (Texas), Anne Dallas Dudley (Tennessee), Pattie Ruffner Jacobs (Alabama), and Madeline McDowell Breckinridge (Kentucky), see Wheeler, ed., *One Woman, One Vote*, p. 316, Wheeler, ed., *Votes for Women!*, pp. 162–63, and Wheeler, *New Women of the New South*, 145–48; on the race issue during this "second stage" of the movement, see Wheeler, *New Women of the New South*, pp. 125–32.

26. Ibid., pp. 125–32; see Wheeler, ed., *Votes for Women!*, pp. 290–92.

27. Elna Green has claimed that use of the race issue as a statistical argument indicated the relative liberalism of the white southern suffragists; that is, by insisting white women would save white supremacy by outvoting black women, they indicated their willingness to allow *some* black women to vote—as opposed to conservatives who wanted blacks disfranchised completely. However, the white suffragists employing this argument were well aware that most black women would not be allowed to vote since the adoption during the 1890s of new restrictions. Green, *Southern Strategies*, pp. 92–94.

28. Wheeler, *New Women of the New South*, pp. 102–12, 127–31, 162; on Jacobs testimony, see Kraditor, *Ideas of the Woman Suffrage Movement*, p. 156.

29. A bill calling for a state suffrage amendment was introduced also in Mississippi, but it was *not* initiated by the state suffrage leaders, and it may have been the work of opponents who wished to raise the issue and vote it down. Wheeler, *New Women of the New South*, pp. 161–71.

30. Wheeler, ibid., pp. 159–62; Wanda A. Hendricks, "Ida B. Wells-Barnett and the Alpha Suffrage Club of Chicago," in *One Woman, One Vote*, ed. Wheeler, pp. 268–70; Terborg-Penn, *African American Women in the Struggle for the Vote*, pp. 130–31; Kraditor, *Ideas of the Woman Suffrage Movement*, 167–70.

31. Terborg-Penn, *African American Women in the Struggle for the Vote*, pp. 149–58, especially 155–56; Terborg-Penn, "African American Women and the Woman Suffrage Movement," pp. 151–54; Darlene Clark Hine and Christie Anne Farnham, "Black Women's Culture of Resistance and the Right to Vote," in *Women of the American South: A Multicultural Reader*, ed. Christie Anne Farnham (New York: New York University Press, 1997), p. 214.

32. Farnham, p. 214.

7

FEMALE OPPOSITION

The Anti-Suffrage Campaign

Thomas Jablonsky

It may be difficult for Americans in the twenty-first century to compre-
hend how a sizable group of women could spend a half century in organized opposition to the right of women to vote. The notion of refusing
to embrace political equality is the antithesis of history's direction since
the American and French Revolutions. Yet the saga of America's female
antisuffragists reveals not only the subtleties of our political tradition but
also the evolution of women's place in U.S. society.

The women who opposed woman suffrage did so for decades. Both
the individuals involved and the reasons for their opposition changed
over time. Antisuffragists saw the female franchise as a threat to the
United States and to themselves as women. Thus, they banded together
to publish and lobby and debate in a protracted struggle to stop female
enfranchisement. Antisuffragists established state organizations and,
eventually, a National Association Opposed to Woman Suffrage. Some
of the local affiliates were dynamic and well developed, while others were
organizations in name only. In the end, when the Nineteenth Amendment became the law of the land in 1920, some antis adjusted with remarkable ease. Others found the new political world of the twentieth
century more than they could accept and continued a belated fight to
turn back the clock.

Throughout their half-century of activism, antisuffragists remained
consistent in their perceptions of what could be tolerated as appropriate
political behavior for women, but they changed over time in their ac-

knowledgment of what roles women could undertake in the world beyond their doorsteps. Some fought for access to higher education for women; others thought such intellectual pursuits to be physically and psychologically harmful to women. Some insisted that women should become journalists or public servants working to make society a more wholesome place to live; others contended that only marriage and managing families were proper careers for women. Some antisuffragists appeared to be intrigued by prospects for the twentieth century; others could see no benefit to humankind from a rejection of long-established traditions, a few of biblical origins. What the antis shared was a preference for a "separate but equal" political world, wherein they would address only civic issues that were vital to women. They valued power when it was accorded to them. And, they understood that men were not likely to treat women as equals in the dirty little world of turn-of-the-century politics. Antis fought to maintain gender behavior unchanged with regard to political justice while, at the same time, they strove to improve the moral and social conditions of twentieth-century America in a manner befitting their sex.

The first evidence of organized anti-suffrage sentiment among women came just a few years after the Civil War. In 1868–1869, a proposal supporting woman suffrage was introduced in the Massachusetts state legislature. About two hundred women countered this petition with a "remonstrance," urging their elected officials to resist any effort to force the ballot on the Commonwealth's female citizenry. The elective franchise, they insisted, would "diminish the purity, the dignity and the moral influence of woman, and bring into the family circle a dangerous element of discord."[1] Their perspective on this issue was embraced by male legislators. No action was taken on the pro-suffrage proposal.

Fourteen years later, remonstrants (the early title for antisuffragists, especially those in New England) once again voiced their concern when another woman suffrage proposal came before the Massachusetts legislature. This time, rather than disband immediately following their response, the antisuffragists stayed together under the name of the Boston Committee of Remonstrants. They intended to serve as a "vigilance committee" prepared to take any necessary action. At first, they periodically but demurely submitted written commentary to the state legislature through male representatives. But, with time, they became emboldened in the defense of their political separateness and would, by the late 1880s, speak their own minds before legislative sessions. Increasingly, they became organized and forceful. By 1890, they established an annual publication (which eventually became a quarterly), entitled *Remonstrance*, so that their conservative viewpoint could be consistently heard not only across the Bay State but in other sections of the country as well.

In 1895, Massachusetts remonstrants were called to battle a legislative proposal that not only asked for a male vote on the suffrage issue but asked women for their unofficial opinion as well. Fearful that only feminists would go to the ballot box to express their beliefs, antisuffragists organized in the most comprehensive fashion to date. Since they refused to consider the possibility of voting even if it was to register their opposition to suffrage, the antis took the position that every single female who *did not vote* on election day was to be designated a ballot *against* the franchise. In order to get their message across to both men and women, Massachusetts antisuffragists organized a statewide campaign of parlor meetings, published circulars, and newspapers advertisements. Of the women who did vote in November, 96 percent supported the franchise for their sex; however, less than 4 percent of women voted and, therefore, the remonstrants boasted that 96 percent of Massachusetts women had, in fact, opposed the franchise. Since male voters had done the same by a two-to-one count, the final decision—for the moment, at least—had been laid to rest.

While Massachusetts continued to be the best organized of all the antisuffrage clubs, thousands of women in other states also voiced their opposition to the vote. Some of these groups were visible and energetic in their battles for continued disfranchisement. Other organizations were nothing more than paper creations of individuals who sought lofty titles. In their early years of existence, most of these groups imitated their sisters in Massachusetts by preferring to deliver written remonstrances in the form of newspaper articles or letters to the editor as evidence of their political opinions. In their minds, the printed word was more feminine. With time, some organizations altered their position. As they became more involved in the struggle over political equality, some antis convinced themselves that women had to stand up for what was right, even as they insisted that women had no business in the political arena.

Most anti-suffrage clubs came into existence in response to pro-suffrage activity. In this manner, they were reactive, responding—often belatedly—to the work of women and men who supported the franchise. Because most male legislators in the United States during the nineteenth century did not believe in woman suffrage, the often tardy arrival of petitions opposing the vote did not harm the anti-suffrage position. Some anti-suffrage groups remained in existence after a particular proposal had been defeated either in the state legislature or statewide in a political referendum. Also, over time, a handful of antisuffragists, such as Josephine Dodge and Minnie Bronson, both of New York, became quite well known nationwide for their speaking abilities. They traveled by train lending their voices to the cause of continued disfranchisement.

This ongoing presence led to the formation in 1911 of the National Association Opposed to Woman Suffrage (NAOWS). Headquartered in New York City under the leadership of Josephine Dodge with Bronson as general secretary, NAOWS had its core allegiance in the urbanized, industrialized East. Here could be found the strongest state chapters. Here could also be found some of the most interesting remonstrants including Kate Gannett Wells of Massachusetts, a prominent figure in the Commonwealth's women's club movement, and the earliest anti to step forward to personally address the legislature in Boston. Of even more untraditional vintage was New York's Jeanette Gilder, who climbed trees as a youngster, clung to the end of horse-drawn carts, and loved baseball. Her career was in journalism and her autobiography was entitled, appropriately, *The Autobiography of a Tom-Boy*.

Wherever antisuffragists organized, they deluged legislatures, colleges, women's clubs, granges, libraries, and the general public with thousands of pieces of literature. Bolder antis dared to appear before labor union conferences, grange meetings, and even state party conventions as the twentieth century unfolded. The most daring of all antisuffragists came from New York, where the remonstrants took their cause to the meeting rooms of pro-suffrage clubs. Although they were met with heckling and laughter, the antis' boldness demonstrated the political evolution occurring among these conservative women. In turn, anti-suffrage meetings were periodically disrupted by pro-franchise agitators, who asked embarrassing questions or applauded at the wrong times. Curbside evangelizing by suffragists even took place on the doorstep of the New York Anti-Suffrage Association. In retaliation, antisuffragists tore down pro-suffrage banners and posters. On one occasion, franchise supporters accused antis of dumping lemons, wet sponges, rolls of ticker tape, bags of water, and garbage pails on innocent suffrage supporters parading outside the anti-suffrage offices.

Even the more sedate Massachusetts antis came to life during a 1915 referendum. Anti-suffrage speakers crisscrossed the state appearing at women's clubs, grange meetings, county fairs, and rural crossroads warning their parsimonious Yankee audiences that doubling the electorate by enfranchising women would double the cost of each and every election. Ads were placed in the Harvard Freshman Red Book and an anti-suffrage theme song ("Anti-Suffrage Rose") found its way into nickelodeons, where it played as background to an anti-suffrage slide show. Season schedules for the Boston Red Sox and the Boston Braves were distributed with batting averages and photographs of baseball heros Tris Speaker and Johnny Evers interspersed among anti-suffrage essays.

Most anti-suffrage activity was centered around state referenda on woman suffrage. Legislatures frequently left it to the male electorate to determine whether wives, mothers, and daughters should be allowed to vote. At other times, the choice was made in the State House alone. The first referendum on woman suffrage was held in Kansas in 1867. In the half century that followed, proponents of "Votes for Woman" waged nearly five hundred campaigns aimed at persuading legislatures to hold referenda on the franchise issue. Fifty-six times the suffragists were successful in requiring these elections. Remonstrants could claim credit for defeating the suffrage proposals in only a handful of the more than four hundred times legislatures refused to order a vote on woman suffrage. Even when politicians refused to schedule a vote on the franchise, legislators and antis alike could anticipate yet another suffragist drive during the following session. Most states north of the Mason-Dixon line eventually held at least one vote on the issue of woman suffrage after 1890. Some anti-suffrage clubs contested these measures when they were first introduced before the legislature. Others failed to rally until a referendum had already been scheduled.

Promotion of the anti-suffrage position during referenda campaigns came through the usual assortment of posters, fliers, and pamphlets. Materials ranged from single-page handouts to sample ballots to quotations from famous individuals such as Daniel Webster, Herbert Spencer, G. K. Chesterton, and Cardinal James Gibbons in denouncing the female franchise. Remonstrants also festooned their publications with the names of nationally prominent women who had enlisted in their ranks, including Mrs. William Howard Taft, Mrs. Thomas J. Preston, Jr. (widow of President Grover Cleveland), and muckraker Ida Tarbell. Antis purchased double-spaced columns in local newspapers. In a more inventive approach to campaigning, Ohio antis traveled about the state in an automobile speaking at rural gatherings. After NAOWS, the national association of antisuffragists, was founded in 1911, they adopted the red rose as a symbol of their cause. Antis subsequently used pink and rose as "their" color. Appropriately, in New York City during the 1915 referendum, pink roses, pink paper, pink enrollment cards, and pink leaflets were scattered around the city. Letters were enclosed in envelopes with "Vote No On Women Suffrage" printed in bold type on the front covers of the envelopes. Posters on subway station kiosks and elevated trains carried reminders that New York women enjoyed special advantages under the benevolence of male suffrage. In contrast to pro-suffrage speakers, who were alleged to have depicted wedding rings as relics of barbarism, antis said that their organization stood for "Home, Heaven, and Mother."

In 1893, Colorado became the first state to enfranchise women through a popular election. Shortly thereafter, Idaho followed suit. (Wyoming in 1890 and Utah in 1896 enfranchised women in their first state constitutions.) Until 1910, a dry spell followed for suffragists. In that year, women from the state of Washington were granted the vote and thereafter until 1919 (except for 1915–1916), at least one additional state granted women either partial or complete suffrage every year. As suffragists slowly accumulated victories from California to New York, remonstrants could take satisfaction in suffrage defeats in a number of states. Even in the others, the very presence of a female opposition appears to have provided a soothing tonic to men who stood against the "politicalization" of women. The simple visibility of a few well-known women allied against the vote belied the existence of a united female thinking on the issue of suffrage. For some American men, both within and without the legislature, this presence of a female opposition was sufficient excuse to question the wisdom of the female franchise.

Until 1917, the struggle over equal political rights was largely a state level matter, with the suffragists taking the initiative and the antis responding. The problem for the suffragists, though, was the unending routine of this strategy. Every defeat, whether within the legislature or at a referendum, meant another year's campaign just to be heard. However, during the middle of the second decade of the twentieth century, as America moved toward participation in World War I, suffragists changed their approach. In harmony with the increasingly national tone of reform—in matters such as labor laws, supervision of food and drugs, and monetary policy—suffrage proponents took their case to the national legislature and to President Woodrow Wilson. This shift in approach by the suffragists alarmed antis because it squarely placed the center of the fight on Capitol Hill between two sets of males only. Instead of dozens of combinations represented by bicameral state legislatures, with the beginning of 1918, only the House of Representatives and the U.S. Senate stood between women and the possibility that every legislature would have to make a final determination about supporting the female franchise. Heartache and disappointment loomed ahead for the remonstrants as the struggle shifted to our nation's capital.

Antisuffragists had considered President Woodrow Wilson a "typical" southern gentleman, who viewed the role of women in modern society as a continuation of past restraints and limited responsibilities. However, during the course of 1917, the president slowly moved toward a position that, at first, took federal enfranchisement of women under consideration and, later, fully supported such action. The following year he became increasingly public with this evolution. He openly offered the personal observation that enfranchisement meant justice as he endorsed the Susan B. Anthony amendment. This endorsement was soon followed by passage of the suffrage amendment by the House of Representatives. Although the United States Senate did not quickly follow their colleagues in the lower house, the remonstrants were clearly shaken. Whereas antisuffragists had competently combated suffragism on the state level among elected officials, who may very well have been their neighbors or social acquaintances, they never could get comfortable with the large-scale pageantry surrounding political arm-twisting in the U.S. House and Senate. Except for a few empty, futile communications to the Senate, the antisuffragists simply let history take its course.

During Senate debates in late 1918, remonstrants, resplendent in hats and gowns, filled the front rows of the gallery, offering visible support to their male supporters. Defeat of the suffrage amendment in that session heartened their cause, but this was followed in June of the following year by a narrow suffrage victory. The antis immediately called a three-day conference to consider their options. Representatives from twenty-six states attended. Their only substantive decision was a meaningless decision to move the national headquarters back to New York City from the District of Columbia. The national leadership of anti-suffragism was failing their cause even at the movement's most critical moment.

Meanwhile, states such as Wisconsin, New York, and Kansas ratified the Nineteenth Amendment. Remonstrants strove to have their voices heard by sending telegrams and printed announcements to state legislatures, as consideration of this suffrage amendment reverberated across the land. The antis were simply overwhelmed. Only in the South did a regional organization of antisuffragists, the Southern Women's League for the Rejection of the Susan B. Anthony Amendment, succeed in having their viewpoint presented on a consistent basis. In this region, racism played a role as remonstrants warned their listeners that a federal suffrage amendment would enfranchise African-American women as well as Southern ladies.

Eventually, it came down to a final contest in Tennessee during the summer of 1920. Thirty-five states had ratified the Nineteenth Amendment. One more was needed for passage. As the legislature assembled, the scene smacked of Mardi Gras and Barnum and Bailey. The Hermitage Hotel became the site of a "War of the Roses," with suffragists bedecked in yellow, purple, and white clothing, and yellow roses to match their flags and banners. Antis wore their familiar red roses and went about singing "Keep the Home First Burning." Each side tried to outdo the other by pinning yellow or red roses on the overwhelmed legislators.

Only nine days after the special session convened, the Tennessee legislature put the Anthony amendment over the top. Anti-suffragism became a historical footnote. It had clearly been outmaneuvered by the suffrage camp with the shift to a national strategy that focused on Congress, instead of dozens of state legislatures with their parochial peculiarities. Suffragists had increasingly emphasized the sociopolitical benefits of the franchise for the nation, in contrast to earlier emphases on the justice of the vote. The linkage of enfranchisement with progressive reform mollified some anxious males. No longer was the emphasis on what seemed to be a sexual revolution. Instead, woman suffrage became a tolerable manifestation of twentieth-century social change. Along with electricity and the automobile, voting rights for women came to be seen as a modern convenience.

After passage of the Susan B. Anthony amendment, a handful of diehards transformed NAOWS into the Woman Patriot Corporation which, throughout the twenties, continued its anti-suffrage battle in the guise of anti-socialist, anti-bolshevik, and anti-radical rhetoric. Mary Kilbreth, the last president of NAOWS and the main figure leading the Woman Patriot Corporation, warned Congress that women who supported disarmament in the twenties promoted the cause of Lenin and Trotsky. She also fought against an Equal Rights Amendment, a Uniform Marriage and Divorce Law, a Child Labor amendment, and a department of education. For most remonstrants, however, enfranchisement became the new way of life—and they learned to accept it. In mobilizing their "majority" of right-minded women, remonstrants through the decades had developed a complex set of rationalizations that, for them, vindicated the rejection of what suffragists contended was "an inalienable right." Through monographs, magazine articles, letters to the editor, debates, pamphlets, press releases, and polite jawboning, antisuffragists wove an ideological tapestry that portrayed their intertwined assumptions about women and American society. Beneath the surface of these positions rested their underlying principles: duty, nature, and stability. Upon these elements were built whatever wrong-headedness or insight the antisuffragists were able to generate. Around these principles developed an intricate set of arguments, some universal in character, others expedient and contemporary.

When viewing the national landscape in the late nineteenth and early twentieth centuries, suffragists and remonstrants alike perceived the same unacceptable conditions: horrific housing arrangements in American cities, brutal working conditions for children in the nation's mills and mines, and inadequate educational programs for a majority of the country's offspring. The nation's welfare demanded that every citizen, regardless of sex, contribute his or her full measure of wisdom and devotion. Both suffragists and antis agreed on these points. Their differences arose in terms of appropriate paths to reform.

Antisuffragists believed that elected officials drew their insights regarding legislative decisions from the court of public opinion. Lawmakers were simply the instruments of the public mind. Therefore, women could effect change without holding political office by molding public opinion through their discussions with one another and through their influence on male members of their families. In addition, their absence from the hurly-burly of political life allowed them to remain untainted by political loyalties. By being nonpartisan, they could demand change—industrial safety legislation or a children's bureau, for instance—based purely on the merits of the case, not on political associations. Women had duties to improve society, especially as the United States moved inexorably toward a modern state filled with factories, cities, and modern conveniences. But by what strategy could they best complete their civic duty, asked the antis? Complete immersion in the unkind, uncouth, and unprincipled behaviors of daily political life was not a reasonable or effective way to produce positive change, they argued. Rather they felt that the purity of their position vis-à-vis political parties had to be maintained through nonpartisanship and behind-the-scenes campaigning.

Furthermore, early remonstrants believed that this civic duty had to be accomplished away from the tumult of the political arena because women by their nature were different from men. Antis took pride, as the years unfolded, in the host of legal, educational, and even economic advances achieved by women in the latter half of the nineteenth century. Annie Nathan Meyer, an energetic New York anti, was not only the first woman to own and use a bicycle in the city of New York, but she was also a key proponent behind the establishment of Barnard College and a college trustee until her death in 1951. A Massachusetts anti, Agnes Irving, served as the first dean of Radcliffe and was a driving force behind the school's determination to institute a doctoral program. And, Emily Bissell, a nationally renowned anti, founded the Christmas Seal campaign in 1907 and later became one of the first child labor commissioners in her home state of Delaware. Occasionally, remonstrants even conceded that at some point in the future, women might be ready to share the extra burden of the franchise with their male counterparts. But, for the moment, they were willing to live in an age in which "separate but equal" pertained to sex roles as well as race relations.

Remonstrants insisted that the separate but equal worlds of women and men grew out of the inevitability of natural law. They argued that natural law required a two-part professional structure whereby the sexes were matched in their valuation as to intellectual gifts and moral virtue, but applied their specialized attributes in distinctly different fashions. Simply put, men did their naturally assigned tasks to the best of their abilities and women completed their own to the best of theirs. If both progressed within specialized spheres of responsibility, problems associated with child labor, impure foodstuffs, and epidemic diseases could be eradicated.

These women insisted that members of their own sex had intellectual capacities and vocational proclivities that were the true equal of any man, only different in function. Women best exemplified this co-equal role by a mastery of their own sphere of influence: the home. This private sphere became theirs through both the evolutionary process and a divine command. Remonstrants, for the most part, were earnest believers in a male Christian godhead. This supreme being had placed humanity on earth with specific duties in mind, duties that were to be completed by following his natural order. As "mothers of the race," women, according to antisuffragists, realized their highest calling through the perpetuation of moral ideals within their families. In this fashion, home became not only a man's refuge from an unclean secular world but also a woman's place of business—both civic and familial.

During the early decades of the twentieth century, the focus of the anti-suffrage argument drifted from an emphasis on the natural differences of women and men toward perspectives that addressed contemporary sociopolitical issues. Early in the fight against the vote, Massachusetts remonstrants had been motivated by anti-Catholic bigotry, fearful that legions of Catholic women would march to the polls under the directions of their priests. As the decades passed, their prejudices shifted focus to women of color, especially African Americans. Unlike the more cautious prejudice that they harbored against the recent immigrants from Eastern and Southern Europe, remonstrants were never hesitant to abuse racial minorities whom they openly described as "ignorant." Antis highlighted the efforts of suffragists to organize African-American women and of the latter to attain political equality. They constantly reminded southern legislators of the danger inherent in enfranchising female ex-slaves, particularly for counties in which African Americans possessed a numerical superiority.

On occasion, racist arguments were embedded in a political debate over states' rights. Especially after 1917, when the suffrage strategy increasingly emphasized federal enfranchisement over state enfranchisement, southern remonstrants voiced alarm over the survival of constitutional government. "The right of a state to create and control its own electorate is the cornerstone of its autonomy," cried Virginian Mollie Seawell. Where a question of race was involved, she added, states' rights became "the rock upon which its civilization rests." The Civil War and Reconstruction had proven, she continued, the harm of federal domination of political electorates. Now the suffragists, acting as their abolitionist ancestors had a half century earlier, were attempting to subvert the foundations of America by erecting a dual electorate: one controlled by the states and one by the federal government, the latter including two million African Americans.[2]

Even as woman suffrage was debated, the antis claimed, the security of the nation had to be guaranteed. Women had the indulgent opportunity to discuss the pros and cons of women's rights because the armed forces of the United States protected them from foreign invaders and domestic anarchy. How could women ever provide the muscle necessary to safeguard freedom if they were permitted to design national policy through the ballot box? To remonstrants, men had always provided the brute strength and military competence needed to preserve democracy. In an age of labor strife with socialist legions rising up across the nation and overseas, nations survived, the antis argued, only through the fighting skills of their male constituents. How could women enforce the laws they enacted? Could women serve as the cavalry in the West, the police in New York City, or the navy in the Pacific? The antis frequently voiced with great indignation what they considered the trump card in this line of argumentation: What if women declared war and sent men out to die for the sake of women's supposed equality? The stronger sex had to carry out the responsibilities of protecting the liberties of all Americans. The antis urged women to pay attention to their own assigned tasks and leave the defense of their nation to their brave husbands, fathers, and brothers.

Unlike the suffragists, who needed to convert the American public to their way of thinking, anti-suffrage women articulated cultural values that were perfectly in keeping with this nation's traditions. Antis put into words what society had believed for a long time and had practiced for generations. The world of women, according to remonstrants, was blending too quickly with the world of men, especially in the political arena. A group of malcontents, according to the antis, now preached a new gospel of womanhood, one that threatened a national catastrophe. Those who wished to maintain a "loyalty" to their feminine heritage were called to the state associations opposed to woman suffrage during the decades from 1868 to 1920. Most antis wanted neither an inflexible society immobilized by the past nor an anarchic future fractured by selfish individualism. In molding the wisdom of the past to the demands of the present, remonstrants relied heavily on the safety of what had been rather than what could be. The two opposing camps of women both professed love for their nation, but drew apart—at times contentiously—as they sought to address the end of the nineteenth and the beginning of the twentieth century. The antisuffragists ultimately became part of history's forgotten "losers."

NOTES

1. Harriet Robinson, *Massachusetts in the Woman Suffrage Movement* (Boston: Roberts Brothers, 1881), p. 101.

2. Mollie Elliot Seawell, "Two Suffrage Mistakes," *North American Review* (March, 1914): 368–73.

8

CARRIE CHAPMAN CATT AND THE LAST YEARS OF THE STRUGGLE FOR WOMAN SUFFRAGE

"The Winning Plan"

Robert Booth Fowler & Spencer Jones

The most satisfying moments in Carrie Chapman Catt's life were those when she saw her dream of woman suffrage fulfilled. The moment had two vivid expressions. The first came when the Tennessee legislature passed the suffrage amendment in 1920. This decision brought into the fold the last state needed for the three-quarters majority of states necessary to ratify constitutional amendments and give women nationwide the right to vote. Knowing that the outcome of the legislative vote was uncertain in the border state of Tennessee, Catt had been lobbying the state's delegates for weeks and was in Nashville during the vote. Victory left her overjoyed but exhausted and eager to return to her home in New York.

The second moment came when Catt returned to New York and was met at Grand Central Station by supporters who recognized her strategic contributions to victory. Many in the crowd were veterans of the movement who had fought the suffrage battle with her, while others were politicians, like New York's governor Al Smith, who came to pay homage. A photograph from the event shows a smile suffusing the face of the essentially shy and serious-minded Catt. It was the triumphant and joyous expression of victory by a woman who had long believed that without her "Winning Plan" there would have been no woman suffrage in 1920 or for many years after.

The formative years of Carrie Catt's life reflected the combination of personal independence, tough-mindedness, and determination that resonated throughout her career as a woman suffrage leader. Carrie Lane was born in 1859, in the birthplace of the Republican Party, Ripon, Wisconsin. Catt's parents, well educated for the time, settled in Charles City, Iowa, with Carrie in 1866. Their daughter early expressed her distaste for her mother's acceptance of the traditional female role in a patriarchal household. During elementary school she also displayed her dislike for male dominance. Seven-year-old Catt successfully thwarted a troop of schoolyard boys who habitually chased girls with snakes by threatening her tormenters with a snake of her own and watching in pleasure as the frightened boys ran. Catt was equally tough when she walked up to a young bully tormenting another girl and slapped his face. "They had respect for us girls after that!" Catt would fondly recall, even seventy years after the incident.

Catt's independent streak continued after she completed high school. Against her parents' wishes, she decided to attend college. In the face of derisive comments about her being a "silly woman," Catt completed her formal education at Iowa State University in 1880, the only woman in a graduating class of seventeen. After a short stint as a schoolteacher, Catt was named superintendent of schools in Mason City, Iowa, a highly unusual post for an unmarried young woman to occupy in the late nineteenth century. She left the superintendent job in 1885 to marry her first husband, Leo Chapman, and to work with him on his newspaper. Although it may seem surprising that Catt would give up her hard-earned independence for marriage, Catt wanted to be married—but only if she was an equal partner with her husband.

The Chapmans' political views were similar and through the newspaper, the *Mason City Republican*, Carrie Catt edited a "Woman's World" column focused on serious issues she judged especially relevant to women, including woman suffrage. Her initial foray into public debates—the latter a form of oratory she had learned at college—proved short lived, however, as financial reverses led Leo Chapman to move to California to make a new start. Catt planned to join him as soon as possible, but Leo Chapman died of typhoid fever soon after his arrival in California. At twenty-seven, Catt suddenly found herself a widow with neither financial resources nor a profession. Like most middle-class American women in the late nineteenth century, Carrie Chapman had accepted the breadwinner's ethic—that is, that husbands supported their wives financially and emotionally. Her husband's death, however, marked the last time that Catt would entrust control of her life to anybody but herself.

In the 1880s as a widow she moved west and worked at several jobs, usually connected to newspapers. While she was working for a San Francisco newspaper soliciting advertising, a male co-worker sexually harassed Catt. Many women of this period accepted such humiliations, but not Catt. The incident sparked her commitment to achieve equal dignity for women in the workforce.

Catt returned to Iowa in 1887 and began a career in public speaking, often on the subject of woman suffrage. Among others, Lucy Stone, Susan B. Anthony, and Elizabeth Cady Stanton had demonstrated that lecturers who commanded large enough audiences could earn a living from the podium. At the same time, Carrie Lane Chapman became reacquainted with a successful structural engineer, George Catt, whom she married in 1890. Their union was decidedly unconventional for the time. For example, Catt set as a precondition for accepting George Catt's proposal that she was to have at least one-third of each year free to pursue her public goals, including woman suffrage. By making her career a central part of her life and insisting she have the independence to pursue it, Carrie Catt made herself available to continue to serve and, eventually, to lead the Iowa Woman Suffrage Association.

Catt was elected secretary and head of field organization of the Iowa Woman Suffrage Association in 1889. Her efficacy as an organizer soon earned her rave reviews from officers in the Iowa branch of the National American Woman Suffrage Association (NAWSA), but she had a larger, national battlefield in mind. In 1890, Catt marshaled support for a South Dakota referendum on woman suffrage. This was Catt's debut in front of the national leaders of the NAWSA. Though the referendum lost, the national leaders, impressed with Catt's organizational skills, her administrative ability, and her zealous commitment to the cause, invited her to speak at the annual NAWSA convention in 1890. It was at this convention that the reunification of the American Woman Suffrage Association and the National Woman Suffrage Association occurred and the two organizations merged into one association for the final offensive for the vote.

After her successful leadership of the Colorado suffrage struggle in 1893, Catt was appointed to the important post of "national organizer" of NAWSA. By 1895, she had worked her way up to chair of the National Organization Committee, a position she held from 1895 to 1900. Disagreeing with veteran suffrage leaders, she strove to shift the woman suffrage movement away from the noble and yet impractical idealists who surrounded the aged Susan B. Anthony. In the inner sanctums of the movement, she struggled to reorganize the suffrage organization and to turn it into a more effective machine promoting votes for women.

Her long-term objectives were clear in her blunt report to the 1895 national convention on its organizational failures. Ever the pragmatist, Catt was impatient with those who did not understand the practical realities necessary for the passage of a federal amendment guaranteeing woman suffrage. But the ratification of such an amendment required adopting modern strategies of fund-raising and lobbying.

By the late 1890s, Catt's leadership position within the elite group of women running the NAWSA was clear. Her colleagues viewed her as the new "General" of the movement, a general with a considerable amount of political acumen. Catt's climb into the NAWSA hierarchy did not come without controversy. For example, Catt had the temerity to criticize women suffragists in the field who proved ineffective or pessimistic, labeling them as weaklings. To be sure, she strongly favored a program of proximate steps toward victory, such as acceptance of municipal suffrage and local statutes permitting women to vote in school board elections. But guided by what she saw as practical realism, she insisted that the larger, long-term goal of woman suffrage for all was an expectation that would come true—and no one should doubt that.

Catt's criticisms raised the hackles of the "old guard" elite of the suffrage movement, but its matriarch, Susan B. Anthony, came to regard Catt's energy and organizational techniques as essential to the success of woman suffrage. Anthony admired Catt's ability to listen and learn from others, especially those in the various states whose campaigns required a knowledge of local circumstances. Both Anthony and Stanton also recognized in Catt a woman without the encumbrances of children, who could devote all her considerable energy to the cause. As Anthony wrote to another suffragist in 1901, referring to Catt, "I know of no other woman with leisure, with no children, with a husband who backs her morally and financially, with the brains and disposition to do for the sake of the cause, and seemingly no personal ambition, but Mrs. Catt."

The election of Carrie Catt to the presidency of NAWSA in 1900 confirmed the triumph of her program of pragmatic organization within NAWSA. Anthony bestowed her mantle of leadership not from close friendship or personal devotion. Anthony had her "nieces," women of the second generation of NAWSA with whom she was particularly close on a personal level. Catt was not included in this most favored circle of Anthony's confidants. Moreover, Catt's criticism of the disorganized and unsuccessful Anthony-led NAWSA contributed to the professional, rather than personal, nature of the relationship between the two leaders, as Catt continued to maintain a certain distance from almost all leaders within NAWSA.

A case in point was Catt's relationship with Anna Howard Shaw. An ordained Methodist minister, physician, and accomplished orator with a lifetime of dedication to the suffrage movement, Shaw was a member of Anthony's inner circle, and she expected to be Anthony's successor. Shaw was shocked when Anthony came to the conclusion that Catt's organizational skills superseded the privileged relationship Anthony maintained with her, which included visits to Anthony's home in Rochester. After Anthony anointed Catt as her successor, recognizing the younger woman's "great genius" as an administrator, in 1900, Catt received 254 of the 275 votes for the NAWSA presidency. After Catt's overwhelming election, Shaw was relegated to the vice presidency, the same position that she had held in the Anthony years. She regretted her failed attempt at the presidency. "I will admit . . . I made the greatest sacrifice of my life. My greatest ambition had been to succeed Miss Anthony."

Catt's first tenure as president of NAWSA from 1900 through 1904 proved unremarkable. She had inherited a skeletal organization with serious membership and fund-raising problems. While Catt barnstormed the country tirelessly, using her presidential pulpit in attempts to educate women (and men), to bolster NAWSA membership, and to sway public opinion, her first term saw not one newly enfranchised woman in America. Nor was there any concrete progress toward the adoption of a constitutional amendment for woman suffrage. Catt did, however, raise enough money to place NAWSA on a firm financial footing, while improving her skill and reputation as a national speaker and public representative of the suffrage cause. In 1904, Catt decided not to run for reelection, citing what we would recognize as burnout: "I find a rest has become necessary." Not only was Catt herself ill, but so were her husband and mother. George Catt died in 1905, not long after Carrie Catt turned over the leadership of NAWSA to Anna Howard Shaw.

Anna Shaw presided over NAWSA for the next twelve years. During her tenure, dues-paying members rose from 17,000 to over 200,000 in 1916, and the number of woman suffrage states grew from four to twelve. What also increased during this time period, however, was pressure, especially from younger women within the movement, for much faster progress. That criticism was increasingly directed at Shaw. One significant expression of the dissent came in 1914 when a faction of NAWSA, headed by Alice Paul, broke off to form a more radical organization, which eventually became known as the National Woman's Party.

Carrie Catt used these years to repair her depleted reservoir of energy and recover from a serious depression following her husband's death in 1905. As an affluent widow, she did not have to work and instead devoted her attention toward the emerging International Woman Suffrage Alliance (IWSA). Like most suffrage women who had served at a national level, she had a global perspective on issues that she believed brought women together throughout the world. Catt had been a leader of the IWSA from its creation in 1902, serving as its first and only president until 1923.

As president of IWSA, an organization with branches in twenty-six countries, Catt's resilient nature manifested itself as she roamed the globe, spreading the gospel of woman suffrage. Her travels included one trip around the world from 1909 to 1911 to "organize the women of the world for suffrage." In the process, she expanded her network of influential contacts and her status as a political celebrity soared.

By 1912, however, Catt could no longer resist the lure of the American suffrage movement. She threw her efforts into New York State, now her adopted home, and its suffrage battle. Undaunted by the work of Harriot Blatch, Elizabeth Cady Stanton's daughter, she quickly established a competing umbrella group within the state to coordinate the numerous independent suffrage groups. Catt's immediate efforts failed in New York, when the 1915 state referendum on woman suffrage was defeated. This failure in what was then the most important state in the Union underscored the frustratingly slow pace of progress for the nationwide suffrage movement. The defeat of three more suffrage votes in the same year—in Iowa, South Dakota, and West Virginia—provided more evidence. The voices of impatience increasingly focused on Shaw and led to growing pressure on Catt to return to the presidency of NAWSA. Catt would return to the helm only on her own terms, demanding that she have autonomous control of NAWSA to lead the group in the direction that she saw fit.

That direction eventually came to be known as "the Winning Plan," a strategy that combined efforts at both the state and federal levels and that depended on a winning campaign in at least one southern state along with some midwestern states. In Catt's view, these victories would encourage the U.S. Congress to pass the suffrage amendment. Frustrated by the never-ending appeals to American men, she believed it better to avoid case-by-case state efforts that depended on popular sentiment and referendums and instead turn to federal action by Congress and the president. She knew that in order for the plan to succeed it would still be necessary for the states to ratify the federal amendment, but by that time she calculated that opinion leaders would convince an apathetic ignorant male public

to fall into line. The basic challenge was to overcome the immense ignorance and apathy among the voters.

Catt's plan, with its mandate for aggressive nonpartisan lobbying at the
federal level, was adopted at a 1916 emergency meeting of NAWSA. Deriv-
ing from Catt's realistic understanding that a focus on the state level might
never succeed because too many states lacked enlightened electorates or
had constitutional mechanisms that made attempts at achieving woman
suffrage nearly hopeless, Catt's plan was a calculated gamble. This did not
bother her since she had always been a leader willing to take risks. Catt did
seek to keep up pressure to enact suffrage on the state level, but her heart
was not really in this exhausting effort that dissipated the energies and
resources of the suffrage movement. As she succinctly expressed her idea:
"We care not a gingersnap about anything but that federal amendment."

Combining her cumulative frustrations with the state referendum
process and her fervor for organization, Carrie Catt decided on a single
plan, focusing all efforts on the adoption of a federal amendment, called
optimistically the Sixteenth, to the U.S. Constitution. Catt was always careful to promote her goal in a nonpartisan fashion, a stance that was an
essential part of her winning plan. She believed that supporters must be
encouraged wherever they might be found, and she did not intend to let
suffrage get lost in partisan squabbling. This part of her plan came naturally to a woman who was a born politician, despite her distaste for partisanship. Mainly her approach was a practical one. Had partisan politics
appeared the way to success, the unashamedly pragmatic Catt would surely
have embraced it and supported one party.

The stakes that Catt placed on her plan were great, given inevitably
limited resources, and she secretly vowed to resign if NAWSA failed to
approve her gamble at the emergency meeting of 1916. Thanks in part to
the strong and gracious support of Shaw, however, Catt's plan to shift
the focus of NAWSA from the state level to the federal level passed by a
large margin.

Catt's strategy to realize the federal plan involved five basic elements:
a specific concept of leadership; an intense commitment to a hierarchical, militarylike organization; an efficient publicity machine designed to
sway public opinion; a determined pragmatism; and a steady optimism
that woman suffrage would win and would provide the means to con-
structing a better society. Catt's concept of leadership required someone
able to play a galvanizing role as a charismatic public speaker, while still
dedicating the majority of her efforts to bureaucratic and organizational
matters. Catt had herself in mind, of course, and she strove to fulfill that

role as much as possible, whether on the stump, lobbying in Washington, or centralizing NAWSA under her executive control.

Catt now turned from dealing with resistant local male populations to concentrating on convincing political elites in Washington of the justness of her cause. She shifted the efforts of NAWSA officers to Washington, D.C., where she worked closely with Maude Park Wood on day-to-day federal lobbying. Catt herself was a frequent lobbyist, working the White House and rest of Capitol Hill in a style that combined determination and dignity.

Along the way, Catt successfully overcame her instinctive reluctance to become a "media star." Her position required her to make frequent public addresses, and while she believed that she was not a good speaker, most contemporary accounts do not substantiate this opinion. She routinely infused her speeches with clarity, energy, and, above all, her burning determination. Indeed, by her second presidency, Catt was a commanding speaker, a master of the medium. A typical account of one of her 1917 speeches noted, "again and again salvos of applause stopped her for a moment but again and again the steady rhythm of her strong voice regained control." In 1920, she was the most sought after of the suffrage speakers, traveling over 100,000 miles and delivering a prodigious 7,000 speeches that year.

Yet, while succeeding in the public responsibilities her presidential role required, Catt was true to her plan and devoted the bulk of her presidential energy to the improvement of NAWSA from an organizational standpoint. One crucial feature of this effort was the establishment of "suffrage schools." Recognizing the vital need for well-trained and effective women to occupy leadership positions within NAWSA at all its levels, from the affiliated state organizations to the education committee, Catt started the suffrage schools in order to teach women the history of suffrage, the terms of the current debate, and the procedures of successful participation in the movement. Schools addressed how to work with ordinary citizens and professional politicians, how to deal with (and, if possible, use) the press, and the fundamental techniques of skillful public speaking. Above all, Catt's schools taught women how to organize down to the last practical detail of circulating petitions.

Catt's professional organizers, a network of trained women, eventually penetrated every level of society: state, district, town, city, and village, and often even many precincts. In time, the organizers helped NAWSA recruit a membership of two million to pursue the cause throughout the United States, although efforts in the South often proved an exception.

They also helped achieve another of Catt's organizing goals: uniting every kind of women's group from local associations to important existing national women's groups such as the National Federation of Business and Professional Women's Clubs. In this way, she believed suffrage would become a formidable movement that politicians could ignore no longer.

Catt realized that a broad publicity effort was also essential in order to attract new members and weaken the persistent objection that women did not want the vote. She enlisted a professional editor, Rose Young, to head the NAWSA publicity machine. Press releases flowed out, favorable stories were planted when possible, "false" perspectives were attacked, and endless letters were sent to newspaper editors in an effort to use the press to promote suffrage. Using other advertising approaches, NAWSA also made and distributed numerous pamphlets, leaflets, balloons, and buttons proclaiming the necessity of woman suffrage.

At the same time, Catt sought a quality publication to reflect the organization's views. She successfully negotiated with Alice Stone Blackwell, the publisher along with her father Henry Blackwell of the well-regarded *Woman's Journal*. An earlier attempt to buy the *Woman's Journal* had floundered amid tensions before their merger between AWSA led by Lucy Stone, Alice's mother, and Henry Blackwell's wife, and NWSA. In 1916, NAWSA purchased Blackwell's journal, retaining part of its staff. The publication now became the "Official Organ of the NAWSA," and its name was changed to the *Woman Citizen* in 1917, its new title indicating the transformation that Catt had in mind for women.

Of course, publicity campaigns, suffrage schools, and speaking tours all required money, more money than NAWSA had been able to accumulate in previous presidencies. Catt understood that raising funds had to be an integral part of her "Winning Plan." Searching for support through membership drives, public meetings, and NASWA publications proved an unending task for Catt and other leaders. While they succeeded in raising millions of dollars donated by members and sympathizers from across the country, the organization's needs predictably outpaced its means.

Lack of money had been a problem since its founding. In the Anthony-Stanton period between 1869 and its merger with the American Woman Suffrage Association in 1890, the organization had benefited from several legacies. Then, in 1914, Mrs. Frank Leslie, the widow of a prominent New York publisher, donated almost one million dollars to the cause. Although court battles swirled around the Leslie endowment, Catt succeeded in engineering a legal victory that established the rights of NAWSA to the substantial bequest. She was quick to employ the badly needed Leslie monies, doling out $200,000 for staff salaries and over $400,000 to the *Woman Citizen*, reflecting her belief that for the "Winning Plan" to succeed there had to be a well-oiled, well-funded national publicity machine. Overall, the Leslie bequest put NAWSA on firm financial footing for the first time in its history, and it came at a time when NAWSA needed it most.

Catt's pragmatic focus determined her stance on other issues and Progressive reforms. Convinced that victory would prove elusive if enemies of the cause were able to brand her or her organization as politically extremist or anti-American, she publicly abandoned her pacifism (to avoid having the suffrage cause labeled unpatriotic in World War I), her belief in black civil rights and equality (to win southern white votes for suffrage), and her radical feminism (to avoid being associated with the "radical" Alice Paul and the National Woman's Party).

In the eyes of history, Catt's maneuvers regarding African Americans proved to be most controversial. Catt was actually quite liberal on racial matters for her time, indeed, far more so than most Progressive-era reformers. But her racial views were distantly secondary to her suffrage goal. When speaking and lobbying in the South, Catt did not hesitate to complain that (in the North) illiterate blacks had the right to vote, while literate, refined southern white women could not vote. When speaking in the North in places where blacks could vote, she did not hesitate to argue that giving white women suffrage would block the influence of ignorant African Americans. Catt also knowingly condoned racism by holding conventions in southern cities to advance her cause in its weakest region, and she accepted fervent racists for NAWSA offices. At the same time, she also told selected African American audiences that "suffrage democracy" should know "no bias of race color or sex," which was her actual view. Catt played the race card in many ways, but always with the goal of woman suffrage uppermost in mind, and at a time in which white male politicians throughout the United States worked to limit, not expand, racial justice by restricting black male voting.

NAWSA's public stance on the entry of the United States into World War I was another instance of Catt's single-minded approach to the realization of woman suffrage. Although Catt was a member of the Woman's Peace Party and a vigorous campaigner for world peace, who believed that expanding the electorate to include women would foster this goal, she would not jeopardize the suffrage cause by aligning it with an unpopular position. Thus, when the United States entered World War I in 1917, Catt swung behind the war and never looked back. It was just another (if painful) pragmatic decision that the plan required her to make, and she coolly did so. Catt's choice to rally to the American effort and especially her service on the Woman's Committee of the Council of National Defense resulted in her ejection from the tiny and soon besieged Woman's Peace Party, but it saved NAWSA from the accusation that it was unpatriotic.

By this time, Catt suspected that if the woman suffrage movement played its cards right, the war might actually prove an excellent opportunity for NAWSA to move into the mainstream of American life and shed its image as a vaguely radical operation. As suffragists had after the Civil War, she consistently argued that the patriotic service of woman suffragists during the war must be repaid with their enfranchisement at its conclusion. And she drew attention to the irony that some German women could vote.

Moreover, Catt guided NAWSA on a mainstream course by distancing the organization from Alice Paul's National Woman's Party, which sought to pursue a more forceful and confrontational approach to women's enfranchisement. Catt and other established figures like Anna Howard Shaw believed that Paul's militancy hurt the cause, making it easier for opponents to label woman suffragists as radicals and raising fears about what would happen if women got the vote. This was basically a dispute over tactics, but it took on a personal nature as well. At the time, Catt was furious about the Woman's Party picketing of the White House and its partisan positions, which resulted in sensational, unflattering news coverage. Later however she admitted that Alice Paul's tactics may have legitimized NAWSA and assisted the overall cause.

Catt's "Winning Plan" brought results in 1918 when the House of Representatives finally passed the Anthony amendment with the requisite two-thirds margin. Gaining passage in the Senate proved harder than in the House, but the determined Catt and NAWSA saw that step completed in 1919. When the Anthony amendment was sent to the states for approval, Catt switched her focus back to states, correctly predicting that they would follow the example of the federal government. Meanwhile, she mobilized all the elements of her Winning Plan to make sure they did. When Tennessee ratified the Anthony amendment in 1920, Catt's plan had indeed proven to be a winning one.

Implicit in Catt's faith in evolutionary optimism—and in her Winning Plan as an expression of it—was her version of W. E. B. DuBois's contemporary concept of the leading tenth of society. Like many other Progressives, she believed that on the road to evolutionary change there must be elites who worked for, and in association with, the masses they led. For Catt, there was no doubt that she and her fellow laborers in the suffrage battle represented a stage in the progress of humanity, a step in the evolution of society toward the common good. Giving women the vote opened the door to achieving many social reforms, she insisted, from improving the lives of individual women and children to advancing world peace. Frequently, Catt noted that gaining the vote was "no more than an episode in an age-old battle" toward a better society.

Catt lived for twenty-seven more years after the suffrage amendment passed, and in those years she personified some of the postvote reactions among suffrage women. The most lasting achievement Catt gained after the passage of the Anthony amendment was the creation of the League of Women Voters (LWV). Catt lent her name as symbolic chair of the LWV but quickly turned actual management of the organization over to Maude Wood Park. In its beginning years, the LWV reflected Catt's political goals; it was run by women but for the common good; it was all about education for informed citizenship. It focused on rational issue discussions, was nonpartisan, and avoided elections and electoral campaigns.

But now that suffrage was won, Catt's own distaste for party politics disappeared. She had no hesitancy about reentering political battles—even partisan ones—when she felt called to do so. The competitive—and political—Catt rarely resisted, especially since she never forgot her enemies and did not hesitate to focus her opposition on them. In 1926, she attempted to defeat New York Senator James Wadsworth, a major foe of woman suffrage, whose wife had been the national leader of anti-suffrage women. Wadsworth compounded his sins in Catt's eyes through some of his political stands in the 1920s, including his opposition to a constitutional amendment forbidding child labor and to Prohibition (an idea that Catt, for the most part, endorsed). Catt swept into the campaign against Wadsworth with all her typical energy and employing all her wiles. She was exultant when he lost.

After 1920, Catt was encouraged to provide a historical record of the woman suffrage crusade to prevent its enemies from distorting its history and falsely characterizing her role. The result was the book, *Victory: How Women Won It: 1840–1940*, which Catt oversaw and contributed to, along with other former leaders in the woman suffrage movement. Catt's postsuffrage reputation reached its height with her establishment of the Woman Centennial Congress of 1940 and when her friend, Eleanor Roosevelt, honored the eighty-two-year-old Catt at a gala ceremony in 1941. But she was also criticized for her support of peace initiatives. In the 1940s, Catt faded from public life and died of heart failure in 1947.

Catt's reputation in our time suffers since she is often accused of being a manipulative politician, as well as an unethical compromiser of important values. Such charges are nothing new regarding Catt. She was the object of these during her lifetime. But Catt made up her mind early in her career that she had no interest in such critical perspectives from those she viewed as abstract ideologues who accomplished little. She wanted to win woman suffrage, which she thought (too optimistically, perhaps) would advance the vision she always held in her heart: treatment of women as human beings equal to men. Even after the passage of the suffrage amendment, in areas such as the workplace, marriage and divorce law, women's position in society was hardly that of equals. In her last years Catt remained as optimistic about the future as ever. The future, like woman suffrage, was there to be won. What was needed was effective leadership such as that she had provided the suffrage movement and the determination by a new generation of women to grasp it with "a winning plan."

9

AMERICA AND THE PANKHURSTS

Christine Bolt

All over America the Suffragists declare that they have gained hope and inspiration from our great British movement. In the early days of our long struggle it was we who drew inspiration from them. Our movements act and react on each other. We and the world have much to gain from our joint effort.

E. Sylvia Pankhurst, 1911

The three British militant suffragettes,[1] Emmeline Pankhurst and her daughters Christabel and Sylvia, were famous throughout the world by the time votes for women were won in America and Britain. Born in Manchester in 1858, Emmeline Goulden had, as a schoolgirl, been influenced by the city's early support for woman suffrage and by her parents' sympathy for the cause. Her marriage to an established reformer, Richard Pankhurst, had helped to radicalize her further. Widowed early, Emmeline was of necessity drawn further into affairs beyond the home. She also shared with her children an ardent desire to make a difference in the world, and in due course she did so through founding a suffrage society in 1903—the Women's Social and Political Union (WSPU)—whose members and methods were to render the Pankhurst name notorious.

To spread the suffrage message, Mrs. Pankhurst and her two elder daughters eventually toured the United States: Emmeline in 1909, 1911, and 1913; Sylvia in 1910–1911 and 1912; and Emmeline and Christabel during World War I, when British but not American militancy was abandoned. For the Pankhursts and their American hosts alike, the encounters proved both exciting and rewarding, and for subsequent observers, they shed valuable light on the radicalization of British and American suffragist methods, in the first decades of the twentieth century, and on the always complex Anglo-American relationship.

It is not surprising that British and American suffragists took a keener interest in one another's activities than they did in those of the rest of the world. Both movements selectively drew on Enlightenment thought, on the tenets of Social Darwinism and imperialism, and on the shifting emphases of liberalism and socialism. Both flourished in nations with a fairly permissive political environment and took off in the 1860s, when hopes soared that legislation enfranchising men would be extended to women.

The course of American and British suffragism was also similar, with both campaigns producing elaborate organizations, such as the National American Woman Suffrage Association in the United States and the National Union of Women's Suffrage Societies in Britain. Both movements provided their supporters with a political education that propelled them onto the public platform and forced them to cultivate an ever-larger array of political friends, in order to reply effectively to their intermittently mobilized but constantly vocal political enemies. Both movements offended powerful conservative interest groups and found it impossible to win meaningful support from the major political parties. Both were tested by personal and tactical disagreements; and both endured decades of drudgery before a promising political setting for women's enfranchisement materialized during World War I.

And throughout their struggle the two movements exchanged ideas, inspirational literature, and personnel. Both played a key part in organizing the regular conferences of international feminism from the 1880s. American activists were therefore well placed to detect and debate any new tactics that emerged in Britain, while British campaigners were similarly alert to the value of securing support for such developments among their American sisters.

When militant British suffragettes began to visit the United States in the first decade of the twentieth century, they showed the good timing that is an essential part of success in any undertaking. As the new century dawned, on both sides of the Atlantic, more women than ever before were going to college, working outside the home, being drawn into labor organizations, and supporting an elaborate array of reform institutions and causes, including female suffrage. Women had even improved their political skills through firsthand experience, exercising local franchises in both countries and enjoying the vote in Wyoming, Colorado, Utah, and Idaho by 1896. The number of female voters remained small, however, not least because the suffrage states were thinly populated, and because in the United States partial suffrage was generally seen as an unacceptable half-loaf.

In Britain, the frequent association of local politics with domestic—and hence feminine—issues such as education and health made it harder for women to argue their case for the national suffrage. As a result, the changing circumstances of women in Britain and the United States by the early twentieth century only served to make campaigners aware of how much remained to be done before full female enfranchisement could be achieved.

Acting on this awareness, the British and American suffrage movements set out to increase their following among working-class women, to shake politicians out of their intransigence, and to take advantage of the period of greater political radicalism associated with the Progressive movement in America and the advent of a reforming Liberal government in Britain in 1906. To secure suffragist ends, fresh tactics and intellectual emphases were adopted. And they were applied first by British women, most famously in the WSPU, which pledged itself to "deeds not words" in seeking votes for women.

The tactics adopted by WSPU leaders built on the more confrontational methods used by groups of radical British suffragists from the 1890s, including the open-air, mass direct action favored by a range of working-class groups during the nineteenth and early twentieth centuries. In the Pankhursts' case, sympathy with such action was also nurtured by immersion in Manchester (where they were raised) radical politics that Christabel believed provided them with tenacity in the face of obstacles and in resistance to diverting side issues.

Although there is some truth in the popular opinion of the time that wherever the Pankhursts were, there was the focal point of the movement, militant suffragism was neither a simple phenomenon, nor one totally controlled by the Pankhursts. Its adherents in Ireland, Scotland, and the English provinces showed considerable independence; and the most famous suffragette "stunt"—Emily Davison's plunge under King George V's horse during the Derby race in 1913—was not the work of an unquestioning Pankhurst devotee, but the calculated act of an independently minded WSPU militant, who was sustained by her own "women's community" of "friendship, love and support."

The WSPU actions were bold. Yet its members asked for the vote on the same terms as men, a compromise claim that, if successful, would have enfranchised only some women and which was supported by many moderate British suffragists. Moreover, militants often employed the conventional pressure group tactics used by moderates and saw the need for words as well as deeds. Accordingly, suffragettes were at pains to stress women's difference from men. They emphasized the transformative power of women's superior morality "in the great struggle for upward human evolution"; the innate justice of their assertion that "a Government can only rest upon the consent of the Governed"; and the quasi-religious nature of their cause, which was "for the good of our own souls, and for the improvement of the souls of men."[2]

The fact remains, however, that the militants commanded attention because of their distinctiveness, because of their determination to utilize new methods and blaze new trails. The suffragettes' early campaigns involved refusal to pay taxes; heckling politicians at public meetings; urging electors to vote against the government at by-elections; and sending representatives to the House of Commons. Politicians and the public were startled and dismayed by the WSPU's ability to bring growing numbers of women out onto the streets, where they literally made a spectacle of themselves. Theatrically attired in the suffragette colors of purple, white, and green to emphasize female solidarity, and wielding striking banners and placards proclaiming their identity and goal, the suffragettes quickly won the attention they wanted.

Energized by noisy crowds, vigilant police, fines, and imprisonment, by 1909, WSPU activists had progressed to still more dramatic tactics. After resisting increasingly rough handling from the police and bystanders, suffragettes embarked on the carefully orchestrated destruction of public and then private property. Although militancy was suspended for most of 1910–1911, so as not to jeopardize the passage of compromise suffrage measures before Parliament, it was resumed when conciliation efforts failed. The attacks on property, including window smashing and arson, were stepped up. And the suffragettes proved their toughness when jailed by demanding to be treated as political prisoners, hunger striking, opposing as well as enduring the brutality of force feeding, and coping with harassment under the 1913 Prisoners' Temporary Discharge (or Cat and Mouse) Act, a measure that allowed the government to release sick militants from prison only to rearrest them when they had recovered. Emmeline, Sylvia, and Christabel Pankhurst were among those jailed for their beliefs, and over 1,000 suffragettes were imprisoned. A few of these intrepid women subsequently died as a result of their experiences. Though some did resort to physical violence, no men were seriously injured or killed by militants.[3]

Of course, the actions of the WSPU reverberated not only throughout Britain and the United States but also in continental Europe, where suffrage leaders maintained regular contacts with each other until the disruptions of World War I. Nonetheless, for a number of good reasons, the Pankhursts chose to lecture in America rather than, say, Germany or France, whose feminists were aware of and sometimes applauded WSPU methods. Despite the French-educated Mrs. Pankhurst's love of Paris and Christabel's direction of the WSPU from that city after 1912 (to avoid arrest in Britain), the two women recognized that militant links—like suffrage links generally—were strongest with their American sisters.

Britain's radical suffragists of the late nineteenth century, who sustained the Women's Franchise League and favored the full emancipation of all women, had benefited from the presence in their circle of the fearless American suffragist, Elizabeth Cady Stanton, and her daughter Harriot Stanton Blatch. Harriot's 1882 marriage to an Englishman led to a long period of British residence, during which, Ellen DuBois has shown in chapter 10 in this volume, she underwent a gradual shift toward "a more democratic and socialistic approach to women's rights." Blatch later recalled that "Mrs. Pankhurst and I, burdened as we were by young children and domestic cares, were the admiring neophytes" of this radical circle.[4]

When Mrs. Pankhurst first contemplated lecturing abroad in 1909, it was natural that she should turn for help to Mrs. Blatch, who had moved back to New York in 1902. Suffragettes visiting the United States could look forward to bigger audiences, larger fees, and more vigorous publicity than were to be found in any other country. British travelers and lecturers of every kind had long crossed the Atlantic. Moreover, there was a well-established lecture circuit in America, and its women had been accepted on the public platform far longer than their British counterparts.

For militants like Emmeline and Sylvia Pankhurst, who were engaged in strenuous campaigning and constant brushes with the law in Britain, the journey to and from the United States provided an opportunity for physical and mental recuperation from the fatigue incurred from a lecture tour, which entailed traveling frequently and performing up to three times a day. On reaching America, Emmeline and Sylvia experienced "the relative repose of speaking in full security from re-arrest."[5] Since suffragettes believed that the British press tried to avoid giving them helpful publicity, they were understandably jubilant about the extensive news-paper coverage of the Pankhurst visits. The two militants delighted in the "open-handed American hospitality [,] . . . forthcomingness, . . . [and] frankly expressed pleasure in meeting [a reporter]."[6]

Mrs. Pankhurst was not a mercenary woman, but she needed money for her family as well as for suffragism. She was naturally thrilled to meet her personal needs and gratefully advertised the fact that she returned home from her second tour with "a very generous American contribution [over £4,500] to our war chest." She was similarly quick to report that "everywhere I found the Americans kind and keen, and cannot say too much for the wonderful hospitality they showed me."[7]

If the Pankhursts' visits thus afforded them personal and material grati-fication, there were more substantial gains for militancy in both Britain and the United States. Essentially, the tours allowed Emmeline and Sylvia to spread their message abroad while embarrassing the British government and rallying their followers at home. Aware that hostile British comments on militancy had crossed the Atlantic, Mrs. Pankhurst was determined to explain the phenomenon to American skeptics and so help radicalism to develop in the American suffrage movement.[8]

Standing before a huge New York audience in 1909—dainty and digni-fied, small and immaculate—her first words were: "I am what you call a hooligan." Carnegie Hall erupted with laughter, and having thus broken the ice, Mrs. Pankhurst set out to show that neither she nor other suf-fragettes were acting irrationally. She carefully explained why women had abandoned peaceful, educative methods, resorting instead to "violence and upsetting the business arrangements of the country" in their alleg-edly "undue impatience to attain their end." They had done so, she de-clared, like many men had done before them, because "England is the most conservative country on earth." All the party political work undertaken by British women had been accepted by British men, "but they never offered any kind of payment." It therefore remained extraordinarily hard to produce a female suffrage bill acceptable to the various sections of the House of Commons. Some MPs objected to restricted measures, which would enfranchise primarily prosperous and single women, while others feared any enlargement of the electorate or dreaded the impact of female voting on established party priorities, on "women's social position," and on the men who remained disfranchised.[9]

Mrs. Pankhurst stressed that it was only after meeting with politicians' ingratitude and conservatism that normally law-abiding British women— many blessed with the time and means to agitate—were forced to adopt militant tactics in order to obtain their own freedom and to redress the "intolerable grievances" they endured because British men upheld a double standard of morality for the sexes. Americans were assured that suffragettes did not seek martyrdom and were not being imprisoned simply for destroying property. Rather, they were in conflict with the government over many political protests and demands, including "the right of peaceful petition."

In seeking sympathy as well as respect for the militants, Mrs. Pankhurst appealed to the class instincts of her often prosperous listeners. Accordingly, she pointed out that in its dealings with the militants—"many of them eminent in art, in medicine and science, women of European reputation"—the authorities subjected them to "treatment that would not have been meted out to criminals." She noted that British politicians became insulted when heckled by women but accepted interruptions from men as a matter of course.

Mrs. Pankhurst also recognized the value of flattering the Americans, underpinned by just a hint of reproach. Thus, she asserted that freedom fighters have traditionally relied on "happier parts of the world for support and sympathy." She assured Americans that "all my life I have looked to [the United States] . . . with admiration as the home of liberty." Just as the American patriots had turned to France for help during their country's founding revolution, so British suffragettes now turned to the Americans, whose memories of their revolutionary and abolitionist crusades should surely enable them, "of all people . . . to see the logic of our reasoning." They too had once fought to be heard around the world in a quest for freedom, and all that women militants asked of them now was "to back us up. We ask you to show that although, perhaps, you may not mean to fight as we do, yet you understand the meaning of our fight . . . for the betterment of the human race."

Pankhurst's thoughts on her American trips were consolidated in the life story that she published in 1914, with the aid of an admiring American journalist, Rhoda Childe Dorr. What the readers of her life and the audiences in the United States received was propaganda: seizure of the moral highground, a reply to commonly raised criticisms of militancy, and a simple claim that suffrage was needed both to free women and to enable them to realize their reform objectives. Nor was Mrs. Pankhurst's justification of violence entirely successful in the United States, and Sylvia noted that many American supporters were appalled by the resort to stone throwing. But Mrs. Pankhurst did acutely judge and effectively exploit Americans' radical past, their conservative anxieties amid the turmoil of the Progressive era, and their enduring strain of anti-British sentiment.

Emmeline and Sylvia Pankhurst both found things to censure in the United States. Mrs. Pankhurst on her 1909 tour criticized American suffragism for its "curious state of quiescence," while Sylvia at first recoiled from the "harsh, rude extremes" of the country and exhorted American women to seek the vote so that they could remedy evident social evils. Nevertheless, both women recognized the need to conceal negative feelings about the United States at a time when they were asking its citizens for financial and moral support. And so Sylvia extolled America's "scope and opportunity for young people" and "receptivity to new ideas," while Mrs. Pankhurst praised American women's reform activities, their eventual conversion to militancy, and the "respect, courtesy and chivalry" showed to women in the one state she visited where they were enfranchised.[10]

The American response cheered the British women. In the first place, Emmeline Pankhurst's charisma was such that she made an immense impact wherever she went. The prominent American suffragist, Carrie Chapman Catt, spoke for the majority when she remarked on Mrs. Pankhurst's stage presence, her "gentle face and slight figure in stark contrast to her turbulent and heroic story."[11] These attributes challenged the contemporary caricature of suffragettes as loud, unattractive she-men. As the ghostwriter of her autobiography recalled fondly, "I have known many Americans, editors, correspondents, business men, who were almost hysterical in their denunciations of [Mrs. Pankhurst's] . . . deeds, wanted her excluded from the United States, but who simply crumpled as soon as they saw her."[12]

Americans warmed to two other qualities possessed by Mrs. Pankhurst, namely, her bravery and her eloquence. In the words of one New York daily newspaper, she had confounded the opponents of woman suffrage by demonstrating "the courage to go to jail. When she came out of jail, too feeble to walk, she had the courage—splendid, moral, spiritual courage—to continue her fight for women's rights and her denunciation of injustice."[13]

As an orator, Mrs. Pankhurst's strengths were her wonderful voice, her ability to speak spontaneously, her ease with questioners, and her awareness that Americans did not understand her militancy, so that she would have to explain it courteously and at length. Her confidence before audiences was the more remarkable since she was a typical woman of her day. Indeed, she once declared herself incapable of public speaking. Even to utter 'I second the resolution,' was a tremendous ordeal to her. Altogether, Christabel's tribute to her mother appears to have been borne out in the United States: "she kindled others; she lit their flame from her own."[14]

To the personal qualities of Mrs. Pankhurst must be added her attraction as the widowed head of a reform family noted for its impressive teamwork. Her husband's interests had ranged from law reform and working people's education to woman suffrage, and he had worried that his children might repudiate the values that he and Emmeline held dear. He need not have worried. All three Pankhurst daughters became feminist activists, and Mrs. Pankhurst recalled that Christabel and Sylvia as children had wanted to attend suffrage meetings.

The family had always been extolled as the cement in America's fluid society, and the maternalist strain in American feminist ideology was strong. Hence, the family solidarity of the Pankhursts appealed to many who heard them speak in the United States: Sylvia and Christabel were clearly daughters of whom any mother could be proud. In Sylvia's case, "youth and earnestness," combined with artless simplicity and femininity, gave her "great [audience] appeal." While for her part, Christabel seemed to be "the symbolic modern girl, full of natural courage, attractively "slim . . . [and] delicate, [with a] high English color, hard brilliant mind, earnest, eloquent."[15]

The Pankhurst family feuds that would eventually separate Sylvia from her mother and sister were kept from the general public, and even American observers who knew about the divisions among British suffrage campaigners were willing to concede that they were unified in their fight for suffrage. Moreover, Mrs. Pankhurst's deliberate courtship of the young and Sylvia's youthful idealism attracted female college students—a much larger group in the United States than in Britain, and one that was increasingly politicized and supportive of major suffrage events.

There were several other reasons why the Pankhursts were successful in America. As the United States moved inexorably toward world power, some of its citizens were responsive to the argument that they should epitomize modern trends, believing that suffragism represented "a great moment in the world's history," and that they had the "Tendency of the Time on our side."[16] Great moment or not, militancy was undeniably news. The suffragettes sold newspapers and, in turn, the news media helped to make them famous. Thus, Sylvia Pankhurst could count on meeting all manner of luminaries and on commanding audiences everywhere—from lecture halls to women's clubs. And since Mrs. Pankhurst was regarded as a celebrity in the United States, she was treated accordingly, although Harvard refused her its halls for a speech, thereby providing further advertisement and ensuring that she played to a full house of Harvard and Radcliffe students when she found an alternative location.

However, the Pankhursts' successful use of militant techniques was the main reason for the American suffragists' interest in them. Given the friendly contest between the British and American woman's movements for the leadership of international feminism, it was generous of Mrs. Catt to endorse Mrs. Pankhurst's proud claim that England was the "storm centre of the worldwide women's movement," spreading "the militant spirit" throughout the world. Mrs. Pankhurst did not hesitate to assert in New York in 1913 that helping British suffragettes "will be the hastening of your victory. It has not as yet been necessary in the United States for women to be militant in the sense that we are, and perhaps one of the reasons why is that we are doing the militant work for you. And we are glad to do that work. We are proud to do that work."[17]

Ignoring the touch of vanity displayed here, many American feminists used the Pankhurst visits as an opportunity to honor the suffragettes, to hear about their methods firsthand, and to win more attention and support for their own efforts. Such speakers "were a sound business venture," according to Mrs. Blatch. For example, Mrs. Pankhurst's 1909 Carnegie Hall meeting alone brought in $1,000 after all expenses had been paid. But tidings of the militants' direct action had reached the United States well before Mrs. Pankhurst lectured there.

As early as 1906, Lucy Stone's *Woman's Journal* was giving the fresh techniques sympathetic publicity, as well as covering the speeches of a few lesser-known British suffragettes at meetings around the United States. By World War I, a handful of young and fearless American women like Alice Paul and Lucy Burns, after working in Britain for the militants, had returned home to apply what they had learned to the national crusade. The result was the foundation in the United States by Paul and Burns of a similar sister's militant organization, first called the Congressional Union (1913) and after 1917 known as the National Woman's Party.

From such varied sources, American activists came to see that "spectacular events carried suffrage messages to the masses of the people" in a way that "suffrage appeals to reason never could." They soon appreciated the effectiveness of "processions, pageants, meetings out under heaven's blue sky"[18] and emulated their British sisters on these occasions by mobilizing bands, "floats, heralds, horsewomen, banners and contingents of professional women and graduates in gowns." British posters were used in American campaigns; American suffragists welcomed the imported feminist drama, *Votes for Women*, written by Elizabeth Robins, the American author and actor who worked for the British suffragettes. As it had in Britain, the boldness of the new tactics encouraged in many elite women the confidence and personal security to flout convention.

In time, American suffragists deployed a number of the more extreme tactics of the British militants, notably picketing, obstruction, willingly going to jail, declaring their political prisoner status, and hunger striking. Stirring tales of suffragette agitation ignited American activism in previously inactive or hostile areas, and readers of the WSPU journal, *Votes for Women*, were assured that appearances by Emmeline and Sylvia Pankhurst before American political and judicial bodies, together with suffragette exploits in Britain, had inspired the militant struggle in the United States. Finally, the stupidity of the American government in its treatment of militants picketing the White House enraged and radicalized many of the country's women, who had not believed that American politicians could behave like their British counterparts.

Yet there were differences between American and British militancy. American critics' basic objection to British militancy in its violent last phase after 1909 was that the suffragettes had allegedly become irresponsible vandals and lawbreakers, instead of the morally superior creatures women were meant to be. Such critics were not moved by tales of the use of violence during the American Revolution. Instead, they recoiled from the suffragettes as dangerous radicals, symbolic of a world changing not for the better but for the worse. Although suffragist-labor links were in fact problematical on both sides of the Atlantic, it did not help in the United States that the movement was associated with a pro-labor stance.

As a result of these objectionable features, British militancy played a significant part in the growth of anti-suffragism in the United States, just as it did in Britain. Until the years before World War I, American anti-suffrage activities had ebbed and flowed depending on whether and where the suffragists were mounting serious campaigns. Hence, Mrs. Pankhurst, who relished testing herself against vocal opposition, positively welcomed the prospect of the American "antis" becoming more prominent. Unfortunately, she underestimated the strength of conservatism in the United States and the power of the "antis" who associated suffragists with "proletarian mob rule" and prostitution to undermine her own and Sylvia's personal triumphs there. Despite the attraction of anti-suffragism for elite men and women, the latter often moving into public roles, the "antis" also managed to disparage the suffragettes as spoilt society women trying to graft their latest fad onto suffragism.[19]

Xenophobia was another key factor in discrediting the American suffrage movement. With immigration running at an all-time high between 1901 and 1910, and nativist groups clamoring for restrictions, Mrs. Pankhurst's tour actually sparked off an attempt to exclude her from the United States as a foreign criminal. She was summoned before a Board of Special Inquiry at Ellis Island, New York's center for processing disembarking immigrants, and was confronted with a large dossier about her operations, probably provided by Scotland Yard. The charge she faced was "moral turpitude," something with which no British jury had ever charged her. The exclusion attempt failed, however, after prominent American suffragists rallied in Mrs. Pankhurst's defense, appealing her case to President Wilson, who ordered her release. Meanwhile, free publicity had been given to militancy, and Mrs. Pankhurst, notwithstanding her threat of a hunger strike, had charmed her keepers on Ellis Island into giving her a tour of its excellent facilities and generally putting "themselves out . . . to make my detention agreeable."[20]

If the Ellis Island incident turned into "a triumphal progress" for Mrs. Pankhurst and a snub for the implicated British authorities, it was not so easy to contain the negative impact of militancy on American feminists themselves. While some campaigners, like Anne Miller of the Geneva (NY) Political Equality Club, were convinced after a visit from Emmeline Pankhurst that there was "nothing to forgive and everything to be thankful for," doubters remained.[21] Gloomily they argued that visiting suffragettes returned home with money needed in the American campaign and that, far from helping local efforts, they in fact divided activists and distracted attention "from our issues and our methods."

Many American suffrage workers felt that they had to find their own way forward and could not tolerate the kind of autocratic body that the WSPU had inexorably become.[22] NAWSA's outspoken Dr. Shaw even complained that British militants had not shown American suffragists visiting Britain the courtesies that British suffragettes received when they crossed the Atlantic. "I have been there repeatedly," she exclaimed. "Mrs. Catt has been there, other presidents of our organization have been there. But I have yet to know of a luncheon or dinner or reception being given by Mrs. Pankhurst or her society for any of us."[23]

American moderates were on much stronger ground when they contended that the wholesale adoption of British suffragette tactics was inappropriate in the American political context. Suffragists correctly perceived that the British focus on by-election campaigns and holding the party in power responsible for women's disfranchisement had only limited relevance in the United States. After all, British activists wanting the national franchise had to focus on a single legislature, formed by regular national and sometimes highly politicized by-elections, and dominated by a single party that might be turned out of office. By contrast, American campaigners could seek the national vote either from the individual states or through an amendment to the federal constitution. But they faced a situation where the ruling party might not control all three branches of the federal government and could not be called to account in the same way as the British parliament.

American suffragists were equally correct in maintaining that, given the American stress on government by law and on the importance of public opinion, activists desiring constitutional changes would have to appeal in a law-abiding manner to voters who had never responded to violent demands for the extension of the suffrage. Nor did American suffragists have before them any extremist precedent comparable to that provided in Britain by the Irish clamor over Home Rule. Furthermore, the conservative views on women of the American South, and the southern suffragists' decision to work within the prevailing mores of their region, made the deployment of militancy there unthinkable. All told, as Mrs. Blatch noted, no suffrage society in the United States had supported the use of physical force.

An additional difficulty in the American suffrage movement sprang from the Woman's Party's adoption of militant methods later than in Britain, and its consequent reluctance to abandon them once the United States was drawn into World War I. The result was an increasingly angry public reaction to the militant suffragists, who from 1917 picketed the White House, seeking to expose President Wilson's hypocrisy in posing as the defender of democracy abroad when he denied it to women at home. For patriotic Americans, militancy, and indeed suffragism as a whole, came to be associated unhelpfully with pro-Germanism. By contrast, Emmeline and Christabel Pankhurst—hostile to Germany's male-oriented culture, confident that the vote was coming, and shrewdly determined not "to take advantage of the national danger to win a selfish gain at the risk of our soldiers' lives"—reinvented themselves as promoters of the British government's war effort and toured the United States in the hope of encouraging its involvement in the conflict and the subsequent peacemaking process.[24]

The mixed response of Americans to British militancy and its most famous exponents illustrates how, even in an international movement like woman suffrage, national political conditions and structures, styles and emphases were crucial. British and American women alike sought the vote as a right and because of their distinctive qualities, roles, and interests as women in politics. They sought the vote because they felt they were fit for it and would use it not only for their own benefit but also to improve the world at large. They contended that suffragism was a cause whose time had come; that the vote was desired by ever increasing numbers of women; that suffragists were not motivated by hatred of men; and that votes for women would not destroy the sanctity of home and family.

Common challenges and problems confronted American and British suffragettes. The militant campaigns of both countries relied heavily on the actions and appearances of a few ruthless and nationally known individuals, notably Emmeline and Christabel Pankhurst in Britain, and Alice Paul and Alva Belmont in the United States. Yet in both countries these leaders had to take account of local circumstances and of the thousands of lesser-known workers who kept their campaigns going. On each side of the Atlantic, the suffragettes found it difficult to consolidate their early appeal to working-class women, though that appeal was sustained longer in Britain. There, radical suffragists sought to make common cause with the labor movement, emphasizing that women's enfranchisement would only arrive as part of an adult suffrage measure that gave the ballot to the substantial number of men who remained voteless before 1918. Militancy frequently came to be regarded by working women as an indulgence that only their elite sisters could afford, just as the "antis" alleged. While the Pankhursts were careful to stress the wide social appeal of their crusade, they were unable to change the image of the suffragettes as members of a small and privileged cadre, an image quickly acquired by militancy's shock troops in the United States.

Still, for all their differences, this transatlantic collaboration had benefited both groups in their struggle for the ballot. As the Pankhursts—mother and daughters—proudly proclaimed, their militant exploits have not been forgotten on either side of the Atlantic.[25]

NOTES

1. The term "suffragette" was first used by the *Daily Mail* on 10 January 1906 and was employed by British militants to distinguish themselves from more moderate campaigners for woman suffrage.

2. Quotation about the Pankhursts from the journal of the International Woman Suffrage Alliance, *Jus Suffragii*, 15 December 1908; Ann Morley

with Liz Stanley, *The Life and Death of Emily Wilding Davison, with Gertrude Colmore's The Life of Emily Davison* (London: Women's Press, 1988), 153, 184; and Cliona Murphy, *The Women's Suffrage Movement and Irish Society in the Early Twentieth Century*; (Hemel Hempstead: Harvester Wheatsheaf, 1989); Leah Leneman, *A Guid Cause: The Women's Suffrage Movement in Scotland* (Aberdeen: Aberdeen University Press, 1991); L. Leneman, "A Truly National Movement: The View from Outside London," in *The Women's Suffrage Movement: New Feminist Perspectives*, ed. Maroula Joannou and June Purvis (Manchester: Manchester University Press, 1998); Constance Rover, *Women's Suffrage and Party Politics in Britain*, 1866–1914 (London: Routledge and Kegan Paul, 1967), 26.

3. Emmeline Pankhurst, *My Own Story* (London: Virago Press, 1979), 186–87.

4. Ellen DuBois, *Harriot Stanton Blatch and the Winning of Woman Suffrage* (New Haven: Yale University Press, 1997), 73, 69–82, 87.

5. Christabel Pankhurst, "Unshackled," in *The Militant: Christabel Pankhurst*, ed. Marie Mulvey Roberts and Tamae Mizuta (London: Routledge, 1995), 258.

6. Viscountess Rhondda, *This Was My World* (London: Macmillan, 1933), 240.

7. E. Pankhurst, *My Own Story*, 161, 326; see also Sylvia Pankhurst, *The Suffragette Movement* (London, Virago Press, 1977), 348.

8. E. Pankhurst, *My Own Story*, 15, 36, 54, 65, 160–61, 168, 180–81, 187–88, 281, 310, 349–50; Jane Marcus, ed., *Suffrage and the Pankhursts* (London: Routledge and Kegan Paul, 1987), 153, 156, 160–62; letter quoting Mrs. Pankhurst, entitled "A Reassurance," in suffrage clippings file, Alice Morgan Wright Papers, Sophia Smith Collection, Smith College; *Votes for Women*, 16 September 1910; *Woman's Journal*, 5 September 1908.

9. Brian Harrison, *Separate Spheres: The Opposition to Women's Suffrage in Britain* (London: Croom Helm, 1978), 31; Lilian Lewis Shiman, *Women and Leadership in Nineteenth-Century England* (London: Macmillan, 1992), 126.

10. S. Pankhurst, *The Suffragette Movement*, 350; E. Pankhurst, *My Own Story*, 161, 185, 201; *Votes for Women*, 24 March, 28 April, 27 October 1911; 16 February 1912; *Woman's Journal*, 28 October 1911.

11. Mary Gray Peck, *Carrie Chapman Catt: A Biography* (New York: Octagon Books, 1975), 140.

12. Peck, *Catt*; E. Pankhurst, *My Own Story*.

13. C. Pankhurst, "Unshackled," 259; E. Sylvia Pankhurst, *The Life of Emmeline Pankhurst: The Suffragette Struggle for Women's Citizenship* (London: T. Werner Laurie, 1935), 29; *Votes for Women*, 3 November 1911.

14. C. Pankhurst, "Unshackled," 259.

15. Harriot Stanton Blatch and Alma Lutz, *Challenging Years: The Memoirs of Harriot Stanton Blatch* (New York: G. P. Putnam's, 1940), 138; Vera Britain, *Pethick-Lawrence: A Portrait* (London: George Allen and Unwin, 1963), 205; undated manuscript on Christabel Pankhurst, 2, and Lucy Burns to Doris Stevens, 31 December 1958, both in Doris Stevens Papers, Schlesinger Library, Radcliffe College; *Votes for Women*, 27 January, 3 March, 21 April 1911; *Woman's Journal*, 11 March 1911.

16. Angela John, *Elizabeth Robins: Staging a Life, 1862–1952* (London: Routledge and Kegan, 1995), 162.

17. Mrs. Pankhurst's New York speech of 21 October 1913, in Marcus, ed., *Suffrage and the Pankhursts*, 161–62.

18. Blatch and Lutz, *Challenging Years*, 205; Carrie Chapman Catt and Nettie Rogers Shuler, *Woman Suffrage and Politics* (New York: Charles Scribner's Sons, 1923), 241.

19. *The Reply: An Anti-Suffrage Magazine*, 1 (May 1993); Blatch and Lutz, *Challenging Years*, 178; Doris Stevens, *Jailed for Freedom* (1920; reprint, New York: Schocken Books, 1976), 31; article on Doris Stevens in *Time and Tide*, 26 October 1928, 2.

20. S. Pankhurst, *The Suffragette Movement*, 493; E. Pankhurst, *My Own Story*, 324–26; C. Pankhurst, *Unshackled*, 259; E. Sylvia Pankhurst, *The Life of Emmeline Pankhurst*, 137–38; Blatch and Lutz, *My Own Story*, 201–2, 205.

21. Robert A. Huff, "Anne Miller and the Geneva Political Equality Club, 1897–1912," *New York History* (October 1984), 340; Ida Husted Harper, ed., *History of Woman Suffrage* vol. 6 (New York: J. J. Little, 1922), 855; *Votes for Women*, 23 May, 24 October 1913.

22. Blatch and Lutz, *Challenging Years*, 137, 202–4; *Woman's Journal*, 5 September 1908; Sharon Hartman Strom, "Leadership and Tactics in the American Suffrage Movement: A New Perspective from Massachusetts," *Journal of American History* 62 (1975), 306, 312.

23. Blatch and Lutz, *Challenging Years*, 202; DuBois, *Harriot Stanton Blatch*, 113–4.

24. E. Sylvia Pankhurst, *The Life of Emmeline Pankhurst*; C. Pankhurst, *Unshackled*; David Mitchell, *The Fighting Pankhursts* (New York: Macmillan, 1967); Andrew Rosen, *Rise Up Women! The Militant Campaign of the Women's Social and Political Union, 1903–1914* (London: Routledge and Kegan Paul, 1974); Christabel Pankhurst, *America and the War* (WSPU, 1914), 3, 15, 17; and Christabel Pankhurst, *International Militancy* (WSPU, 1915), 12, 18.

25. Mitchell, *The Fighting Pankhursts*, parts 4 to 7; Barbara Castle, *Sylvia and Christabel Pankhurst* (Harmondsworth: Penguin, 1987), 151.

10

THE NEXT GENERATION

Harriot Stanton Blatch and Grassroots Politics

Ellen Carol DuBois

By the late nineteenth and early twentieth century, a second-generation of suffrage women were replacing the early pioneers of the movement, bringing to the struggle new arguments for the necessity of the vote as well as innovative tactics and strategies. All were virtual daughters of the pioneers; some were literal descendants. Among them were Alice Stone Blackwell, the daughter of Lucy Stone and Henry Blackwell, and Lucy Anthony, the niece of Susan B. Anthony, who with Blackwell engineered the merging in 1890 of the two national suffrage organizations into the National American Woman Suffrage Association. This chapter tells the story of a crusade by one of these women of the second generation.

The battle for women's rights had begun in the state of New York, the birthplace of Elizabeth Cady Stanton and the longtime home of Susan B. Anthony. In Seneca Falls, New York, the Declaration of Rights and Sentiments had been rousingly proclaimed in 1848. In Albany, both Stanton and Anthony testified in the 1850s before the New York Senate's Judiciary Committee. There they argued, with some success, for changes in state law to establish women's guardianship rights over their children, grant property and earnings rights to married women, and deliver woman suffrage. In 1915, nearly seventy years later, the struggle, now led by a new generation, had come to focus on woman suffrage. Fittingly, Harriot Stanton Blatch, Elizabeth Cady Stanton's daughter, led this major effort to win woman suffrage in its home state. But even in the early twentieth century, success was uncertain.

Harriot Stanton, the second daughter and sixth child of Elizabeth Cady and Henry Brewster Stanton, inherited her role as a defender of her sex from her mother. She was born in Seneca Falls in 1856, during a period when Elizabeth Cady Stanton was immersed in women's issues and the development of a convention movement to publicize concerns as revolutionary as liberalizing divorce. Young Harriot was raised to be a reformer. While other Victorian girls followed their mothers into quiet lives based on family service, Harriot was taught to be assertive and independent. She was surrounded by activist women, including her mother's political partner, Susan B. Anthony. Her mother prepared her daughters to go out into the world not only to make their individual marks on it but also to embody her convictions about women's untapped capacities. Elizabeth Cady Stanton rejected all weakness and dependence in women, and although such expectations could make for a harsh discipline, Harriot accepted the challenge.

During the Civil War, Harriot moved with her family from Seneca Falls to New York City and soon after to nearby Tenafly, New Jersey. In 1874, she enrolled at Vassar, the first all-female college established in the United States. There, she elected an unconventional course of study focused on science, politics, and history. Upon graduation, she became a member of the first generation of women college graduates, one of only a few thousand women in the United States who held a bachelor's degree. Two years after graduation and a brief stint as a professional lecturer, twenty-four-year-old Harriot Stanton went to Europe to continue her education and pursue a vocation. On a return trip to the United States in 1882, to help her mother edit *The History of Woman Suffrage*, she met William Blatch, the handsome, accommodating son of a wealthy brewer from Basingstoke, Hampshire, England. Harriot and William married in 1882, and the couple's first child Nora (named after the heroine of Ibsen's *A Doll's House*) was born in England the next year. A second child Helen, born in 1892, died of whooping cough in 1896. Like her mother but with fewer children, more money, and a compliant husband, Harriot Blatch managed to combine marriage and motherhood with an energetic commitment to reform activities. She joined with veteran British women activists to revive the British suffrage movement. Having inherited from her father a readiness to turn to political parties for reformist ends, she pressured the British Liberal Party to support women's rights. In 1890, she joined the socialist Fabian Society, where she fought for, but failed to win, strong support for women's rights. For two decades as an ex-patriot in Edwardian

England, she honed her political skills and updated her mother's feminist convictions, speaking at meetings, writing for suffrage journals, and becoming involved in local politics as a member of the Women's Local Government Society.

In 1902, with her daughter Nora grown and studying engineering at Cornell, and her husband Henry able to retire, Harriot Blatch moved permanently to New York to take up the task she had inherited—leadership of the American suffrage movement. She joined the Women's Trade Union League, a pioneering effort of elite settlement house women and female wage earners joined together to empower, not patronize, working women. There she came to see that to be modern and effective the suffrage movement in the United States must unite women across the classes in a militant effort. She also saw, as other women activists did not, that women's growing interest in electoral politics was crucial to the reinvigoration of the suffrage movement. Like the English suffragist Emmeline Pankhurst with whom she had worked in England and whose visit to the United States in 1909 Harriot sponsored, she was committed to forcing the political parties to address the suffrage issue and winning from them the political support necessary to gain victory. The setting for this crusade was New York State.

To enact her vision of a militant, democratic suffrage organization based on a coalition of working-class and middle-class working women, Harriot Blatch organized the Equality League of Self-Supporting Women in 1907, renamed the Women's Political Union (WPU) in 1910. Although it gradually moved away from reliance on wage-earning women for its most active participants, the WPU went on to spearhead a political effort to force the New York legislature to pass a bill authorizing a referendum to amend the state constitution to grant women suffrage.

The WPU suffrage campaign, which ran from 1910 to 1915, involved an exhausting and elaborate two-pronged effort: first, both houses of the state legislature had to pass a bill authorizing a referendum on woman suffrage, and then the state's all-male electorate had to approve the referendum. For politicians who opposed suffrage, there were thus two opportunities to defeat the women's vote. First, they could employ familiar legislative gambits to delay or defeat enabling legislation for the suffrage referendum. If that failed, they could then organize to defeat the suffrage referendum at the polls. Still suffragists in New York took hope from a narrowly won suffrage victory in California in October 1911, which involved similar innovative tactics and a multiclass coalition. By 1912, California was the sixth state in which women were voting in the presidential election. Blatch and her followers were determined that New York women would do the same in the next presidential election.

The WPU came to Albany in late 1910 to begin its lobbying campaign for the suffrage referendum. Blatch and her coworkers spent their first year learning the intricacies of legislative procedure and assessing where various politicians stood on woman suffrage. During the 1911 session, in which a new generation of Democratic politicians unseated the longtime Republican state bosses, the women learned how to maneuver their way through, even find opportunities in, partisan conflict. In 1912, determined to move the referendum measure through the legislature, Blatch inaugurated the suffragists' third year of lobbying on a theatrical note. To demonstrate the female patience and forbearance that women had maintained throughout the many decades of the suffrage movement, pairs of suffragists were posted as "silent sentinels" outside the Judiciary Room. As a second-generation suffragist, Harriot understood the necessity of such endurance better than most. But she was also determined that hers would be the last generation to have to fight for the vote.

Harriot Blatch had a talent and taste for partisan politics that was unusual in the movement. Although many of the new generation of suffragists were college-trained professionals, Mary Beard, the historian and a close friend, wrote of Blatch that more than others, "she worked steadfastly to root the suffrage movement in politics, where alone it could reach its goal."[1] She certainly had the lineage. Her mother and Susan B. Anthony had immersed themselves in party politics. From them, from her father, and from her years in England, Harriot had come to see that if suffragists were ever to win, they would have to go behind the scenes and engage in precisely the political maneuvering and lobbying that women had traditionally repudiated as the unhappy consequence of the male monopoly of public life. While such openly political methods distressed many older women reformers, they invigorated Harriot.

In one episode, which became a staple of suffrage legend, Harriot and other WPU leaders tracked down a particularly elusive senator. By this time, opposition to suffrage had moved from ridicule to avoidance. "The chase led up and down elevators in and out of the Senate chamber and committee rooms." Finally, they ferreted out his hiding place and cornered him; he could no longer avoid the issue. The WPU account reversed the standard metaphors of gender to emphasize the senator's humiliation at the hands of women. "Of slight build," he was literally overpowered by the suffragists. "With Mrs. Blatch walking on one side with her hand resting ever so slightly on his sleeve [sic]," the women led him into the committee room and got his vote. "I'll never forgive this," he told Blatch. "Oh yes, you will, "she responded, "some day you will be declaring with pride how your vote advanced the suffrage resolution."

The WPU won a similar battle with Robert Wagner, the new Democratic majority leader of the state Senate and one of the most determined opponents of suffrage in the New York legislature. To prevent Wagner from once again employing the delaying legislative tactics of moving to table or returning the referendum resolution to committee for another year, Harriot arranged for three hundred New York City suffragists to go to Albany to pressure him to set a date for a vote. Some fifty or sixty women crowded into the committee room, with the rest gathered in the corridor outside. When Wagner moved to take his place in the chair at the front of the room, the aisle filled with suffragists. "There were no antisuffragists to rescue him," wrote Harriot later. "There were only all about him, the convinced and ruthless members of the Women's Political Union." He grudgingly agreed to set a date for the state Senate to vote on the suffrage resolution.

In both episodes, the WPU's power rested not only in numbers but also in its willingness to exploit the gendered meanings of power. Wagner yielded because he could not afford to let it be known that he had been physically and politically outmaneuvered by women. The newspapers predictably reported what the women requested, and Wagner graciously granted a date for the Senate vote. But at a time in which accounts of British militant suffragists smashing windows were prominently featured in American papers, the sense of sexual warfare, of women besting men, was close to the surface and hard to overlook.

The Senate debate and vote took place on the date Wagner had guaranteed. Harriot and her followers watched from the gallery. Like good politicians, they had carefully counted their supporters, knew that they had just the right number of votes with not one to spare, and "were full of confidence" that the referendum would carry. Across the hall, the lower house was giving them an unanticipated victory. It looked like the legislative battle might actually be won. But at the last moment "a perfidious" senator abandoned the public pledge he had given the WPU, shifted his vote, and denied them their victory.

With this undeserved defeat uppermost in her mind, Blatch went to the people. The WPU had organized parades twice before, but the 1912 New York City parade was by far the most carefully organized street demonstration in U.S. suffrage history. The WPU spared no effort at recruiting and educating a large number of marchers and alerting the public to the meaning and significance of the parade. Pledge cards were circulated, committing marchers to take to the streets. Newspapers eagerly covered the clever "stunts" that suffragists devised to advertise the parade: suffragists at the circus, "suffragette hats" for sale at department stores, recruitment booths behind the Public Library.

Harriot was determined that the parade give evidence of a massive, disciplined army of women with which politicians would have to come to terms. She paid great attention to the details of the march, the numbers of marching columns, and the spacing of the lines of marchers. Women were instructed to dress simply, walk erectly, and keep their eyes forward. The spectacle was to be an emotional and sensual evocation of women's power. Opponents, according to Blatch, should be converted through their eyes. "The enemy must see women, marching in increasing numbers year by year out on the public avenues, holding high their banner, Votes For Women." On the appointed day, more than ten thousand took to the streets: women college graduates in their academic gowns, working women by trades and industries, prominent wealthy women, even some men. The president of the national suffrage society marched with a banner that read "Catching Up with China"—a reference to reports that insurgent nationalists in one of China's provincial legislatures had declared women enfranchised. Public demonstrations of this sort were new and a bit daunting to many women. "I marched the whole length," one demonstrator proudly reported to a friend.

In 1912, the emergence of a third national political party, the Progressives, affected the task of getting a suffrage referendum. While Progressive leaders begged women for their support, Blatch was disappointed with the tepid role the party had played in a woman suffrage referendum in Ohio earlier in that year. And former president Theodore Roosevelt, the party's candidate for president in 1912, repeatedly embarrassed himself and his party by sexist declarations that suffragists were "indirectly encouraging immorality." Still, the Progressive Party's support was crucial for the WPU's plans in New York because of the leverage it gave in prying support out of the Republicans, who were struggling to keep voters from bolting to the new party. First the Progressives and then the Republicans endorsed the submission of the suffrage referendum to New York voters at their state conventions. All that was left was to win over the Democrats, and Harriot saved the "terrible tiger" of Tammany, the very embodiment of partisan corruption, for herself. In a private meeting with Charles Murphy, the leader of the city's Democrats, she declared, "I felt it was high time for me to come to the boss." "You are something of a boss yourself," he responded, a comment that so delighted her that she repeated it in her autobiography.

The two bosses came to an understanding: the Democrats followed the other two parties in urging submission of the referendum. Victory, at least in the legislature, was assured. The election of 1912 swept the Democrats, including Harriot's nemesis Robert Wagner, into power in the state, and, under the leadership of Woodrow Wilson, into the presidency as well.

There was a last-minute complication when the Republicans added a clause to the referendum subjecting immigrant women, who were citizens by marriage, to special requirements for voting, and the Democrats objected. The issue was a difficult one for Blatch. On the one hand, she had lost her American citizenship by virtue of her marriage to an Englishman and was sympathetic to women whose citizenship was altered by marriage. On the other hand, like her mother decades before, she had her own nativist prejudices, as did many of her middle-class followers. In the end, she decided the issue politically: keeping the clause would gain the referendum more upstate Republican votes than it would lose downstate Democrats.

Party leaders followed her lead, and in January 1913, both houses passed legislation proposing an amendment to the state constitution striking out the word male and enfranchising citizens over twenty-one "provided that a citizen by marriage should have been an inhabitant of the United States for five years." Blatch had worked three years for this moment, a long time for a single bill. And even with this victory, the most difficult task lay ahead—the winning of the referendum itself. Now the suffrage leaders would have to convince a majority of New York men to vote for woman suffrage.

Harrriot Blatch and the leaders of the WPU had no illusions about how difficult this might be. "The task we must accomplish between now and election day 1915 {when the referendum would appear on the ballot} is a Herculean one, compared to that we have just completed," the Executive Committee of the Women's Political Union declared. In their legislative efforts, they had had only to persuade 151 men in the Assembly and Senate. "Now we must convert the male electorate of New York to woman suffrage." Harriot had her misgivings about immigrant voters, with their "Germanic and Hebraic attitude toward women," but she counted on the democratic logic of the situation, believing that men who were being allowed to exercise the franchise could be convinced to vote in favor of women's demand to share it. Winning the referendum would be harder, and in many ways less exciting than the legislative part of the campaign; it would require what Blatch described as a "dead frontal attack . . . labor [which] is limitless, vague, unindividualized."

But a great deal was riding on the New York referendum. "If we win the Empire State all the states will come tumbling down like a pack of cards," she promised. To cultivate the voters, the WPU played on its strengths. It based its suffrage advocacy on the proliferating devices of modern mass culture—forms of commercial recreation, methods of advertising, and the pleasures of consumerism. Californians had used billboards, automobile caravans, and suffrage postcards to bring their cause before the electorate in their successful campaign of 1911. New York women had to do the same. "If we are to reap a victory in 1915, we must cultivate every inch of soil and sow our suffrage seed broadcast in the Empire state," declared Harriot.

Such an approach conformed to Harriot's view of democracy which, she believed, should be based on the heart rather than the head. Emotions were the key to popular democracy, not reason. "We learned . . . as we toiled in our campaign," she later wrote, "that sermons and logic would never convince. . . . Human beings move because they feel, not because they think." This was not an expression of any special contempt for either women or working-class voters; on the contrary she considered men (especially politicians) more irrational than women and the rich more prejudiced and conservative than the poor. She believed particularly that changes in women's status and in power relations between the sexes could never be reduced to rational arguments and dispassionate appeals, even to venerable principles of American democracy such as equality and civic virtue.

"Democracy was the keynote" of the grand suffrage ball that the WPU sponsored in January 1913 to inaugurate the referendum campaign. Extensively advertised, it took place in New York City's Seventy-first Street Armory, which was barely large enough for the eight thousand men and women who attended. Rich and poor, working-class and society women alike paid fifty cents to dance the turkey trot and other popular new dances. The event proved, as the WPU put it, "that love of liberty and democracy did not belong to one class or one sex but is deeply rooted in human nature itself."

In January 1913, the Women's Political Union also began publication of a biweekly two-penny suffrage newspaper, the *Women's Political World*. The *World* offered analyses of suffrage politics, notices of suffrage events, reviews of new books, discussions of sexual morality, and reports of labor activism. Its format was lively and featured up-to-date cultural references. Suffrage workers sold the paper on the streets of New York's cities and towns. Labeled suffragette "newsies," the women themselves emerged as an additional source of publicity for the cause.

Given Harriot's appreciation for the role of emotions in mass politics, she was especially intrigued by new technologies of mass communication. "I stand for the achievements of the twentieth century," she declared. "I will make use of . . . anything which civilization places at my command." Lee de Forest, her former son-in-law (Nora's brief marriage to him had ended after a year), was one of the pioneers of modern radio broadcasting, a term he may have borrowed from the suffragists, who used it to characterize their mass propaganda work. At his invitation, she delivered a radio talk on woman suffrage from the newly opened broadcasting station in downtown Manhattan.

Moving pictures represented another new technology with political possibilities. The WPU arranged for a commercial movie company to produce *The Suffragette and the Man*, a romantic comedy in which the beautiful young heroine, forced to choose between her suffrage principles and her fiance, first picks principles and then overcomes an anti-suffrage competitor and wins back her lover.

In 1913, the WPU collaborated on a second movie entitled *What 8,000,000 Women Want*. This time the romantic triangle did not involve good and bad men fighting for a heroine's heart but good and bad politics fighting for the hero's soul. Newsreel footage of actual suffrage parades was interspersed with the dramatic action. Harriot played herself and brought to the screen her self-confident authority and her genuine pleasure at conducting the struggle. Suffragists all over the state were encouraged to arrange for the movie to be shown in parks, halls, and the new commercial movie houses that were springing up everywhere.

An especially effective suffrage device was the so-called voiceless speech: a silent suffragist stood in a shop window with a series of simple suffrage messages on large cards, displayed one-by-one to crowds who stopped to watch. While suffragists gave plenty of regular speeches, the voiceless speech's success lay in its novelty. The crowds that gathered to look were so large that one WPU activist was arrested and charged with causing a crowd to block the sidewalk. The charges were dropped, but not before the affair generated wonderful publicity.

Small inexpensive commodities were also used to advertise the cause as well as to raise money. Suffrage paraders in 1912 and 1913 were urged to purchase inexpensive "suffrage hats," which also added uniformity to the marchers' ranks. Midtown department stores were willing to lend their windows for the display of the hat and other suffrage items, but they refused their employees' request for time off to attend the parade. Harriot protested that "the Department store is a woman's store and they must wake up to the fact of recognizing us."

By 1913, the WPU was experimenting with its own "suffrage shops." Suffragists rented a downtown storefront and organized a daily program of suffrage speeches and events for workers' lunch hours. In 1914, the organization bought a used horse-drawn lunch van and turned it into a roving shop, selling suffrage buttons, pencils, and even suffrage cigarettes. Wrote Blatch in 1913, "We have ceased to put much energy into discussing the pros and cons of democracy with doubting women in the chimney corners and have instead gone out on the street corner to appeal to men, to the voters."

In 1913, as in previous years, the most spectacular suffrage event was the parade, organized by the WPU. Each year, the parades had become more stunning affairs, symbolically conveying both the diversity and the unity of modern women. The 1913 parade was one of the high points of Harriot's suffrage leadership. "We will muster an army fifty thousand strong this year," she predicted. The marchers were arranged by divisions. At the head were two dozen female marshals mounted on horseback and dressed in stylish adaptations of men's evening wear, black cutaways and silk hats with streamers of green, purple, and white, the WPU's colors and those of the movement in England. Leading them, dressed in white and astride a white horse, was Inez Millholland, "the official beauty of the parade." The intention was to provide unforgettable visual images of all kinds of women marching shoulder to shoulder together. "In these times of class wars," Harriot observed, could men really afford "to shut out from public affairs that fine spirit of fellowship" that suffragism represented?

The effectiveness of the parade as political propaganda infuriated antisuffragists, for whom the spectacular aspect of the movement was proof positive of the social and cultural upheaval that votes for women threatened. The antisuffragists charged that the bold stance of the marchers smacked of the deliberate exploitation of "sex appeal." The *New York Times* echoed the antis' charge that the parades marked a "lowering of women's ideals" and "a distortion of the sex question." Harriot Blatch found the charges amusing. "Funny idea of sex appeal. Twenty thousand women turn out on a hot day. 87 degrees and march up Fifth Avenue to the blaring music of thirty-five bands; eyes straight to the front; faces red with the hot sun. . . . If it had been mellow moonlight . . . But a sex appeal set to brass bands! That certainly is a new one. " The WPU was determined to finesse the conventional notions of female beauty that had so long restrained women's public activities. Suffragists were not immoral or disreputable; they were charming and beautiful, just too modern to abide by such outdated cultural mores any longer.

During the legislative lobbying years from 1910–1913, Harriot and the WPU had not faced much organizational opposition within the New York suffrage movement. The state suffrage organization was small and ineffective. But once the referendum campaigning began in earnest, the Woman's Political Union, led by the blunt, sometimes undiplomatic Blatch, came into direct conflict with the other great figure of New York suffragism, the moderate, circumspect Carrie Chapman Catt. Within the woman's movement, Catt embodied the progressive faith in organizational structure and administrative centralization. In contrast, Harriot celebrated individual initiative, modern invention, and personal freedom. Notwithstanding lofty suffrage rhetoric about the unity of all womanhood and the solidarity of the sex, these two were bound to clash.

Rising to prominence in the 1890s as the head of the newly formed Organization Committee of the National American Woman Suffrage Association, by 1900, Catt had become Susan B. Anthony's hand-picked successor for president. In 1904, she gave up the post to concentrate on international suffrage work and in 1909 returned to New York to found the Woman Suffrage Party, the chief organizational rival to Blatch's WPU. Catt was always more concerned to unify and reconcile all existing suffragists than to reach out and create new ones. While some activists believed that Blatch was autocratic and high-handed, the ever-diplomatic Catt prized harmony within the movement above all things. Catt's efforts went to creating internal order rather than tackling external obstacles. Unlike Blatch, Catt had little skill or interest in the intricacies of partisan politics and legislative maneuvers.

Catt's plan was to bring all the suffrage societies in New York (and there were at least four including the College Equal Suffrage League) together under one wing, but the Women's Political Union, crucial to her efforts and the richest organization in the state, refused to subsume itself under Catt's leadership. From the beginning, the WPU's Executive Committee was determined to keep their organization unfettered, autonomous, and innovative, which they were convinced was required for victory in New York State.

By 1914, it was clear that two parallel suffrage campaigns would be conducted in New York, one by Catt's Empire State Campaign Committee and the other by Harriot Blatch's Women's Political Union. Both raised money for the referendum effort; both sent paid agents around the state; both set up separate offices, sometimes generating considerable conflict among activists in smaller communities in upstate New York. The suffrage movement had survived previous internal divisions and would face others in the future, but in the context of the prolonged, hard-fought New York campaign of 1915, it is hard to know whether these factions strengthened the cause by encouraging more intense commitment or weakened the campaign by duplicating efforts.

In the last six months of the campaign, the WPU flooded the state with publicity-generating gimmicks and stunts. Suffragists played both ends of the gender divide to demonstrate that they could join in traditional male activities as good fellows and at the same time retain their female virtue. On Suffrage Day at the Polo Grounds, New York suffrage organizations competed with each other to sell tickets to a benefit baseball game between the New York Giants and the Chicago Cubs. At the same time, they organized a series of events that emphasized their enthusiasm for the roles of wife and mother. To span the generations, the WPU held a Grandmother's Day at the suffrage shops, where grandmothers and granddaughters together advocated suffrage as well as holding a baby contest. To counter the anti-suffrage claims that they were bitter women who wanted the ballot as compensation for their inability to find husbands, they even held a series of "married couple days," in which husbands and wives declared their mutual happiness and support of votes for women. At the end of the campaign, Harriot devised a megastunt: A special suffrage torch, to symbolize "the freedom we are seeking," was carried back and forth across the state, from Montauk Point on eastern Long Island to Chautaqua County at the western end of the state.

Ten weeks before the end of the campaign, Harriot's single-minded attention to the cause was shattered by the sudden death of her husband, William Blatch, who was accidentally electrocuted. She announced that she would have to return to England to tend to her husband's estate. Before leaving, she took advantage of one benefit of widowhood and resumed her U.S. citizenship. Harriot's decision to leave the country so close to the end of the 1915 campaign is something of a puzzle. She could have postponed the trip a few months. Moreover, England was already at war with Germany, and the transatlantic trip was dangerous. Perhaps she was growing weary of the unrelenting labor of trying to convert New York voters, or perhaps she sensed that she was losing her position as New York's foremost suffragist to Carrie Chapman Catt.

By the time she returned in mid-October, the Empire State Campaign Committee, marching with its banners of blue, gold, and white, had taken over organization of the final suffrage parade. The Women's Political Union, assembled under its own colors of green, purple, and white, held a much smaller demonstration through the streets of the lower East Side to recall its self-supporting roots.

Harriot had one last resource to marshal on behalf of her claim to leadership: her maternal legacy. Three days before the election, the WPU held an elaborate luncheon, with a thousand people in attendance, in honor of Elizabeth Cady Stanton's hundredth birthday. The event was Harriot's ways of dedicating the entire, exhausting political effort of the referendum, and hopefully the victory of woman suffrage, to the memory of her mother. Carrie Catt's refusal to attend cemented Blatch's lifelong resentment of her.

As election day approached, all suffrage leaders predicted victory. Catt forecast a 50,000 vote margin, while Harriot thought suffrage would win by a much smaller majority. In a stunning reversal of its usual policy of opposition, Tammany Hall, the New York City arm of the Democratic Party, declared itself neutral, thus freeing city Democrats to vote as they wished on the measure. Perhaps someone should have paid more attention to New York bookies, however, who were giving two-and three-to-one odds against passage.

November 2, 1915, the day toward which Harriot Blatch, Carrie Catt, and thousands of other New York women had been working for years, was the kind of warm, sunny day for which hard-working campaigners pray. When the polls opened at 6 A.M., several thousand suffrage activists were in their places as pollwatchers, guarding against any effort to cheat them of their victory. In New York City, many polls reported that the majority of their votes had been cast before noon. In some polling places, voting machines were used for the first time, and since woman suffrage was at the end of the ballot, the results on the amendment came out first.

By midnight, it was clear that the woman suffrage amendment had been defeated. Out of 1,200,000 votes cast across the state, woman suffrage had been defeated by 190,000 votes, about 16 percent of the total. All the boroughs of New York City voted against woman suffrage as well as fifty-six of the state's sixty-one counties.

Most New York suffragists kept the bitter disappointment they felt to themselves and declared the referendum a moral triumph. "On the whole we have achieved a wonderful victory," Carrie Chapman Catt proclaimed. "It was short of our hopes but the most contemptuous opponents speak with newly acquired respect for our movement." Catt's wing of the campaign announced the day after the election that a second referendum campaign would begin as soon as state law permitted. Thousands of dollars were pledged immediately for this second effort.

Harriot Blatch was one of the few suffrage leaders who dared to react with open anger. She was "disgusted at the conditions which had forced women to campaign in the streets" and humiliated at having to appeal to immigrant men to gain her native-born rights as an American citizen. She vowed she would never make another street-corner speech. Her retreat into this outraged elitism recalled her mother's reaction to her own crushing disappointment at the failure of the Reconstruction constitutional amendments to include women. Blatch also blamed the suffrage forces themselves for the defeat, at least the Catt wing of the movement, which she thought had neglected upstate New York. She believed a second referendum would be a mistake because the antisuffragists would be even better organized for the next round.

In this she was wrong. In 1917, a second voters' referendum was victorious in New York, thus winning an incalculably important political prize in the battle that was intensifying nationwide. Yet Harriot was correct in a larger way. The era of state suffrage referenda was over; with the exception of New York, no other state was won by this method after 1915. From this point on, attention, energy, and political initiative shifted to the federal arena, to the constitutional amendment Elizabeth Cady Stanton and Susan B. Anthony had first introduced and which had been stalled in congressional committee for almost fifty years. In less than five years, the amendment was moved onto the floor, secured a two-thirds vote in the House and three years later in the Senate, and was ratified by three-quarters of the state legislatures to become the law of the land.

Like many other bold and determined leaders of this "next" generation, Harriot Blatch moved on to the work of gaining suffrage at the federal level. Here again her trademark political sensibility was much in evidence. "Those who have done the actual work of appeal to individual voters," she commented, "prefer henceforth to deal with legislators." In pioneering this approach to politicizing suffrage and in using modern techniques of appealing to public opinion, she represented other women of this generation, some of whose names have been forgotten, others of whom like Alice Paul, are remembered as significant contributors to the extension of political rights to women. Harriot Blatch had succeeded in meeting her obligation to her mother's generation and in providing a legacy to younger women, who would superintend the final act of the American suffrage battle.

NOTE

1. All quotes in this chapter are from Ellen Carol DuBois, *Harriot Stanton Blatch and the Winning of Woman Suffrage* (New Haven: Yale University Press, 1997), 122–87.

11

ALICE PAUL AND THE POLITICS OF NONVIOLENT PROTEST

Linda Ford

The National Woman's Party (NWP) was both militant and radically feminist in its battle for a national woman suffrage amendment between 1913 and 1919. Years of effort in state suffrage fights by the major organization, the National American Woman Suffrage Association (NAWSA), had yielded little result, and by 1912, the issue was a stagnant one. Only five western states had given women the vote, and virtually nothing was being done for a national suffrage amendment to the U.S. Constitution. Anna Howard Shaw, NAWSA president and heir to pioneer Susan B. Anthony, was proving an ineffectual leader, and unlike her nineteenth-century predecessor, did not have a militant bone in her body. Seeking to breathe life into the complacent movement, the new suffragists looked elsewhere for inspiration, adopting the British brand of militancy to the American situation in their own particular nonviolent style.[1]

Led by its "Chairman" Alice Paul, the NWP (first called the "Congressional Union") tried a spirited but unsuccessful campaign of aggressive congressional lobbying, and then organized women of the western states to vote in a bloc against the Democratic Party in the 1914 and 1916 elections. As the National Woman's Party, they confronted the Wilson administration with incessant picketing and protests, resulting in eventual imprisonment.

By 1917, these suffragists were joined by hundreds of committed women, including a large and enthusiastic contingent of radical women from the political Left. One of the first groups ever to employ tactics of classic nonviolent resistance in their protests, the Woman's Party intended their methods to provide a "female" contrast to the ongoing "male" violence of World War I. The NWP's insistence that their struggle for women's rights took precedence over war patriotism culminated in their becoming victims of violent government suppression. The resulting dramatic publicity of their protest helped win the day for woman suffrage.

It seems contradictory to call the Woman's Party both "nonviolent" and "militant" in their cause, but it is accurate. "Militancy" is defined here as pertaining to aggressive defiance, to resistance of authority. NWP militancy evolved from a "militant state of mind," as they called it, such as engaging in an aggressive style of action within the political system, to acts of "overt" or "real" militancy, steps taken with a willingness to break the law. This use of the term "militancy" was essentially the way in which it was used by NWP leaders, including Chairman Alice Paul and her Woman's Party co-leader, Lucy Burns. Paul and Burns differentiated between militant feelings and overtly militant actions. In fact, they did not call themselves "militants" before 1917. "Real" militancy, according to Paul, was reached in June of that year when women faced imprisonment for breaking the law in defiance of authority.

Woman's Party suffragists may have disagreed on exactly how to define "militancy," but all agreed that it involved defiance of and resistance to authority. Western NWP leader Anne Martin, for instance, insisted the Party did not use "militant tactics" but that militancy was used *against them* [emphasis added].[2] And party organizer Hazel Hunkins described the NWP as the "least militant" of groups, one which was led by a woman who "did not like violence," the Quaker Alice Paul. So when nonviolent means were used in civil disobedience to resist authority, women demonstrators were, by definition, both militant and nonviolent.[3]

Alice Paul, the leader of the Woman's Party, was deeply influenced by earlier American feminist activists, as well as contemporary British militant suffragists. Born into a Quaker middle-class family from New Jersey, she was provided with an excellent education, culminating in a doctorate from the University of Pennsylvania. Paul soon tired of the usual career choice for a woman with her qualifications—social work. She instead wanted to work for a moral cause and found that life's work in women's rights, first for woman suffrage and then for an Equal Rights Amendment. Idealizing Susan B. Anthony, she identified with the defiant, no-compromise spirit defining Anthony and the nineteenth-century National Woman Suffrage Association (NWSA).[4] NWSA activists practiced isolated militant acts of civil disobedience for suffrage in the 1870s. The NWP's historian Doris Stevens stressed how Anthony's act of civil disobedience of 1872 inspired the women

Anthony
voting. arrest 1872 = example

activists who followed her. In order to publicize the cause, Anthony had voted in Rochester, N.Y., and was subsequently arrested and tried (and released). This precursor of twentieth-century suffrage militancy would serve as a source of practical policy, as well as inspiration for the Woman's Party. In fact, their nonviolent protests showed recognition of what Stevens insisted Anthony had always known: "[T]he attention of the nation must be focused on minority issues by dramatic acts of protest."[5]

A more immediate inspiration was provided by the dramatic protests of the British Women's Social and Political Union (WSPU). According to Christabel Pankhurst, the WSPU brand of suffrage protest was born on the occasion of Susan B. Anthony's visit to London in 1900, when Pankhurst had been seized with a desire to win woman suffrage for the eighty-year-old pioneer American suffragist.[6] As young women, Alice Paul, Lucy Burns, and Anne Martin all had extended terms of service with the WSPU, and many more American suffragists were influenced by their briefer sojourns in England or by hearing a Pankhurst on tour in the United States.[7] Burns and Paul came directly from their British apprenticeships to revive the woman suffrage struggle in America. The English experience initiated them into protest marches and demonstrations, as well as jail, hunger strikes, and forced feedings. It also taught them the use of publicizing those actions in order to create public sympathy. Suffering violence at the hands of British police served to fuel an angry feminism that underpinned the founding of the Woman's Party.

British suffragists had brought their struggle to the point of violence, or as they called it, guerrilla warfare, by the time the National Woman's Party was founded in the United States. After marches on Parliament and heckling government leaders had no effect, the British suffragists' frustration culminated in escalating acts of civil disobedience. Believing the situation there warranted such "violence," Paul and Burns participated in breaking windows and slapping bobbies. In England, the public atmosphere, the tone of government, and the attitude of the man in the street, were all thought to be more resistant to change and more violent toward women, than in America. Emmeline Pankhurst always insisted that suffrage reform in England came only because of "outside agitation." Her daughter Christabel argued that as with previous agitation: "For Women denied the right of petition by deputation the only thing left is violence— only stones could get into meetings."[8] But in response, greater acts of violence were inflicted on the woman demonstrators as punishment.

In 1913, Alice Paul and Lucy Burns founded an activist woman suffrage organization, inspired by the British type of suffrage militancy, but prac-

tically adapted to what American feminists saw as their much more promising political situation. Emmeline Pankhurst acknowledged that "in a
way" Alice Paul and Lucy Burns were her children, especially in that they
learned in England that if men would not give women rights they would
take them, which was the essence of militant, radical feminism.[9] The
Woman's Party was continually compared to the WSPU and indeed considered itself, to some degree, the counterpart of the WSPU in the United
States. It was the "spirit" of the Pankhursts and of Susan B. Anthony to
which the fledgling Woman's Party continually referred, and it would
be that "militant spirit" which governed the years of political action between 1913 and 1916. In 1917, after the failure of those political tactics, "actual" militancy, as Alice Paul put it, began—protests, arrests, and
imprisonment—which continued until the suffrage amendment was
passed. But even the NWP's actual militancy was quite different from
the "violent" militancy in which Paul and Burns had been involved in
England.

Launching a congressional committee under the auspices of the mainstream suffrage organization, NAWSA, Paul and Burns attempted to revive the idea of a woman suffrage constitutional amendment and infuse
the movement with a more aggressive spirit. Always conducting their campaign in a ladylike manner, NAWSA had, as noted, settled into a long and
tedious struggle to gain woman suffrage on a state-by-state basis until
Catt's "Winning Plan" shifted the focus. Paul and Burns' aggressive lobbying was totally foreign to the group that evolved from Elizabeth Cady
Stanton and Susan B. Anthony's original radical movement. The women
of the new congressional committee were saddened when NAWSA eventually expelled them. They were expelled for several reasons, first, because
of territorial jealousy over members and money, but second and more
important, over large tactical and philosophical differences. NAWSA's
Carrie Chapman Catt called Paul and Burns "Pankhurst imitators" and
feared their militant strategies would antagonize male allies.

By 1914, the independent "Congressional Union" (CU) had become quite
distinct from NAWSA. Members of the CU initially believed that they could
work within the democratic American political system without resorting
to British-style militancy. They immediately started lobbying congressional
members and presidential candidates about their cause. They soon found
that logic and determination would not so easily move congressmen or a
president, who continued to insist that woman suffrage should be decided
by the individual states. In 1916, Lucy Burns explained that when the CU
cross-examined President Wilson, which the press called "heckling," that

it did not in itself constitute English-style militancy, but that it was an American's right to "rebuke a representative who denied [her] justice."[10]

Certainly, NWP leaders believed in the optimistic spirit of the Progressive era, a time of political reform to further democracy, which helped give credibility to Woman's Party arguments for women's participation in government. In England, the only means the unenfranchised had of gaining a hearing was petitioning Parliament, but the atmosphere of democratic reform in America made getting a hearing for a woman suffrage amendment seem logical and reasonable.

Then, in 1916, the CU expanded its membership and took the campaign for political reform in a new direction. They decided to use the political clout that women already had in western states to form a Woman's Party of Western Voters. By then, Alice Paul and her fellow militants believed that the government (and President Wilson) could only be moved by the force of strong public opinion, persuasion through lobbying, and then, most important and quite differently from NAWSA, through organizing women who already had the franchise to vote in a bloc against Wilson Democrats. In this way, the women wielded available political power, the votes of the women of western states, to affect the electoral process and consequently the government's stand on woman suffrage. This new policy of "holding the party in power responsible" came under severe attack because it was associated with the Pankhursts and seemed as bloc voting un-American, even though the NWP argued correctly that Anthony and Elizabeth Cady Stanton withheld their support from parties not supporting women's rights. During the 1916 electoral campaign, some of the Woman's Party 's optimism began to fade as party activists encountered violent opposition and were even assaulted by Democratic Party supporters in some cases.[11]

The dramatic turning point toward real militancy began when socialist activist Inez Milholland Boissevain became seriously ill while participating in the western campaign against a persistently recalcitrant Wilson in the fall of 1916. Milholland died in late November after collapsing during a speech, gasping as she fell: "How long must women wait for liberty?" When President Wilson remained unmoved by a memorial to Inez Milholland Boissevain in December, saying only that the women should go out and "concert public opinion," many of the NWP suffragists had had enough.[12] Even after a half-century of organized activity, the president and Congress were not yet moved to pass a woman suffrage amendment. In fact, many legislators strongly objected to the CU on the grounds that its militant purpose was to organize women for *power*. The NWP responded that they *were* "in a sense . . . being strong, positive and energetic," and that their policies were merely reflecting an American tradition of using the power of the vote and trying to change public opinion. In March of 1917, the Congressional Union combined with the Women's Party of Western Voters to officially become the National Woman's Party in order to strengthen their number and their cause.[13] At this point, they decided to use acts of "real" militancy and civil disobedience and call themselves militants.

In 1917, the leaders of the NWP began to defy authority by picketing the White House, even after America entered the war in April. When they were arrested and jailed, the NWP "displayed their militancy." Yet even when victimized by mob attacks and government-sanctioned police violence, Woman's Party suffragists did not use violence but confined their protests to acts of symbolic pageantry, picketing, and holding public meetings and demonstrations. To do so, Alice Paul drew on ideas and protest techniques of earlier militant suffragism, American labor activism, especially picketing, and her own heritage of Quaker pacifism.[14] Working with a small circle of advisors, she sometimes mapped strategy on a day-to-day basis with no grand scheme in mind. Members of the NWP intended to embarrass the stubborn Wilson, who would no longer see their delegations, with a constant lobbying effort in the form of peaceful picketing and pointedly worded banners.

One thing seems certain about Alice Paul's philosophy. She, like other prominent Progressive women such as Charlotte Perkins Gilman and Jane Addams, believed that women were different from men in that they were inherently more peaceful and temperate. Paul and organizer Hazel Hunkins had privately urged Congresswoman Jeanette Rankin to vote against the war, as a woman. To Alice Paul it was clear that "women were the peace-loving half of the world and that by giving power to women we would diminish the possibilities of war."[15] Accordingly, Paul's organization did not stop its efforts for women's rights after war broke out in 1914 or their picketing once the United States entered the war in April 1917, and the situation for demonstrators became much more dangerous.

To be sure, the United States was not faced with as threatening a situation as Great Britain. Woman's Party leader Abby Scott Baker argued that the British and American situations were "not analogous" because England was "stripped for a death struggle."[16] But even so, the contrast of American suffrage policy with the actions of the WSPU on the war was striking. By the time the war began in 1914, the Pankhursts had thinned their group to those revolutionaries committed to a policy of guerrilla warfare. Their policy had become a highly moralistic sex war of Good (women) versus

Evil (men). The official reasons given for the WSPU's giving up the battle against the Liberal government was that its militancy was "less effective" in the face of war violence, and patriotism demanded that suffragists join the war effort. British militants transferred their battle to another theater. This new "evil" seemed quite appropriate since as Christabel Pankhurst pointed out, "German *Kultur* means the supremacy of the male carried to the point of obscenity."

In the United States, most militant leaders did not approve of the Pankhursts leaving the field of the women's rights battle. Some NWP leaders, notably Harriot Stanton Blatch and writer Rheta Childe Dorr, disagreed with what they considered the NWP's "unpatriotic" policy, eventually leaving the Woman's Party for that reason. Yet Alice Paul insisted that the Woman's Party must continue to work for women's rights only, although members should feel free to work for war or peace in other organizations. Nevertheless, many members left over the issue in the spring of 1917.[17]

To Paul, the feminist struggle had to come first, but most especially in wartime, when woman's influence was sorely needed and, she argued, might have prevented war in the first place. As usual, each step in the new militancy and civil disobedience was taken very cautiously, with Paul gaining the consent of her advisors and support of the membership before instituting any new policy.[18] But these women revealed a new willingness to suffer. It was not male Evil so much as the "autocracy," hypocrisy, and wrong-headedness of a particular administration and president that the NWP fought, as they went into the streets in front of the White House during the war. They carried banners comparing "democratic America" unfavorably with Russia and Germany.

In June 1917, citing the danger to the White House, police and bystanders began to rough up the women and then arrested them for criminally "obstructing the sidewalk." In contrast to the stage of militancy characterized by the destruction of property that the British militants reached, American deeds of propaganda were always careful models of nonviolence. At the height of their struggle, the WSPU dynamited railways, slashed paintings, and burned down the prime minister's home. However, the WSPU stressed that they maintained woman's "moral superiority" by never using violence against persons, only property.[19] In the United States, the NWP did no damage, even to property, and used no weapons. Instead, these women willingly sacrificed themselves, along with their health, jobs, and reputations.

The National Woman's Party was one of the first organizations ever to use nonviolent resistance for a political cause. Bolstered by the Quaker tradition, numerous women's pacifist organizations such as Jane Addams's Women's Peace Party (now the Women's International League for Peace and Freedom) and Woman's Party advisor Crystal Eastman's American Union Against Militarism already existed. The nonviolent politics of protest against what women suffragists were by then calling an autocratic government appealed to women pacifists and leftist activists.

When NWP women were beaten, arrested, and jailed, they found a great deal of sympathy from the American Left, which was experiencing similar treatment for harboring antigovernment views during the world war. The war against Germany, coupled with the November 1917 internationalist Bolshevik Revolution in Russia, had made American leaders anxious about political dissent. In October 1917, Congress passed the Espionage Act against "abetting the enemy," and in May 1918, the Sedition Act, which punished those expressing antigovernment and "disloyal" opinions. On November 22, the *New York Tribune* reported that the Department of Justice was looking into links between *militant suffragists* [emphasis added] and "pacifists, anarchists and anti-war agitators."[20]

The National Woman's Party, which is still considered elitist by some historians, actually had very close ties with segments of the American Left during its struggle for woman suffrage. In turn, the women of the Left had an important impact on the strategies of the NWP's protest struggle. The Woman's Party not only drew membership from among socialists and labor organizers, as well as working-class women themselves, but also attracted enthusiastic support from left-wing organizations. During the earliest years of NWP activity, when the organization was spearheading an aggressive but fairly traditional campaign, leftist women were leery of hobnobbing with "plutocrats," such as CU executive and major benefactor Alva Belmont, although some socialist groups did support the NWP's efforts from the beginning. There had long been controversy among socialist and working women over whether or not to join the "bourgeois" suffrage movement at all. To most socialist women, women's rights were of secondary importance to the class struggle. Although this controversy remained, socialists (especially those in the western U.S.) remained among the most loyal and hardworking friends of suffrage, especially of militant suffrage.

In turn, National Woman's Party leaders viewed working women, or more specifically, factory workers and "industrial women," as a valuable addition to their processions, parades, and delegations. Many leftists were activists for the NWP between 1914 and 1916; they served as speakers, lobbyists, and representatives throughout the country. Two major figures with ties to labor were part of the original founding CU Executive Committee: historian Mary Beard and reformer Crystal Eastman. Famed as a Progressive reformer who investigated industrial accidents, Eastman had close ties to the Greenwich Village Left and strong views about the problems of class *and* sex discrimination. Many other leftists worked tirelessly as Woman's Party organizers. Rose Winslow, for instance, was a former factory worker and union organizer who spoke on woman suffrage to groups of workers in the West. In fact, the CU billed her as "one of [the workers'] own people." But she eventually complained to Paul that perhaps the woman suffrage issue was "too upper and middle class" for her.[21]

When the NWP began their militant political demonstrations against an "autocratic" Wilson government in 1917, and its members were harassed and maligned, then jailed and force fed by government authorities, leftist women readily identified with them. Eleven of the 36 (30 percent) jailed recruits of 1917 were socialists, and 13 of the 52 (25 percent) of the 1918–1919 demonstrators had ties to the left.[22] At the height of suffrage militancy, class barriers broke down to form a sisterhood united against what the women saw as the patriarchal power of the Woodrow Wilson government. While other groups of antigovernment dissenters focused their protests directly against war itself, or against the capitalist system which had undertaken a war of "imperialist aggression," antigovernment feminists used nonviolent protests to change the system so that women would have full equality in American society. NWP feminists across the political spectrum shared a radical vision of equal opportunity and were more than willing to fight the Wilson government to achieve at least part of that vision.

In November 1917, Paul stated that the government was trying to "terrorize and suppress" women for merely asking for a share in government. The militants' demands, like those of other dissenters, cast the Wilson administration in a most unfavorable light. But much of the press was still outraged by the woman suffragists' dissent. A *New York Times* editorial in June 1917 linked socialists, draft resisters, and "suffragettes" together as "inciters of rebellion." A journalist in Colorado charged that "German propaganda" sent socialist suffragist Margaret Wood Kessler to picket in Washington. And a *New York Tribune* piece, linking "pacifism and picketing," condemned the suspect NWP's connection to "avowed pacifists" like socialists Inez Milholland and Crystal Eastman. Beginning in 1917, the government's brand-new Secret Service, part of the Justice Department, kept tabs on the NWP all over the country. Western NWP leader Anne Martin was especially plagued by agents in October and November 1917. When the Bureau agent in Los Angeles informed her she could not hold a meeting, she told him America had guarantees of freedom of speech and assembly, and he could come arrest her if she said something "seditious." She was not arrested, but her fellow suffragists were. Between mid-1917 and early 1919, 168 woman suffrage protesters were arrested in various demonstrations, mostly in Washington, D.C.[23]

The government had been jailing militant suffragists since April, but the sentences were not more than a few days in length until mid-August, when the NWP pickets started to carry banners criticizing "Kaiser Wilson." For that, the women started getting sentences of 60 days at the Occoquan Workhouse in Virginia. In September, socialist Peggy Johns started the movement in jail that the suffragists demand to be given status as "political prisoners," which included access to counsel, decent food, and books and writing materials. In late October, showing their impatience with such tactics, government authorities put Alice Paul in a psychopathic ward and force fed her after she went on hunger strike. In turn, Paul wrote acting chair Dora Lewis that things "took a more serious turn" than planned, "but it happened rather well because we'll have ammunition against the Administration, and the more harsh and repressive they seem the better."[24]

On November 10, 1917, more than 150 women picketing the White House were assaulted, brutally beaten, and jailed for protesting Paul's confinement in a mental ward. Determined to escalate their struggle, the militants refused to give their names until they could present their demand to be considered political prisoners to the superintendent. Enraged guards clubbed and beat the women prisoners, from sixty-year-old Lavinia Dock, who was pushed down some stairs, to the youthful writer and activist Dorothy Day, who was beaten and choked.[25] To the Woman's Party protesters, November's "Night of Terror" proved the Wilson government's callousness. Yet they continued their insistence on political prisoner status and all went on hunger strike, which the officials met with more force feeding. As Dorothy Day wrote, this was no easy experience.

> I would have preferred the workshop to hunger striking—to lie there through the long day, to feel the nausea and emptiness of hunger . . . I lost all consciousness of any cause—I had no sense of being a radical, making protest against a government, carrying on a nonviolent revolution. I could only feel darkness and desolation.[26]

Sharing the experience of being beaten, arrested, and jailed by the Wilson government created a sisterhood among NWP members that was not possible in calmer times. New immigrant Nina Samarodin had been a union organizer, Russian teacher, and factory worker in New York since 1914. Coming to America to learn "industrial and political democracy," she said she was disappointed not to find any and so joined the NWP. "Working women of this country arise now and demand your political rights, and prove, that the American woman is strong enough to help herself."[27] Even the revolutionary Louise Bryant, who would later join John Reed in Russia, picketed and was jailed. Her first commitment was to make an important speech opposing American intervention against the Bolsheviks, but she wrote Paul wondering: "If you can arrange an arrest for me after . . . ?"[28] When the civil disobedience campaign of the NWP was in full swing, the party had sympathetic women joining them who took time out from revolutionary struggles, as well as from club luncheons. Woman's Party feminists demanded change not only in women's political role but also in her domestic and economic roles. Therein lay the appeal for feminists of all classes and also the perceived threat to male authorities.

The demonstrations and protests of 1917 continued into 1918. In January, the president finally endorsed a national amendment—the famous Susan B. Anthony amendment—,which was promptly followed by a successful vote in the House. By the following summer, NWP demonstrators were pressuring the Senate by picketing with banners, comparing that body to the German Reichstag. The women held fast to their positions and their banners, and as a result suffered severe police beatings and arrests. At their trials, the nonviolent resisters insisted on their innocence, refused to recognize the court or answer questions, since they were unenfranchised inhabitants of the United States. In late 1918, the women kept demonstrating in even greater numbers, suffering terrible jail conditions in the local D.C. jails. In early 1919, they began to light watch fires "for freedom" and followed this with burning Wilson and his eloquent speeches on democracy in effigy, causing apprehension that even worse (British-style) militancy might follow.[29]

But NWP-style militancy continued to be a classically nonviolent, although aggressive, type of resistance.[30] There was a demonstration staged in Boston in January 1919 "welcoming" President Wilson home from France, in order to persuade him to pressure a Senate still not secured for suffrage. Agnes Morey, demonstration organizer, instructed her "troops" in the same way Martin Luther King might have instructed his: "Don't be provoked to discussion. If you are arrested, offer no resistance and prefer no arguments."[31] Many forms of civil disobedience and noncooperation were exercised in Boston, practices by then common to the NWP. Betty Gram, for instance, had to be dragged by the arresting officer into the patrol wagon. Women refused to give their names, except as "Jane Doe"; they would not answer questions or pay their fines; and in jail, they refused to follow the rules and started a hunger strike.[32] Again, all this overreaction by the authorities was widely publicized. Alice Paul and Lucy Burns were always well aware of the power of the press as third parties to persuade the targeted opponent of the government.

Members of the NWP used the pickets' prison experience skillfully. In early 1919, they added the brilliant touch of a touring "prison train" of the NWP's most "prominent" and respectable "jailbirds." Hundreds were converted to the cause after hearing the jailed suffragists' stories. Americans found it difficult to believe that their government would jail women who were simply demonstrating to win their political rights.[33] Since America prided itself, based its very existence on, the highest principles of human rights, and since Woodrow Wilson advertised himself as a man of principle, drawing attention to hypocrisy was a realistic tactic for American suffrage militants in their nonviolent protests.

Media coverage was essential for what turned out to be the Woman's Party's last demonstration, in New York City in March 1919. This peaceful gathering was met by an unprecedented police attack with clubs. In May, arguably because such demonstrations brought sympathetic press coverage and resulting public pressure, Wilson finally secured the last senator needed to pass the amendment. Still the NWP went back to lobbying to gain enough states for ratification of the amendment, which was finally accomplished by the summer of 1920.[34] Throughout the campaign, American militants had consistently been defiant and aggressive, but unlike the WSPU's "violent" style of militancy, the NWP had instead used noncooperation and nonviolent civil disobedience, believing it more "natural" for woman protesters.

For her book on suffrage militancy in Pennsylvania, the NWP's Caroline Katzenstein of Pennsylvania used a quote from Mahatma Gandhi, in which she drew an obvious parallel between his acts and Woman's Party hunger strikes: "A fast is the sincerest form of prayer. . . . It stirs up sluggish consciences and inspires loving hearts to act. Those who have to bring about radical changes in human conditions and surroundings cannot do it without raising a ferment in society."[35] Woman's Party methods of protest did "stir consciences" and their demonstrations were intended to bring about the radical change for women of political equality. Their militancy and anger were real, but as women and as feminists, Alice Paul and her advisors felt their methods—their most effective methods—should be pacific, even "prayerful."

Perhaps contradictorily, Alice Paul thought nonviolent militancy was suited to woman's peaceable nature, but she also believed women must be militant—determined and aggressive—in pursuit of political rights. As militants, the feminists of the NWP stepped out of their prescribed roles by fighting their own battles to gain power. This struggle appealed to many women, including not only an upper-class elite or even middle-class elite but also working-class and leftist women. The consequences of the women's demonstrations were arrest and imprisonment, but the women picketers decided that it was well worth the hardship since it led to the success of their cause. So much valuable publicity for suffrage was generated by NWP tactics that, together with NAWSA's continuing massive lobbying efforts, Woman's Party efforts have to be given a great deal of credit for the eventual congressional passage of the woman suffrage amendment in 1919. Woman's Party militancy is significant in the history of nonviolent resistance and the feminist rights struggle, not only because it was the first example of an American use of organized nonviolence, but also because the Woman's Party campaign worked.

NOTES

1. Ida Husted Harper, *The Life and Work of Susan B. Anthony* (Indianapolis: Bowen and Merrill, 1898), 654, 678, 683, 945.

2. *New York Times*, July 12, 1917, 11; Martin to James and E. M. Garrett, July 9, 1917, Reel 45 of the National Woman's Party Papers on Microfilm (Wilmington, Del.: Microfilming Corporation of America, 1979), hereafter NWPP; *The Suffragist* (the NWP's journal), July 21, 1917, 9; Hazel Hunkins Hallinan, "A Talk to the Woman's Press Club," Washington, D.C., August 23, 1977, transcribed by Angela Ward, Bancroft Library Oral History of Suffragists Project, University of California, 5; for full explication of militancy and its significance, see the author's *Iron-Jawed Angels: The Suffrage Militancy of the National Woman's Party* (Lanham, Md.: University Press of America, 1991).

3. See Judith Stiehm, *Non-Violent Power: Active and Passive Resistance in America* (Lexington, Mass.: D.C. Heath, 1972), 60–62, describes how nonviolent resistance occurs in groups committed to social justice who have been pushed too far.

4. Amelia Fry, Interview with Alice Paul, 1972–73, "Woman Suffrage and the Equal Rights Amendment," Bancroft Oral History Project, 17–19.

5. See Ellen DuBois, *Feminism and Suffrage* (Ithaca, N.Y.: Cornell University Press, 1978); Harper, *Life and Work*, 954; Doris Stevens, *Jailed for Freedom* (1920; reprint, New York: Schocken Books, 1976), 8.

6. Emmeline Pankhurst, *My Own Story* (1914; reprint, London: Virago Press, 1979), 37.

7. In Burns to Katharine Fisher, May 29, 1915, Reel 16, NWPP, she credits the militants for bringing woman suffrage publicity worldwide.

8. Winsor Report, n.d., Reel 93, NWPP; Alice Paul to Edna Wilson, April 21, 1913, Reel 1; Paul to Bureau of Immigration, September 11, 1913, Reel 4; Paul to Emmeline Pethick-Lawrence, July 10, 1913, Reel 3; Lucy Burns to editor, *Washington Post*, May 14, 1914, Reel 10; *New York Times*, September 14, 1913, 6; *The Suffragist*, July 25, 1914, 4; Pankhurst pamphlet, "Broken Windows," 1, Rex v. Kerr Exhibit, WSPU Papers, Radcliffe College.

9. Emmeline Pankhurst speech of November 23, 1913 on Reel 92, NWPP.

10. Anna Howard Shaw correspondence with Paul and Burns, August and November of Reels 4 and 5, or Carrie Chapman Catt and Nettie Shuler, *Woman Suffrage and Politics* (New York: Charles Scribner's, 1926), 241–48. Burns to *Chicago Post* editor, July 11, 1916, Reel 29, NWPP.

11. Matilda Hall Gardner, "The Attack of the Suffrage Democrats," *Suffragist*, October 21, 1916, 7–10.

12. Letter to author from Milholland's sister-in-law, Anne Boissevain Nusbaum, March 20, 1983; Vida Milholland (sister of Inez) to Paul, October 30, 1916, Reel 35; December Memorial Report, Reel 36, NWPP.

13. Statement from 1914 Newport Convention in Stevens, *Jailed*, 33–34.

14. Amelia Fry, unpublished lecture to a nonviolent association, Washington, D.C., March 1, 1983; author interview with Rebecca Reyher, April 18, 1983 (notes).

15. Fry, Paul interview, 175–76; 551; Report of June 1916 convention, 23, Reel 29, NWPP.

16. Convention Report, March 10, 1917, Reel 40, NWPP.

17. *The Suffragette* (the WSPU journal), May 29, 1914, 120; Christabel Pankhurst's *The Great Scourge and How to End It* (London: E. P. Lincoln's Inn House, 1913); Doris Stevens, "Christabel Pankhurst's Fire Ascends to Heaven," n.d. 1920s? folder 27, box 2, Doris Stevens Papers, Schlesinger Library, Radcliffe College; Anne Martin to Elizabeth Selden Rogers, March 26, 1917, Reel 44; Paul to State Chairmen, February 8, 1917; Ethel Adamson to "Abbie" (Scott Baker), February 8, 1917, Reel 39, NWPP.

18. Fry, Paul interview, ix, 5, 174; for example, Minutes of Executive Committee, January 5, 1917, Reel 87. By the end of July 1917, 101 members were gained, 70 lost for a total number 27,747 members. July 1917 Executive Secretary Report, Reel 87, NWPP.

19. George Dangerfield, *The Strange Death of Liberal England* (London: Constable and Co., 1936), 322; David Mitchell, *The Fighting Pankhursts: A*

Study in Tenacity (New York: Macmillan, 1967); Emmeline Pankhurst, *My Own Story*, 255.

20. Joan M. Jensen, *The Price of Vigilance* (New York: Rand McNally, 1962), 47, 79; Zechariah Chafee, Jr., *Free Speech in the United States* (Cambridge: Harvard University Press, 1946), 52; *New York Tribune*, November 22, 1917, 1.

21. Blanche Wiesen Cook, *Crystal Eastman: On Woman and Revolution* (New York: Oxford University Press, 1979); Ann J. Lane, *Mary Ritter Beard: A Sourcebook* (New York: Schocken Books, 1977); Inez H. Irwin, *The Story of Alice Paul and the National Woman's Party*, 1921, 181; Fall 1916 correspondence between Paul and organizers, and Kessler to Paul and Burns, Reel 16, NWPP.

22. Ford, *Iron-Jawed Angels*, 198.

23. NWP press releases of November 1917, Reel 92, and November correspondence, Reel 52, NWPP; *New York Times*, June 21, 1917, 12; *Rocky Mountain News*, June 20, 1917, 1; *New York Tribune*, November 22, 1917; Martin to Pauline Clarke, October 31, and November 19, 1917, Reel 51, NWPP.

24. Sherna Gluck, ed., *Parlor to Prison: Five American Suffragists Talk About Their Lives* (New York: Random House, 1976), 228, 242–43; Stevens, *Jailed*, 177; Alice Paul to Dora Lewis, November 1917, Reel 53, NWPP.

25. Affidavits of November 23, 18, and 30, 1917 of Eunice Brannan, Mary Nolan, and Alice Cosu, Reel 52; Cora Week affidavit, November 1, 1920, Reel 83; Burns's November 1917 statement, Reel 52, NWPP.

26. Day, *The Long Loneliness* (New York: Harper and Row, 1952), 89–90.

27. Samarodin to Pauline Clarke, October 22, 1917, Reel 51 and September 14, 1917 statement, Reel 91, NWPP.

28. Bryant to Paul, January 27, 1919, Reel 63, NWPP.

29. See Ford, *Iron-Jawed Angels*; Stevens, *Jailed*, for full account.

30. Stiehm, *Non-Violent Power*, 27, again outlines the steps of classic nonviolent resistance.

31. *Boston Transcript*, February 24, 1919.

32. *Boston Record*, February 24, 1919, 1; *Boston Traveller*, February 25, 1919.

33. *Suffragist*, February 1, 15 and 22, 1919; March 29, 1919.

34. Stevens, *Jailed*, 331–32; also see Ford, *Iron-Jawed Angels*, 243.

35. Caroline Katzenstein, *Lifting the Curtain: The Woman Suffrage Campaigns in Pennsylvania as I Saw Them* (Philadelphia: Dorrance and Co., 1955), 344.

EPILOGUE

Anne Firor Scott

Like the movement itself, the written history of woman suffrage has evolved over time. The earliest phase was inaugurated by two suffragists, Elizabeth Cady Stanton and Susan B. Anthony, later joined by Matilda Joslyn Gage and even later by Ida Husted Harper, who gathered documents, memories, clippings, and miscellaneous reports from various parts of the country to create the massive six-volume *History of Woman Suffrage*. Along the way, and after the Nineteenth Amendment was ratified, various participants wrote their own stories—or saw them written.[1] Suffragists created vast quantities of source material, but for a long time academic historians (most of whom were men) paid no attention to the long process that led to the enfranchisement of half the adult population.

Sometime in the late 1930s, a young southern woman, who had a master's degree in history, was teaching in a small college in Alabama. Browsing in the library she came across the *History* and suddenly realized that her historical training to that point had never included women at all. She was inspired to take up the subject. In 1941, with many men off to war, she was admitted to the graduate program at Vanderbilt—she thought she might have been the first woman in that program.[2] Once there, Elizabeth Taylor defied the scorn of faculty and classmates alike to write her dissertation on the suffrage movement in Tennessee. From this beginning, she moved on methodically to examine the movement as it had developed in a number of southern states. Taylor was a careful scholar and a true pioneer, but her purpose was to find out as much as possible about what happened. Speculating or searching for causes or analyzing complex relationships was not her bent.[3]

189

In 1959, Eleanor Flexner, an independent scholar, published *Century of Struggle*, which almost immediately became the accepted narrative. Like Taylor, Flexner was a careful student and when, in the 1960s, women's history began to appear in college curricula, her book was on most reading lists. In 1965, Aileen Kraditor published an intellectual history of the movement that became the basis for a long-running debate. A political scientist and a historian teamed up to produce *One-Half the People: The Fight for Woman Suffrage* (1975), and in 1978 Ellen DuBois's *Feminism and Suffrage* initiated her long-running analysis of suffrage politics.[4]

Then, for a while, in the heady excitement of early ventures into the history of women, suffrage came to seem old hat, stuffy, the work of traditional historians. Other subjects engaged the young scholars, who discovered the pleasures of social history, and who, because politics had for so long been a central focus, often thought anything called "political" must be outdated. Some assumed that all there was to know about the suffrage movement was already known.

However, before long it became apparent that "politics" and "society" do not exist in closed boxes but are parts of a larger whole. In the 1980s, new work examined the ways women had participated in political life, even before they were enfranchised. Much recent research has emphasized the importance of women's associations as the vehicle for women to develop public responsibility and to bring about social change. Voluntary associations are not unique to the United States, but as Toqueville realized so many years ago, they have played a major part in our social development. Women's associations provided the constituency for educational change, as well as for suffrage and for the adoption of innovative public policies, especially in the area of the welfare of women and children.

Other recent scholarship has focused more directly on the political involvement of women, both as partisans and as promoters of certain public policies from the earliest days of the republic. For seventy-two years, between Seneca Falls and the Nineteenth Amendment, the experience of participating in a major political movement, of inventing ways to influence legislators, of developing news of many kinds had a lasting effect on many, many women, as well as on their families, their communities, and American politics. For evidence, one can turn to Mary Beard's *Women's Work in the Municipalities* (1914) or any of several monographs covering women's political activities from the early nineteenth century to the twentieth. Or one might read all the biographical sketches of suffragists in the four volumes of *Notable American Women*.

It is also useful to remember that the right to vote came in stages, beginning with the territory of Wyoming in 1869 and gradually spreading through the western states. By 1912, each of the major political parties had a woman's organization, and Jane Addams's seconding of Theodore Roosevelt's nomination at the Bull Moose convention was said to be worth a million votes. In 1916, women voters in California were praised (or blamed) for having returned Woodrow Wilson to the presidency. These changes began long before women could vote anywhere.[5] While the Nineteenth Amendment represented a great achievement, it was not quite the "great divide" in Nancy Cott's term.

And in consequence, "suffrage history" cannot focus on a single culminating moment but rather must proceed as the study of a long process of women's participation in government. By 1995, a collection of essays by a number of leading scholars was subtitled "*Rediscovering* the Woman Suffrage Movement" [italics added].[6]

This volume is part of that rediscovery and is designed to introduce undergraduates to some of the current work on the subject. Of course, understandings are not static. Historians are carriers of the understandings of their own time and are influenced by place, class, education, and aspiration. When Stanton and Anthony set out to compile a record of the movement, they managed to shape that record in their own image. They paid scant attention to any one whose views or methods differed from their own, and especially did little justice to Lucy Stone and her American Woman Suffrage Association.

Despite all the work that has been done over more than a century, many vital questions have yet to be fully answered. We have only an imperfect idea about how the movement came into being, and how the small groups scattered across the nation were related to the larger, national organizations or how money was raised and spent. It would be important to know more about what it meant to women, who did the work, and just how difficult the task of persuading those who held the power to share it was accomplished. There is considerable information about the national leaders, but we do not know much about the innumerable local leaders or about the men who helped, openly or quietly. While some of the essays in this volume review familiar work, others raise interesting new questions and suggest lines for further investigation.

What difference did suffrage make?

Just as we have much more to learn about the movement as it developed, so too we do not yet have a completely satisfactory analysis of the consequences for American society and politics of the potential doubling of the electorate—"potential" because while we celebrate 1920 as the year when "all" American women were enfranchised, in point of fact, many groups of women were still barred from the polls. Most of us know that African-American women in the South, with a few exceptions, have only been able to vote since the 1964 Voting Rights Act. What we are less likely to know is that women in various other groups—poor white southerners, Native Americans, Asian immigrants, for example—were not immediately included in the electorate.

But beyond the fact that what was hailed as a "victory" took a while to take effect, what can we say with assurance about the ways women's enfranchisement has changed the political and social landscape?

The effort of some historians to divide suffragists into those who had been primarily interested in the vote on principle, and those who wanted the vote as an instrument sets up a false dichotomy. Each woman had her own set of priorities, but it is safe to say that very few wanted the vote solely as a symbol. From the earliest days, these women argued for the right to participate in creating public policy. Similarly, a division between "women's issues" and "social reform" is artificial. Any issue can be a woman's issue, and certainly women have no monopoly on social reform.

Some direct consequences of enfranchisement are obvious. When members of the National American Woman Suffrage Association transformed themselves into a League of Women Voters and set out to educate women and other citizens who might want their help, they were initiating a change in the way the democratic system functions.[7]

Local leagues ran classes, taught citizens state election laws, and otherwise tried to make sure their constituents could exercise the right so long sought. Candidates' meetings became a regular part of each election season. They offered men as well as women a chance to question the office seekers. In various other ways, the LWV has established lasting patterns of what is labeled "voters' service." It is notable that the first nationally televised presidential candidates' meeting took place at the national convention of the league in 1952. As the population expands and the workings of government are more and more complex, efforts to find ways to educate citizens become more important.

Beyond voters' service, local, state, and national Leagues have adopted programs of work and significantly affected public policy at all levels. In many states newly enfranchised women were ready with a legislative agenda, and in some they had remarkable success. It is not an exaggeration to say that organized women were responsible for carrying the social welfare agenda of the Progressive Era into state government in the 1920s.[8] Restricting child labor and improving working conditions of women were among the most frequent issues that engaged women's energies, but there were many others.

The earliest national achievement directly attributable to women voters was the Sheppard-Towner Act of 1921. Despite its wealth and growing power in the world, the United States in 1920 had a dismal record of maternal and infant mortality To attack this problem, newly enfranchised women joined forces to establish a federal-state program, one of the first national programs for social welfare.[9]

The work was accomplished by a Women's Joint Congressional Committee representing ten women's organizations. The opposition was formidable, as various existing groups (including the American Medical Association) accused supporters of the bill of being socialists, if not communists. Antisuffragists reappeared to fight it. Fresh from their success with the amendment, they inundated Congress with mail and engaged in vigorous on-the-spot lobbying. The bill passed, and in due course infant mortality improved. As is true of many pioneering efforts, this early success energized the opposition, and after a few years the law was changed, and the appropriation cut. Still, the idea and the experience did not die and would reappear in New Deal legislation.

As early as 1921 and continuing to the present, another visible consequence of enfranchisement has been the expanding number of women office holders, especially in local and state office. In many local communities women ran for offices. The president of the Mississippi woman suffrage organization led the way when she was elected to the state senate and made a legislative record that elicited extravagant praise from her male colleagues. Many others followed suit. There has been a steady increase over the decades in women office holders. And in some towns and counties, the entire local government has, from time to time, been female. Several women have been governors. Even the U.S. Congress, though it happened slowly, now has a significant contingent of women representatives and senators who, regardless of party affiliation, tend to be more interested in certain issues than their male counterparts.

When Franklin and Eleanor Roosevelt came to the White House in 1933, an extraordinary group of women, suffrage veterans experienced in politics, were appointed to important posts in the federal government. Frances Perkins joined the cabinet as secretary of labor and several dozen others were appointed to various agencies, especially those dealing with health and welfare.[10]

The enfranchisement of women was part of a larger change in the role and status of women in American society that had been developing since the eighteenth century, that had accelerated after the Civil War, and that was clearly visible by the end of the nineteenth century. It became part of the complex of factors that have continued to generate historical change. Suffrage was a tributary flowing into the rich and turbulent river of American social development. That river is enriched by the waters of each tributary, but with the passage of time it becomes increasingly difficult to distinguish the special contribution of any one of these tributaries.

We do not yet have a means for analyzing the complex set of changes that have revolutionized not only relationships between men and women but also the way society, business, and government function. The convention is to attribute these changes to the accelerating urbanization-industrialization of American society and to the ever-increasing productivity which was part of that process. Important as such factors clearly have been, it is not clear exactly how they worked together to create the structural change that made a woman's rights movement possible. The chicken-and-egg question is difficult: in Europe, for example, an active woman's rights movement sometimes preceded widespread industrialization. The improvement of women's educational opportunity was a vital piece of the picture, but what made that change possible? Questions abound; answers must be tentative.

The best we can do is to recognize how interrelated social changes can be and to understand the suffrage movement as part of such a complex of change.

In the twenty-first century, the process continues as the number of women college graduates, Ph.D. holders, lawyers, doctors, financial experts, political analysts, research scientists, and so on increases annually. Children are being raised differently in this generation; the role of fathers in families is also changing—though not always rapidly. Social change, to paraphrase Kierkegaard, moves forward but is only understood backward. Trying to puzzle out that understanding is the historian's task.

NOTES

1. Elizabeth Cady Stanton, Susan B. Anthony, Matilda Joslyn Gage, and Ida Husted Harper, eds., *History of Woman Suffrage*, 6 vols. (reprint, New York: Arno, 1969); Carrie Chapman Catt and Nettie R. Shuler, *Woman Suffrage and Politics: The Inner Story of the Suffrage Movement* (New York:

H.W. Wilson, 1923); Abigail Scott Duniway, *Pathbreaking: An Autobiographical History of the Equal Suffrage Movement in the Pacific Coast States* (New York: Schocken Books, 1971); Inez Haynes Gilmore, *Up the Hill with Banners Flying* (Penobscott, Maine: Traveresity Press, 1964; Sherna Gluck, ed., *From Parlor to Prison: Five American Suffragists Talk About Their Lives* (New York: Vintage, 1976); Florence Howe Hall, *Julia Ward Howe and the Woman Suffrage Movement* (New York: Arno, 1961); Caroline Katzenstein, *Lifting the Curtain: The State and National Woman Suffrage Campaigns in Pennsylvania as I Saw Them* (Philadelphia: Dorrance, 1955); Louise Noun, *Strongminded Women* (Ames: Iowa State University Press, 1969); Maud Wood Park, *Front Door Lobby*, ed. Edna Lamprey Stantial (Boston: Beacon Press, 1960); Doris Stevens, *Jailed for Freedom* (New York: Liveright, 1926); Mary Grey Peck, *Carrie Chapman Catt* (New York: H.W. Wilson, 1944).

2. A. Elizabeth Taylor, "A Lifelong Interest," in Ruthe Winegartem and Judith N. McArthur, eds. *Citizens All: The Woman Suffrage Movement in Texas* (Austin: Ellen C. Temple, 1987).

3. A. Elizabeth Taylor, *A Short History of the Woman Suffrage Movement in Tennessee* (privately printed in 1943; published by Bookman Associates in 1957).

4. Eleanor Flexner, *Century of Struggle: The Woman's Rights Movement in the United States*, rev. ed. (Cambridge: Harvard University Press, 1975); Aileen Kraditor, *The Ideas of the Woman Suffrage Movement 1890–1920* (New York: Columbia University Press, 1965); Anne F. Scott and Andrew M. Scott, *One-Half the People: The Fight for Woman Suffrage* (Champaign: University of Illinois Press, 1978; Ellen C. DuBois, *Feminism and Suffrage: The Emergence of an Independent Women's Movement in the U.S.* (Ithaca: Cornell University Press, 1978).

5. For the antebellum period, see Elizabeth Varon, "Tippecanoe and Ladies Too: White Women and Party Politics in Antebellum Virginia," *Journal of American History* 82 (1995): 494–521. For the years after the Civil War, see especially Melanie Gustafson, Kristie Miller, and Elizabeth I. Perry, *We Have Come to Stay: American Women and Political Parties 1880–1960* (Albuquerque: University of New Mexico Press, 1999). It has a useful bibliography. See also Anne F. Scott, *Natural Allies: Women's Associations in American History* (Champaign: University of Illinois Press, 1991); Robyn Muncy, *Creating a Female Dominion in American Reform, 1890–1955* (New York: Oxford University Press, 1991).

6. Marjorie Spruill Wheeler, ed. *One Woman, One Vote: Rediscovering the Woman Suffrage Movement* (Troutdale, Oreg.: New Sage Press, 1995).

7. Louise M. Young, *The Public Interest: The League of Women Voters 1920–1970* (New York: Greenwood Press, 1989).

8. Kristi Andersen, *After Suffrage: Women in Electoral and Partisan Politics Before the New Deal* (Chicago: University of Chicago Press, 1996).

9. J. Stanley Lemons, *Woman Citizen Social Feminism in the 1920s* (Urbana: University of Illinois Press, 1973), and Carole Nichols, "Votes and More for Women: Suffrage and After in Connecticut," in *Women and History*, no. 5 (Spring 1983): 1–92.

10. Susan Ware, *Beyond Suffrage: Women in the New Deal* (Cambridge: Harvard University Press, 1981).

BIBLIOGRAPHY

Primary Sources

Gordon, Ann, and Tamara Gaskell Miller, eds. *The Selected Papers of Elizabeth Cady Stanton and Susan B. Anthony*, Vols. 1 and 2. New Brunswick: Rutgers University Press, 1997–2000.

Papers of the National Woman Suffrage Association, Library of Congress.

Papers of the American Woman Suffrage Association, Library of Congress.

Papers of the National Woman's Party, Library of Congress.

Papers of Elizabeth Cady Stanton and Susan B. Anthony, 45 reels, microfilm edition.

Stanton, Elizabeth Cady, Susan B. Anthony, and Matilda Joslyn Gage, eds. *History of Woman Suffrage*. Rochester: Susan B. Anthony, 6 volumes, 1881–1922. (Later volumes edited by Ida Harper Husted.)

Secondary Sources

Anderson, Bonnie. *Joyous Greetings: The First International Women's Movement, 1830–1860*. New York: Oxford University Press, 2000.

Anthony, Kathryn. *Susan B. Anthony: Her Personal History and Her Era*. Garden City, N.Y.: Doubleday, 1954.

Bolt, Christine. *The Women's Movements in the United States and Britain from the 1790s to the 1920s*. Amherst: University of Massachusetts Press, 1993.

Buechler, Steven. *The Transformation of the Woman Suffrage Movement: The Case of Illinois 1850–1929*. New Brunswick: Rutgers University Press, 1986.

Buhle, Mary Jo, and Paul Buhle, eds. *A Concise History of Woman Suffrage: Selections from the Classic Work of Stanton, Anthony, Gage and Harper*. Urbana: University of Illinois Press, 1978.

Catt, Carrie Chapman, and Nettie Rogers Shuler. *Woman Suffrage and Politics: The Inner Story of the Suffrage Movement*. New York: Charles Scribner's and Sons, 1926.

Cott, Nancy. *The Origins of Modern Feminism*. New Haven: Yale University Press, 1987.

DuBois, Ellen Carol. *Feminism and Suffrage: The Emergence of an Independent Women's Movement in America 1848–1869*. Ithaca, N.Y.: Cornell University Press, 1978.

———. *Harriot Stanton Blatch and the Winning of Woman Suffrage*. New Haven: Yale University Press, 1997.

Edwards, Rebecca. *Angels in the Machinery: Gender in American Party Politics from the Civil War to the Progressive Era*. New York: Oxford University Press, 1997.

Flexner, Eleanor. *Century of Struggle: The Woman's Rights Movement in the United States*. Cambridge, Mass.: Harvard University Press, 1975.

Ford, Linda. *Iron-Jawed Angels: The Suffrage Militancy of the National Woman's Party*. Lanham, Md.: University Press of America, 1991.

Fowler, Robert Booth. *Carrie Catt: Feminist Politician*. Boston: Northeastern University Press, 1986.

Gluck, Sherna, ed. *From Parlor to Prison: Five American Suffragists Talk About Their Lives*. New York: Arno, 1961.

Harper, Ida Husted. *The Life and Work of Susan B. Anthony*. 3 vols. Indianapolis: Bowen-Merrill, 1899–1908.

Hoffert, Sylvia. *When Hens Crow: The Woman's Rights Movement in Antebellum America*. Bloomington: Indiana University Press, 1995.

Isenberg, Nancy. *Sex and Citizenship in Antebellum America*. Chapel Hill, N.C.: University of North Carolina Press, 1998.

Jablonsky, Thomas. *The Home, Heaven and the Mother Party: Female Antisuffrage in the United States 1868–1920*. Brooklyn, N.Y.: Carlson Publishing, 1994.

Kerr, Andrea Moore. *Lucy Stone: Speaking Out For Equality*. New Brunswick, N.J.: Rutgers University Press, 1992.

Kraditor, Aileen. *The Ideas of the Woman Suffrage Movement 1890–1920*. New York: Columbia University Press, 1965.

Lebsock, Suzanne. "Woman Suffrage and White Supremacy: A Virginia Case Study," in *Visible Women: New Essays on American Activism*. Eds. Nancy Hewitt and Suzanne Lebsock. Urbana: University of Illinois Press, 1993.

Painter, Nell Irvin. *Sojourner Truth, A Life, A Symbol*. New York: W.W. Norton, 1996.

Parker, Alison. *Purifying America: Women, Cultural Reform, and Pro-Censorship Activism*. Urbana: University of Illinois Press, 1997.

Scott, Anne F., and Andrew M. Scott, *One-Half the People: The Fight for Woman Suffrage*. Philadelphia: Lippincott, 1975.